THE

Chriſtian Miſcellany;

OR,

RELIGIOUS AND MORAL

MAGAZINE.

From JANUARY to AUGUST, *incluſive,*

MDCCXCII.

———————————

LONDON:

PRINTED FOR B. KINGSBURY;

AND SOLD BY C. STALKER, NO. 4, STATIONERS-COURT,

LUDGATE-STREET.

MDCCXCII.

TABLE OF CONTENTS.

No. 1.

No. 2.

a

CONTENTS.

No. 5.

No. 6.

No. 7.

No. 8.

THE

Chriſtian Miſcellany,

For JANUARY, 1792.

ARTICLE I.

The Introduction.

OF the praiſe which is due to the benefactors of mankind, it will readily be acknowledged that a diſtinguiſhed portion belongs to thoſe who have ſucceſsfully exerted their abilities in the cauſe of religion and virtue. For a Publication which is deſigned to ſerve this cauſe, and to promote the moſt important intereſts of man, no apology is requiſite. A ſimple ſtatement of the deſign and nature of the Work will prove its beſt recommendation.

The great object of the ſupporters of the CHRISTIAN MISCELLANY is the promotion of religious knowledge, and the practice of virtue. They lament that many of their fellow-creatures are poſſeſſed of but few means of acquiring that inſtruction which is beſt ſuited to their ſtations; and they think that a Work of this kind, publiſhed *periodically*, and at an *eaſy price*, will tend to ſupply this deficiency, and may prove peculiarly uſeful.

B   The

The plan of this Work comprehends Miscellaneous Papers on theology and morals; a Review of books calculated to serve the cause of religion and virtue; and a Catalogue of monthly publications.

The subjects of those Papers which class under theology or morals, will be various. It is the wish, and will be the endeavour, of the friends of this Publication, to render it as interesting as possible; and, with this view, they will avail themselves of every thing of a pleasing nature, which may be at all confistent with the general design. The CHRISTIAN MISCELLANY will include communications on such subjects as the following.

The doctrines, and evidences, of revelation; illustrations of difficult parts of scripture, and practical comments on interesting passages; stated means of religious improvement, public worship, the lord's supper, family prayer, &c. account of the several religions which have been embraced in the world; view of the present state of christian societies; progress of just sentiments on religious subjects; progress of religious liberty; account of the religious sentiments of learned and eminent men; historical articles respecting those who have suffered in the cause of what they deemed to be truth; the right of private judgment; plans for the promotion of knowlege and virtue; proposals for improvements in the constitution of christian societies; accounts of attempts to serve the cause of religious or civil liberty; penal laws in matters of religion; slave trade; duties of human life; instructive tales; account of charitable institutions; education; instructions for youth, for married people, &c. poetry of a religious and moral tendency, &c. &c.

It may be seen, from this lift of subjects, (and many more might be mentioned) that the plan of

this

this part of the Work affords confiderable variety; and that the fupporters of it may reafonably pleafe themfelves with the idea of engaging the *hearts* of their readers, while they are promoting their improvement.

Thefe Mifcellaneous Papers will be followed by an Account of fuch books on theological and moral fubjects, as feem calculated to fecure the attainment of thofe ends which the friends of the CHRISTIAN MISCELLANY have in view. It is hoped that the execution of this part of the plan will, to the lower clafs of people, who are unable to purchafe, or to read, a *great number* of books, be both agreeable and ufeful.

A regular and exact Catalogue of monthly publications, of every kind, will finifh each Number. As this will form a *permanent* part of the work, the poffeffion of it muft, to many perfons, be convenient and pleafing.

Although the materials of the CHRISTIAN MISCELLANY will generally be original, the Editor of it will think himfelf at liberty to introduce Extracts from interefting publications.

The friends of this Work wifh not to make it a theatre of religious controverfy. But, as they do not all agree in opinion upon certain controverted points, admiffion will not be refufed to any Effay which favours a particular doctrine, if the general tendency of the Paper appear ufeful, and if it be written in the fpirit of chriftian charity.

One Number of the CHRISTIAN MISCELLANY will be publifhed regularly on the firft day of every month. Twelve Numbers will make a Volume. The laft Number will be accompanied with an Index, and a General Title.—It is an obvious reflection, that while the fmall price of a Number will render the purchafe of it fo eafy as to place it within the reach of persons of inferior circumstances, it will afford to the benevolent and pious of higher rank, a mean of instructing others, which many have long wished for in vain.

Having thus given an account of the nature of the Work, it will be right to say something of the means which are provided for the proper conduct of it.

The plan of the CHRISTIAN MISCELLANY was suggested at an Annual Provincial meeting of ministers; who, thinking that it would be of service to the interests of religion, appointed a Committee to prepare and receive materials for the Work. A very considerable collection of Papers is now formed; and the Editor has been encouraged to hope for the support and assistance of numerous well-wishers to the design; some of whom are not less distinguished by the admiration of the Public, than by real respectability and worth. With regard to himself, the Conductor of the Work promises the exertion of his best abilities, and the continued application of care and attention. He trusts, that those who know him, will believe it to be his aim to cherish, in every reader, a spirit of virtuous independence, of firm integrity, of humble piety, of well-regulated and unremitted activity. In the rational exercise of his faculties, and in the approbation of his own mind, he hopes to experience a pleasure of all others the most valuable—the pleasure of doing good.

BENJ. KINGSBURY.

ART. II.

ART. II. *A View of the Advantages of the Sabbath.*

TO THE EDITOR OF THE CHRISTIAN MISCELLANY.

SIR,

AMONG the various inftances of inattention to the laws of reafon and religion, I know of fcarcely any which is more general than the cuftom of employing our fervants, and perfons in inferior ftations, on the Sunday. Not fatisfied with the advantage of their labour during the reft of the week, we thoughtlefsly deprive them of that feafon which is fo humanely and wifely appointed for their relaxation and improvement. The truth of this remark is, perhaps, moft evident in the cafe of hair-dreffers. Without farther apology, I fhall, therefore, endeavour to fhew that the cuftom of employing them on Sunday ought to be difcontinued.

I think I fhall do this effectually, if I can eftablifh the following pofition—that the lofs fuftained on the part of the perfon employed, is, beyond all proportion, greater than the advantage accruing to the employer. There is no other way of forming a judgment of the nature and extent of that *lofs*, than by taking a view of the advantages of the chriftian fabbath, efpecially with refpect to the poor and labouring part of the community.

I fhall firft point out the importance of the fabbath with regard to civilization, and the progrefs of knowledge, among the lower claffes of men.

I fuppofe there is no perfon, into whofe hands this paper is likely to fall, who has not both obferved and deplored the ignorance and grofs

barbarity

barbarity which ftill remain among the lower ranks in fociety. I beg him to confider what the cafe would probably be, if the fabbath was to be abolifhed. Indeed, I cannot make even the fuppofition, without feeling a kind of horror at the confequences which, it appears to me, would inevitably follow. One of the writers in the Spectator gives it as his opinion, that the country towns, and efpecially the villages, would prefently be inhabited by fo many favages. I am perfuaded, that, in lefs than a century, the face of the country would be totally changed; and that, inftead of fome appearance of the arts of life, and of knowledge, to be found even among the moft ignorant, we fhould have a profpect which would at once aftonifh and grieve every thinking mind.

If any perfon has a doubt upon the fubject, I would advife him to confider the circumftances which gave rife to the inftitution of Sunday fchools. The generous propofers and patrons of this charitable defign lay it down as a well known fact, and on which they reft the neceffity of Sunday fchools, that the poor in general have no other time at their command, than what the Sunday affords, for acquiring the loweft and moft neceffary branches of knowledge. And, accordingly, the ignorance found among them, was, in many inftances, great and deplorable. I do not know a ftronger argument in favour of the fabbath, or a better proof of its importance, than that it is almoft the only opportunity which the poor enjoy of improvement in knowledge.

There is another view in which the fabbath may be confidered—as a *general refpite* from the cares of life. This is a confideration which will, no doubt, have its weight with every humane perfon. The man of bufinefs may now, without prejudice to his trade, or inconvenience to his cuſtomers, retire from fatigue and hurry, reſt himſelf, and prepare to engage with new diligence in the duties of his ſtation. The huſbandman, wearied with toilſome exertions, may now repoſe himſelf awhile, and, by a ſhort ſeaſon of reſt, refit himſelf for a freſh engagement in the uſeful labours of his calling. I ſhall have occaſion to mention this ceſſation of buſineſs in another point of view hereafter.

I deſire my readers to take particular notice, in the next place, of the *cleanlineſs* with which the obſervance of the Sunday is attended.

Whatever may be pretended concerning the degree of refinement to which the good people of England are arrived, I venture to affirm that there is no one in the higher walks of life, who has had opportunities of making proper obſervations, but muſt have been ſtruck with the foul, uncomfortable, barbarous condition in which many of the lower ranks are ſtill content to live. What the caſe would probably be, without the ſabbath, I forbear to ſay; and am more pleaſed to mention the higher and happier ſtate of things at preſent. No man is ſo filthy as not to think it his duty to purify and cleanſe himſelf on this occaſion. Scarcely any man ſo poor as not to be able to boaſt a change of cleaner and better raiment, by the wearing of which he diſtinguiſhes this day. This general purification, as it well deſerves to be called, probably owes its regularity and conſtancy, at leaſt, to the ſabbath. It is, no doubt, of the utmoſt conſequence to the comfort and health (and ſome have added, to the morals) of the labouring part of the community. My readers may ſmile, but, for my part, I never meet a poor man on a Sunday, in his beſt cloaths, without looking upon him

to

to be advanced, by many degrees, in a state of civilization.

But if we take *religion* into the account, the importance of the sabbath, one should think, will be established beyond all contradiction. The great and glorious doctrine of a life to come gives a degree of significancy and consequence to every improvement in knowledge, virtue, and piety, which it would otherwise want.

Some, perhaps, may think differently, but it has always been my opinion, that the prosperity of religion, and the observance of the sabbath, must stand or fall together. It is no groundless surmise, no imaginary fear, which leads me to apprehend that, without the sabbath, religion itself would be almost entirely overlooked and neglected. At least, it appears true, that by this institution, the *attention* of mankind to that important object is, in the best manner, secured. The regular and constant return of this sacred day, and that general suspension of business which is the consequence of it, serve to remind the most unthinking that there is such a being as God, and such a thing as religion. Without an admonition of this kind, there is reason to fear that such serious considerations would scarcely ever enter into the minds of the busy and thoughtless; and these, I imagine, compose more than half the human race.

But if it is to be feared that the cares of life would absolutely fix the *attention* of mankind, it is equally to be feared that those cares would also engross their *time*, to the exclusion of all concern about God and a future state. The sabbath provides against a danger of this magnitude, and secures proper time for the exercises of devotion; and, particularly, for acquiring the knowledge of God and ourselves, on which they are founded.

Indeed,

Indeed, that religion ought to share in the thoughts and business of *every* day, I am most ready to grant. But how the knowledge of God and of his will, which lies at the foundation of all religion, can be acquired, without some considerable portion of *time* for acquiring it; how this knowledge can be retained through a long period, and amidst many temptations to forget it, without some *season* for recollecting and confirming it; how it can be enlarged and improved without some *opportunity* of improving it;—I am at a loss to conceive. In these respects, religious knowledge, and all other kinds of knowledge, are in precisely the same predicament.

We are not to forget those *public services* of religion which plainly suppose the sabbath, or some *time regularly set apart* for the worship of God. If the observance of the Sunday was not stated and regular, it could not be universal; and if not universal, it would produce confusion in society. As Mr. Paley says, " the buyer would be coming to the shop, when the seller was gone to church." I shall say nothing of the *importance* of these services. I have somewhere met with the observation, that, if an ancient philosopher was permitted to make a visit to the modern inhabitants of Europe, he would be equally surprised and pleased to see a whole nation assembled, at the same instant, to worship their God, and a number of grave divines appointed to read lectures on morality and other important subjects.

As to the exact portion of time to be appropriated to the duties of religion, and as to the observance of the first day of the week, or of the seventh, or of any other particular day, in preference to the rest, I desire it may be noticed, that what I have advanced does not at all interfere with either of those questions.

tions. If it be granted me, that one day in seven is, upon the whole, a due proportion of time to be devoted to the worship of God, and other acts of piety; and if it be farther allowed me, that the first day of the week, being set apart for that purpose by long usage and common consent, may be observed, for the sabbath, as well as any other day;—this is as much as I should ask.

Thus I have given a short view of the advantages of the sabbath; and the oftener I take this view, the more I revere the wisdom of an institution at once consulting the ease, health and happiness, the moral and intellectual improvement, of mankind. Abolish the sabbath, and, from that moment, all *progress* in knowledge, virtue and piety will be at a general stand; and human nature, it is greatly to be feared, if it does not improve, will degenerate.

Let me now call upon those who do not scruple to employ their servants, and the labouring part of the community, on the Sunday, seriously to consider of what it is that they deprive them. Let them compare what is gained on the one hand, with what is lost on the other. Their hair-dressers, for instance, by being employed on the Sunday, are deprived, either in whole or in part, of the only opportunity which they possess of improvement in knowledge and goodness; of the only season which, in the present state of things, they are allowed for recreation and rest. Let them oppose to all this, if they please, the mighty object of being well dressed. I am sure there is no person, in whose heart I desire any place, who will not blush at the comparison.

A. C. L.

ART. III.

ART. III. *Questions and Answers on the Lord's Supper; tending to explain and recommend it.*

Question. What is the Lord's Supper?

Answer. It is a ceremony appointed by Christ to be observed by all his disciples.

Q. Of what does it consist?

A. Of eating bread, and drinking wine.

Q. In what manner was it instituted?

A. Jesus Christ, the night before his death, being at supper with his disciples, took bread, and having broken it, ate of it himself, and gave of it to his disciples, desiring them to eat. He then took wine, and having drunk, gave to his disciples to drink also. He told them that the bread was an emblem of his body which would be broken for them, and the wine of his blood which would be shed for them; it being necessary that he should die to confirm the truth of the doctrines he taught.

Q. What is the design and use of this institution?

A. To preserve in our minds the remembrance of what Christ did and suffered for mankind.

Q. In what other respects may it be useful?

A. It will be a means of keeping alive our gratitude to God for sending Jesus Christ into the world, to instruct us in our duty, and to promise us a future happy life, if we do not depart from it.

Q. What influence will attending the Lord's Supper be likely to have with respect to our behaviour to our fellow-creatures?

A. To join with our fellow-christians in reflecting upon, and returning thanks for, blessings common to all, is calculated to promote benevolent and friendly affections.

Q. How

Q. How is it calculated to promote such difpofitions?

A. When we confider ourfelves as children of the fame great and good God, as difciples of the fame mafter, and as all equally interefted in the practice of virtue to infure our future happinefs, we muft love one another as brethren, and feel difpofed to treat all our fellow-creatures with love and good-will.

Q. What good effects may it have upon our conduct with refpect to ourfelves?

A. It will encourage us in the practice of virtue by the example of Chrift, who chofe rather to fuffer perfecution, and a cruel death, than live by relinquifhing his virtue.

Q. By receiving the Lord's Supper, do we lay ourfelves under any obligations?

A. This, as well as attending public worfhip, praying to God, and every thing by which we declare ourfelves to be chriftians, lays an obligation upon us to act as becomes chriftians.

Q. In what other fenfe does it lay an obligation upon us?

A. As it is a means of making us better, it will be expected of us that we improve it; fince we fhall be judged according to the advantages we have received.

Admitting the above to be a true account of the defign and tendency of the inftitution; is it not plain, rational, and ufeful? And does it not become every fincere chriftian chearfully and thankfully to obferve it?

ART. IV.

ART. IV. *Religious Objections to the Practice of Inoculation Answered.*

TO THE EDITOR OF THE CHRISTIAN MISCELLANY.

S I R,

The following plain arguments in favour of Inoculation were inserted, some time ago, in a provincial paper, in consequence of a proposal made by the medical gentlemen for the introduction of a plan for general inoculation. As they were thought to be productive of some good at the time of their publication, your giving them a place in your useful Miscellany may possibly be the means of rendering them more extensively useful.

Extract from the NEWCASTLE COURANT, of *Saturday, April* 8, 1786.

S I R,

I KNOW not whether it is customary for you to pay much attention to communications which wait upon you in so homely a dress as that which I now venture to send you. I am a plain man, Mr. Printer, and know little about the forms of polite correspondence; but I am one that wishes well to all mankind, and should think myself particularly happy in contributing either to the health, the population, or the prosperity of my country. With this view, I hope you will gratify me by inserting the following plain account of a conversation I lately heard, which, as it made considerable impression upon me, I remember pretty exactly.

You

You know, Mr. Printer, the faculty in this town have just made us an offer of their affistance in the inoculation of our children; and this, you may be fure, affords abundant matter for converfation among us poor people. Some think favourably of their intentions, who do not approve of inoculation; of which number I profefs myfelf to have been one: others, I am forry to fay, feem to have raifed up the old exploded cry againft all medical charities, " that the poor are to be made the fubjects of experiment, for the benefit of the rich;" than which nothing, I am perfuaded, can be more groundlefs and abfurd.

But the religious objections to the practice of inoculation had made, I confefs, no flight impreffion upon me, 'till, being prefent the other day at the chriftening of my neighbour's child, the officiating minifter happened to afk the father, after the fervice was concluded, whether he meant to take advantage of the general inoculation, or fuffer the two fine children, whom we faw playing about the houfe, to run the hazard of dying by the fmall pox in the natural way. And can you, Sir, faid I, who profefs to teach fubmiffion to God's will, can you exhort us to prefume fo far as to take his difpofals out of his hands, and choofe our own time of ficknefs and difeafe? can you, whofe bufinefs it is to preach that all things are fixed and determined by God, perfuade us with a grave face, that we can change his determinations?—" What God has fixed and determined," faid the worthy clergyman, " I do not prefume to declare. In thefe refpects, I fear, we are much more peremptory and particular than becomes us. But this, I think, is very clear, that he has ordered every thing with a reference to fecond caufes, or to that courfe of nature which he has been pleafed to appoint; and I might with equal

equal reafon retort upon you: How dare you take phyfic, when fick? fince you know not but your ficknefs may be the meffenger of death; or if not, are fenfible that God needs not your help towards your recovery: what folly to move out of the way, if a houfe be falling? for if God does not intend you fhould die, it is impoffible for bricks or timber to hurt you: nay, why fhould you eat your dinner, or put on your clothes? for, if it be decreed that you fhall die, your eating will not prevent it; nor will all your clothing keep you warm, if God intends that you fhould be ftarved to death.—See, my good friend, to what abfurdities this principle will lead you.

"And I think," continued he, "you charge me very unjuftly with a want of fubmiffion to providence, for only making ufe of the means which it has appointed for leffening a neceffary evil. I call it neceffary, becaufe, in a large town like this, the fmall pox are conftantly prevalent in fome quarter or other; fo that we can never be certain that our children will efcape them, nay, we are morally certain they will not. And I think I am warranted to call inoculation a means appointed by God, fince the fuccefs of every part of it depends upon his co-operation. As the hufbandman that fows the feed, has no power of making it fpring, but waits for the rain and warmth of heaven to raife up the fruit of his labours; fo here we muft look for God's influence and bleffing, without which the incifion and the matter that we apply, will fignify nothing. Now furely to have recourfe to the means appointed by nature for any end is to have recourfe to the God of nature. And if done with a proper fenfe of fubmiffion to God, and dependance upon him for his favour and bleffing, this method of confulting our children's health and comelinefs, and

and securing their lives, seems as much an act of duty to them, as it is to restrain them, when in danger of doing wrong; rather than, by leaving them entirely to nature, to run the hazard of their contracting a deformity, or suffering a total destruction of their moral principles."

But still, said I, I can by no means think that I may lawfully bring a distemper upon my child.—— "To be sure," said the clergyman, " no man in his senses would make his child sick for the sake of sickness. But to make him sick in such a way as may probably be of service to his health, is not only lawful and right, but what we do every day. When I give him a purge, a vomit, or a blister, I certainly bring on a distemper for the time. Now if I may lawfully do this by giving him something in his mouth, or laying something on his back, why not by putting something into his arm or his leg? Or if I may lawfully make him sick for one day, why not for two days, a week, or more, as the case may require? —And that it does require it, is plain, because there is a perpetual danger of infection in the natural way; from which, though God can preserve my child if he will, I know of no warrant for thinking him secure. And really I must think that he, who, being equally liable to the small pox with others, is continually in the way of them without taking any measures for his safety, however some may call it faith or trust, or by any other splendid name, is chargeable, in fact, with very great presumption. To put the case in the following manner; If I have not had the small pox, there is something, call it what you will, that requires to be expelled; some fermenting matter that wants to be worked off; or some fuel, that wants but a spark to set it in a flame. The air I breathe is full of these sparks: if I take them in by my breath,

the

the fire will burn vehemently, and confume, perhaps, the body together with the fuel; but if I make an incifion in my arm, I get clear of this matter, fuel or ferment, without any, or with a very trifling, hazard. Why, then, muft I wantonly expofe myfelf to danger? Surely the law of felf-prefervation, which is the law of God, requires me to take the fafeft method."

But is it fo certain, anfwered I, that our children will, even thus, be fecure from danger?

" Why that, faid the clergyman, is a ftrange queftion, when the healthieft of us in company are by no means certain of living till we part. Why, then, fhould certainty be looked for here? I once knew a perfon that died by a vomit, and many perfons have died of lofs of blood from the drawing of a tooth; but would any one, for that reafon, refufe an emetic, or fubmit to the torments of a tooth-ach? It is furely fufficient if the chances be very much in favour of inoculation. Now, the faculty have told you in their report that one in fix die of the natural fmall-pox, and one in 500 by inoculation. I believe they have purpofely kept under the truth; for I remember a very capital practitioner once told me that the proportion of deaths was one in five in the one cafe, and one in 700 in the other; that is, that a perfon inoculated has above 130 times the chance of one who takes them in the natural way. A much lefs difproportion would be fufficient, in my opinion, to juftify the practice. And though I fhould doubtlefs be much affected by the lofs of a child by the fmall-pox, as well as by any other diforder, yet as I fhould be confcious that I had adopted the moft likely means of faving its life from a difeafe of uncommon danger, I fhould endeavour to fatisfy myfelf with having done my duty, and humbly refign my child to God, the great beftower of it.

C   " But

" But consider, on the other hand, my friend, (said he, turning to the master of the house) the case of these poor children, and reflect on the nature of the sensations you must feel, if, neglecting this opportunity, you should shortly behold their deformed and lifeless bodies the victims of this cruel disease, and wish, too late, that you had availed yourself of the means which are here so nobly offered to your acceptance."

I need not tell you, Mr. Printer, that we were wonderfully surprised with the good man's discourse, which, to those of us who were parents, appeared so rational and wise, that we agreed to apply immediately at the Dispensary for the assistance of the faculty upon this occasion; and I send you this, in hopes that our poor neighbours, who have been prevented by like scruples, may be induced by it to follow our example.

V. F.

TO THE EDITOR OF THE CHRISTIAN MISCELLANY.

SIR,

IT is to be lamented that, in the present age, the reading of the histories of persecutions is become rather unfashionable. To this circumstance, it is probable, we are, in some measure, to ascribe that general decay of proper religious principle, which has been so much complained of. At rest from persecution ourselves, and not familiarized with the sufferings of others, it was scarcely to be expected that our *attention* should be sufficiently drawn to the great truths of religion, or that we should feel their power. Nothing, it is apprehended, will better enable us to act, in common life, with that superiority which should characterize

terize the chriftian, or to encounter any difficulties which may attend us, than fuch an acquaintance with the hiftories of confeffors and martyrs, as will caufe us to enter into their fentiments and feelings, and to imbibe their fpirit. What trials any of us may be called upon to endure, what peculiar need we may have for the moft powerful principles, God only knows. Should you agree with me refpecting the propriety of introducing accounts of perfecutions into the Chriftian Mifcellany, and fhould the following fpecimen have your approbation, it fhall be followed by feveral articles of the fame kind. I would not confine myfelf to the firft chriftians, nor even to the proteftants who fuffered in the caufe of the reformation; but would take into my view catholics, baptifts and unitarians, who have diftinguifhed themfelves by their attachment to religious principle. Oppofite as were their creeds, they are to be confidered as all fuffering in one great caufe. Their fufferings do not eftablifh the truth of any particular tenets; but, what is more, they eftablifh the power and importance of chriftian views, and profpects.

I have generally referred to my authorities; which I thought right to do, as I have frequently ufed their own words very largely, without marking fuch quotations by inverted commas.

I am,

S I R,

Your's, &c.

ART. V. *Views of the Perfecutions which have been endured by confcientious perfons of different perfuafions.*

NUMBER I.

It was a very juft obfervation of the apoftle John, that his great lord was well acquainted with

C 2   the

the human heart. " He knew" (faid the beloved difciple) " what was in man." The difcourfes and the conduct of Jefus ftrongly confirmed the idea entertained by the evangelift. It was confirmed by the warning which he gave his followers, that men fhould " put them out of the fynagogue, and that the time would come, when whofoever killed them would think that he did God fervice." On hearing fuch an obfervation as this made in the prefent age of the world, one fhould not wonder. Alas! fince the days of Jefus, we have feen fo much perfecution for righteoufnefs' fake, that but a common knowledge of the world is fufficient to apprize us of the evils which a man may undergo in confequence of that untutored zeal with which too many breafts are warmed. Our lord was un-acquainted with thofe dreadful, bloody facts, which, at prefent, ftain every page of ecclefiaftical hiftory. But " he knew what was in man;"—he knew the ftrength of human paffions ; he knew how con-tracted are the views of mortals; he knew their ignorance of the amiable character of almighty God;—and, therefore, he could fay to his dif-ciples, with too much certainty, " the time cometh, that whoever killeth you, will think he doeth God fervice." Aftonifhing truth! that men fhould be fo depraved, fhould be fo infatuated, as to imagine that they could ferve God by mur-dering the excellent of the earth. But it was really fo. What Jefus foretold actually came to pafs. The apoftles were perfecuted. Their fuc-ceffors in the miniftry were perfecuted ; and not thefe only, but even the difciples in more private ftations.

The innocence and virtue which diftinguifhed fo eminently the lives of Chrift's fervants, and the fpotlefs purity of the doctrine they taught, were

not

not fufficient to defend them againft the virulence and malignity of the ruling powers. The priefts and leaders of the jews not only loaded with injuries and reproach the apoftles of Jefus, and their difciples, but condemned as many of them as they could to death, and executed, in the moft irregular and barbarous manner, their fanguinary decrees. The murder of Stephen, of James the fon of Zebedee, and of James furnamed the Juft, furnifh dreadful examples of the truth of thefe affertions. Of the martyrdom of Stephen and the fon of Zebedee, we have an account in the hiftory of the acts of the apoftles; and the melancholy end of James the Juft is fpoken of in ancient ecclefiaftical records. The jews who lived out of Paleftine in the Roman provinces, did not yield to thofe of Jerufalem, in point of cruelty to the innocent difciples of Jefus. We learn from the hiftory of the acts of the apoftles, and from other records, that they fpared no labour, but zealoufly feized every occafion of animating the magiftrates againft the chriftians, and fetting on the multitude to demand their deftruction. But however virulent the jews were againft the chriftians, they wanted, upon many occafions, power to execute their cruel purpofes. This was not the cafe with the heathen nations; and, therefore, from them the chriftians fuffered the fevereft calamities.

The Romans are faid to have purfued the chriftians with the utmoft violence in ten perfecutions; but this number is not verified by the ancient hiftory of the church. For if, by thefe perfecutions, fuch only be meant as were fingularly fevere, and univerfal throughout the empire, then it is certain, that thefe amount not to the number above mentioned. And, if we take the provincial and lefs remarkable perfecutions into the account, they far exceed it.

C 3   Nero

Nero was the firft emperor who enacted laws againft the chriftians. In this he was followed by Domitian, Marcus Antoninus the philofopher, Severus, and the other emperors, who indulged the prejudices they had imbibed againft the difciples of Jefus. All the edicts of thofe different princes, were not, however, equally fevere, or made with the fame view, or for the fame reafons. The judicial forms alfo were very different at different times, and changed naturally according to the mildnefs or feverity of the laws enacted by the different emperors againft the chriftians. Thus, at one time, we fee the moft diligent fearch made after the followers of Jefus; at another, all inquiry fufpended, and pofitive accufation and information only, allowed. (Mofheim, cent. 1. part 1. ch. v.) The emperor Trajan, in anfwer to a letter from Pliny, ordered " that the chriftians " fhould not be fought after; but that, if they " were accufed and convicted of being chriftians, " they fhould be punifhed: fuch only excepted as " fhould deny themfelves to be chriftians, and " give an evident proof of what they faid by " worfhipping the gods." Agreeably to this imperial injunction, Pliny only afked the accufed, Whether they were chriftians? If they confeffed it, he afked the fame queftion again and again, adding threats to his interrogations. If they perfevered in their confeffion, he condemned them to death; becaufe, whatever their confeffion might be, " their ftubbornnefs," (he perfuaded himfelf) " their inflexible obftinacy, deferved punifhment." Thus do men deceive themfelves, and quiet their confciences, by a vain fhew of equity! Yet, in this conduct, the emperor, his mafter, encouraged him. (Chandler's Hiftory of Perfecution, p. 23, 4.)

(*To be continued.*)

ART. VI.

ART. VI. *A Reflection on Suicide, as practised among the Ancients.*

THERE is a principle in man, usually called self-preservation, which appears to be the moving spring of his actions, and the first law of his nature. How is it, then, that he is so often found to plunge the dagger into his own breast with that very hand which was made for its defence and preservation? This absurdity, not to say impiety, the brutes have left to man.

If there be any thing more astonishing than self-murder in this view, it is, perhaps, that false and extravagant notion which the ancients entertained concerning it. This frightful monster they have not scrupled to array, sometimes in the fair garb of conjugal affection; sometimes in the splendid dress of heroism; sometimes in the venerable habit of religion. They have admired it for greatness of mind; they have extolled it for a social virtue; they have mistaken it for piety to the Gods.

Alas for the weakness and folly of human nature!

E. L. L.

ART. VII. *Character of the "History of Sandford and Merton."*

IN consequence of his opinion of the prevailing manners, and with a view to guard the rising generation against the infection of the ostentatious luxury and effeminacy, which, amid many excellent qualities, characterize the present age, Mr. Day wrote the history of Sandford and Merton. Despairing of the effects of reason, or even of ridicule, on those who have already acquired their habits, he hoped to

make

make fome impreffion on the untainted minds of youth. He did not confider the prefent age as defective, but perhaps fuperior to any other, in humane and generous inclinations; although thefe are too often rendered ineffectual by habitual expences and imaginary neceffities: and it did not appear to him, therefore, that the many ingenious books written lately for children, which principally inculcate humanity and generofity, were fufficient and adequate to all the ends required in the forming of youth. The evil which ought principally to be guarded againft, becaufe it is the moft predominant, is effeminacy of manners. In this age we fail more from want of firmnefs and ftrength than of fenfibility; more from the defect of thofe habits of fortitude, patience, and felf-controul, by which men are enabled to *be* what they approve, than from the prevalence of any vicious propenfity. Accordingly, the hero of this excellent novel is not, as in moft of thefe compofitions, a perfon of noble or princely birth in difguife; but a young peafant, whofe body is hardened by toil, who is enured to patience by the fatigues and abftinence of a laborious country life; whofe fortitude is confirmed by the habit of exertion; whofe appetite, whetted by hunger, prefers the plaineft food to the incitements of luxury. Happy in the free and natural exercife of his mind and body, he feels not the want of the fictitious pleafures of an opulent ftation, nor is he dazzled with its fplendor; while humanity, forgivenefs of injuries, and generofity, flow from his breaft without effort. Thefe manly virtues in young Sandford are contrafted by the feebler character of Merton; a boy bred up in affluence, effeminate indulgence, and the pride of wealth and ftation; whofe natural good difpofitions, yielding often to the foothings of vanity, are at laft confirmed

by

by the wisdom of a tutor, and by the example of the superior merit of the little peasant.

It is in this light, of counteracting the effeminacy and imbecility of the present manners, that the History of Sandford and Merton seems, in merit and in effect, to rise above any other work that has been written for children. And it will ever remain a monument of the benevolent and unambitious applications of Mr. Day's genius to the good of mankind. How well he has succeeded in the execution of his design appears evidently from the singular pleasure and interest with which the little readers run over these volumes. The book is written with a warmth that readily diffuses itself into the susceptible minds of youth, and is, indeed, admirably adapted

> To wake the soul by tender strokes of art,
> To raise the genius, and to mend the heart,
> To make mankind in conscious virtue bold,
> Live o'er each scene, and *be* what they behold.
>
> KEIR'S LIFE OF DAY.

P O E T R Y.

ART. VIII. *To the Poor.*

If, pure of hand, and pure of heart,
  To heav'n you lift your humble vows,
And pay, with grateful mind, the part
  Of service due, your lot allows;
The fost'ring influence from above
  Shall on your heads, like dew, descend;
Shall bless you with a Father's love,
  And make you feel your God, your Friend.

The

The confecrated dome to raife,
  And heav'n-ward point the glitt'ring fpire,
With gems to bid rich altars blaze,
  And fill with folemn founds the choir;

To feed with pomp devotion's flame,
  And fhew religion deckt with ftate;—
Thefe cares the high and wealthy claim:
  Then leave them to the rich and great.

Before the Sov'reign of mankind
  All earth-born fplendours fade away.
He feeks the tribute of the mind,
  And afks no more than *you* can pay.

Let thoughts of love and duty rife
  Warm from a guiltlefs bofom's ftore,
And truft in fuch a facrifice;
  Not crowns nor mitres offer more.

Dr. Aikin's Poems.

Art. IX.   *A Hymn.*

Hast thou beheld the glorious fun
Through all the fkies his circuit run,
At rifing morn, at clofing day,
Or when he beams his noon-tide ray?

  Say, didft thou e'er attentive view
The evening cloud, or morning dew,
Or, after rain, the watery bow
Rife in the eaft,—a beauteous fhow?

  When darknefs had o'erfpread the fkies,
Haft thou e'er feen the moon arife;
And, with a mild and placid light,
Shed luftre o'er the face of night?

  Haft thou e'er wander'd o'er the plain,
And view'd the fields and waving grain,

The

The flowery mead, the leafy grove,
Where all is melody and love ?

Haft thou e'er trod the fandy fhore,
And heard the reftlefs ocean roar,
When, rous'd by fome tremendous ftorm,
Its billows rofe in dreadful form ?

Haft thou beheld the lightening ftream
Thro' night's dark gloom, with fudden gleam,
While too the bellowing thunder's found
Roll'd rattling through the heav'ns profound ?

Haft thou e'er felt the cutting gale,
The fleety fhow'r, the biting hail ;
Beheld bright fnow o'erfpread the plains,
The water bound in icy chains ?

Haft thou the various beings feen,
That fport along the valley green,
That fweetly warble on the fpray,
Or wanton in the funny ray ;

That fhoot along the briny deep,
Or under ground their dwellings keep,
That thro' the gloomy foreft range,
Or frightful wilds and deferts ftrange ?

Haft thou the wond'rous fcenes furvey'd,
That all around thee are difplay'd ?
And haft thou never raifed thine eyes,
To him who bad thefe fcenes arife ?

'Twas God who form'd the concave fky,
And all the glorious orbs on high ;
Who gave the various beings birth,
That people all the fpacious earth.

'Tis he who bids the tempeft rife,
Or rolls the thunder through the fkies :
His voice the elements obey ;
Through all the earth extends his fway.

His

His goodnefs all his creatures fhare,
But man is his peculiar care :
Then, while they all proclaim his praife,
Let man his voice the loudeft raife.

ART. X.   *On a Grove of Poplar Trees.*

I.

The Poplars are fled; and adieu to the fhade,
And the whifp'ring found of the cool colonnade :
The winds play no longer, and fing in the trees,
Nor the eye in its furveys its image receives.

II.

Twelve years had elaps'd fince I laft took a view
Of my fav'rite field, and the bank where they grew ;
When, behold ! on their fides on the grafs they were
    laid,
And I fat on the trees under which I had ftray'd.

III.

The blackbird has fought out fome other retreat,
Where the hazels afford him a fcreen from the heat ;
And the fcene where his note has oft charm'd me
    before,
Shall refound with his fmooth-flowing ditty no more.

IV.

My fugitive years are all hafting away ;
And I muft myfelf lie as lowly as they,
With a turf on my breaft, and a ftone at my head,
Ere another fuch grove rifes up in its ftead.

V.

The change both my heart and my fancy employs ;
I reflect on the frailty of man and his joys :
Short-lived as we are, yet our pleafures, we fee,
Have a ftill fhorter date, and die fooner than we.

THE

THE REVIEW.

Art. 1. *The Meaning which the word, " Myftery,"
bears in the New Teftament*; confidered and applied, in a Sermon, preached to an Affembly of
Minifters, on the Thurfday Morning's Lecture,
at Exeter, May 4, 1791. By Jofhua Toulmin,
M.A. 8vo. pp. 22. 6d. Johnfon. 1791.

Of the various obftacles to the general reception
of religious truth, a belief that the fcriptures contain doctrines which cannot be underftood, and
which muft not be examined, is, perhaps, the moft
powerful, and the moft common. In fupport of
particular tenets, expreffions which were once
plain and familiar, have been mifapplied and dif-
torted; till, at length, by the aid of cunning and
credulity, they have formed " a kind of facred
veil," which few have courage and good fenfe
enough to draw afide. This is remarkably the
cafe with the word, *myftery.*

It muft be very evident, that, where this prejudice is formed, an attempt to enlighten the underftanding refpecting thofe fubjects to which its
influence extends, will univerfally prove fruitlefs.
If we wifh mankind to entertain right opinions
concerning any object, we muft firft perfuade them
to behold it. If we would lead them to think
juftly, we muft previoufly engage their attention.

The defign of Mr. Toulmin in this fermon
(from 1 Cor. ii. 7.) is to promote the interefts of
religion both among chriftians and unbelievers,
by proving that the gofpel does not countenance
the fuppofition of its containing any doctrines
which cannot be explained or underftood. With
this

this view, he inquires into the origin of the word, *myftery*, examines the places in the New Teftament, where it occurs, and fhews ' that it fignifies, not an incomprehenfible doctrine, but a truth which had been hidden and concealed from mankind, but was, at length difcovered and made known. It denotes nothing more than a fecret; or, a point on which men had, for fome time, received no information. " And in the fame manner as the word, *fecret*, is ftill made ufe of, after it is divulged; (as, when we fay, the fecret is well-known;) fo the word, *myftery*, is ufed to fignify the doctrines of the gofpel, even after they had been publicly taught and explained."*

This account of the meaning which the word bears in fcripture, lays a foundation for fome very ferious and important obfervations, with which the difcourfe clofes.

The fubject of this fermon, and the manner in which it is treated, will render it ufeful to every clafs of readers. Good fenfe, and a fpirit of moderation, are every where apparent. While it proves the fallacy of that fuppofition which has excited the derifion and contempt of the unbeliever, it will encourage the fincere and upright chriftian to *fearch* thofe *fcriptures which teftify of* Chrift; to examine and to judge for himfelf.

* Ben Mordecai's Letters, 8vo. vol. 2. p. 895.

Art. 2. A Charge delivered to the Clergy of the Diocefe of Landaff, June, 1791. By Richard Watfon, D.D. F.R.S. Lord Bifhop of Landaff, 4to. pp. 20. 1s. Evans. 1792.

Various as are the religious opinions embraced by the profeffors of chriftianity, it would be happy if all were agreed in the unreferved declaration of
their

their fentiments, and in the exercife of candour and liberality towards others. An example of this temper, fo pleafing to the friend of truth, and to the benevolent difciple of Jefus, is exhibited in the prefent publication.

The author is a firm friend to our conftitution both in church and ftate. He admires it " as a " glorious fabric of civil and religious freedom;" and, while he thinks that fome parts require alteration, is anxious to preferve it from being rudely and indifcriminately levelled to the ground. His great defign, in this Charge, is to point out fome alterations in the ecclefiaftical conftitution of France, which merit our notice and approbation. Under the laft head, he thus ably pleads the caufe of toleration and free inquiry.

' It muft be admitted as a fundamental truth, derived from the equality in which we all ftand to Chrift our common mafter, that no fociety of chriftians whatever, or however diftinguifhed by rank, power, wealth, numbers, learning, can have the leaft claim to any juft authority of compelling others by threats, or calumnies, or penalties of any kind, to a fellowfhip of worfhip. You, they ought to fay to all who diffent from them, are as free as we are. We affect no dominion over your faith. We are not the lords of God's heritage. Go and worfhip the Creator and Confervator of the univerfe in your own way; but fuffer us to worfhip God in our way. Let neither of us find fault with the other; but, preferving good-will, practifing courtefy, interchanging good offices, let us all be perfuaded that, at the laft day, our different fervices will be accepted by him, whom God hath appointed Judge of all, with equal regard to the rectitude of our feveral intentions, and to the means we have ufed in acquiring information concerning the truth.

One

One of the beſt means we can uſe for the attain-ment of this end, is to keep our minds unpreju-diced, open to argument, and free from every de-gree of acrimony of ſentiment or expreſſion, againſt thoſe who differ from us on any point either of doctrine or diſcipline.

'In fine, my brethren, you, perhaps, will think it to be your duty, and I am convinced that it is mine, to endeavour to ſecure the protection of God in another world, by propagating the pure goſpel of his ſon in this; and the purity of that goſpel can by no mean be ſo well aſcertained as by a modeſt and ſincere inquiry into what has been written by the evangeliſts and apoſtles, rather than into what has been delivered by Calvin or Armi-nius, by Sabellius or Socinus.'

What man is there, poſſeſſed of a liberal and candid mind, who, however different his opinion on other ſubjects, will not approve ſuch ſentiments as theſe? Who is there that is not convinced that ſuch is the temper of the humble and benevolent chriſtian?

Art. 3. A View of the Character and Public Ser-vices of the late John Howard, Eſq. LL.D. F.R.S. By John Aikin, M.D. 12mo. pp. 248. 3s. 6d. Johnſon. 1792.

Juſtly as well as beautifully, has it been ſaid, that "Howard, in the gloomy cells of priſons, found glory, and made the peſtilential effluvia of dungeons perfume and preſerve his name.* If diſtinguiſhed integrity, benevolence and perſeverance can merit our approbation, and deſerve *to be had in everlaſt-ing remembrance,* few perſons have had a better claim
than

* Monthly Review for Dec. 1791, p. 389.

than Mr. Howard to be enrolled in the records of fame, and to be decorated by the grateful praifes of his fellow-men.

In this tributary offering to the memory of the friend of mankind, Dr. Aikin, whofe intimacy with Mr. Howard, and whofe literary abilities un-queftionably qualified him for the undertaking, has prefented us with a " portrait of him, modelled upon thofe circumftances which rendered him emi-nent; difplaying, in their rife and progrefs, thofe features of character which fo peculiarly fitted him for the part he undertook, the origin and gradual developement of his great defigns, and all the fuc-ceffive fteps by which they were brought to their final ftate of maturity. The readers of the Chrif-tian Mifcellany will be gratified by the following particulars of his birth, fecond marriage, and con-duct during his refidence at Cardington.

' John Howard was born, according to the beft information I am able to obtain, about the year 1727. His father was an upholfterer and carpet-warehoufeman in Long-lane, Smithfield, who, having acquired a handfome fortune, retired from bufinefs, and had a houfe firft at Enfield, and after-wards at Hackney. It was, I believe, at the former of thefe places that Mr. Howard was born.

' In 1758 he made a very fuitable alliance with Mifs Henrietta Leeds, eldeft daughter of Edward Leeds, Efq. of Croxton, Cambridgefhire. With this lady, who poffeffed in an eminent degree, all the mild and amiable virtues proper to her fex, he paffed, as I have often heard him declare, the only years of true enjoyment which he had known in life.'

At Cardington near Bedford, to which eftate he returned three or four years after his marriage, he fteadily purfued thofe plans, both with refpect to

D   the

the regulation of his perfonal and family concerns, and to the promotion of the good of thofe around him, which principle and inclination led him to approve. Though without the ambition of making a fplendid appearance, he had a táfte for elegant neatnefs in his habitation and furniture. His fobriety of manners, and peculiarities of living, did not fit him for much promifcuous fociety; yet no man received his felect friends with more true hofpitality; and he always maintained an intercourfe with feveral of the firft perfons in his county, who knew and refpected his worth. Indeed, however uncomplying he might be with the freedoms and irregularities of polite life, he was by no meas negligent of its received forms : and, though he might be denominated a man of fcruples and fingularities, no one would difpute his claim to the title of a gentleman.

His charities were not confined to thofe more immediately connected with his property; they took in the whole circle of neighbourhood. His bounty was particularly directed to that fundamental point in improving the condition to the poor, giving them a fober and ufeful education. From early life he attended to this object; and he eftablifhed fchools for both fexes, conducted upon the moft judicious plan. The girls were taught reading, and needle-work in a plain way; the boys reading, and fome of them writing, and the rudiments of arithmetic. They were regularly to attend public worfhip in the way their parents approved. The number brought up in thefe fchools was fluctuating, but the inftitutions were uninterrupted. In every other way in which a man thoroughly difpofed to do good with the means providence has beftowed upon him, can exercife his liberality, Mr. Howard ftood among the foremoft.

In

In thefe inftances, and in many others, which will be evident to thofe who confult the volume itfelf, the fubject of it is very properly held up to our notice as poffeffing qualities ' not lefs to be ' imitated, than admired.'

Art. 4. *The Duty of Forgivenefs of Injuries*; A Difcourfe intended to be delivered foon after the Riots in Birmingham. By Jofeph Prieftley, LL.D. F.R.S. &c. 8vo. pp. 42. Pref. 8. 1s. Johnfon. 1791.

In whatever light we view Dr. Prieftley's theological fentiments, the truly chriftian fpirit which he has manifefted under his late perfecution will be allowed, by every candid obferver, to merit approbation and applaufe.

In this difcourfe, which was read to the congregations of both the Old and New Meeting at Birmingham, Dr. Prieftley enforces the duty of forgiving the inftigators and actors in the horrid fcenes they had witneffed, from the confideration of their *ignorance*, or thoughtlefsnefs; from the example of Chrift; and feveral other particulars immediately refpecting themfelves. He then proceeds to fhew what they might learn from, and what they ought to do in, their prefent circumftances.

' Let thefe calamities, like all others to which we are fubject in this ftate of trial, teach us the ufeful leffon of the uncertainty of all temporal enjoyments, and the importance of habitually looking forwards to fomething more ftable. The change of our condition from the moft pleafing to the moft difaftrous, was indeed fudden, and moft unexpected. As to myfelf, I did not know that I had five minutes from the firft intimation of danger to that of the neceffity of flying for my life, and of leaving behind me every thing that, next to my own life, and the lives of thofe who were moſt dear to me, I moſt valued in the world, viz. the fruits of my labour during a great part of my life. In this our adverfaries, I find, rejoice not a little. But may they never be brought into the fame alarming circumſtances, or fuftain equal loffes.

'Seeing, then, (he adds with the pholofophy of a chriftian) the inftability of all things in this world, let the event remind us of a country in which we fhall have nothing of this kind to dread; a country which will be the feat of wifdom, of virtue, and benevolence; where the voice of the oppreffor fhall no more be heard; but where the recollection of thefe fcenes, as having been the means of improving our virtue, and of promoting an extenfive good, will afford us the greateft fatisfaction.'

Surely every one who reads this well-written difcourfe with an unbiaffed mind, will, whatever be his particular views of religious truth, acknowledge that it contains much good fenfe, and that the Author has, in a very important inftance, fulfilled the great chriftian maxim, "do unto others as ye would that they fhould do unto you!"

A CATALOGUE

A CATALOGUE OF BOOKS,

PUBLISHED IN JANUARY, 1792.

THEOLOGY, MORALS, *and* POLEMICS.

Curfory Remarks; or an Enquiry into the Expediency and Propriety of Public or Social Worfhip. Infcribed to Gilbert Wakefield, B.A. By Eufebia. 6d. Knott.

A Charge delivered to the Clergy of the Diocefe of Landaff, June 1791. By R. Watfon, D.D.F.R.S. Lord Bifhop of Landaff. 1s. Evans.

Sermons, Chiefly intended to promote faith, Hope, and Charity. By Vicefimus Knox, D.D. 8vo. 6s. boards. Dilly.

The Sufferings of Revelation. A Sermon. By W. Turner, jun. 6d. Longman, &c.

The Forgivenefs of Injuries; a difcourfe intended to have been delivered foon after the Riots in Birmingham. By Jofeph Prieftley, LL.D.F.R.S. 1s. Johnfon.

The Spirit of perfecutors Exemplified; and the Conduct to be obferved towards their Defcendants. A Sermon, delivered at George's Meeting-Houfe, Exeter, Nov. 5. 1791. To which are prefixed, Some Obfervations upon the Caufes of the late Riots at Birmingham. By T. Kenrick, 8vo. Johnfon.

A Second Letter addreffed to the Inhabitants of Warwick, in Reply to the Remarks upon the Firft Letter, and upon a Letter to the Printer of the Birmingham Gazette, by the Reverend the Vicar and the Curate of St. Nicholas in Warwick. By W. Field, Minifter of the Diffenting Chapel in High-ftreet, Warwick. To which is added, a

Copy

Copy of the Letter to the Printer of the Birming-ham Gazette. 1s. Johnson.

POLITICS *and* POLICE.

High Church Politics, being a seasonable Appeal to the friends of the British Constitution, against the Principles and practices of High Churchmen, as exemplified in the late Opposition to the Repeal of the Tests Laws, and in the Riots at Birmingham. 3s. 6d. Johnson.

A Vindication of the Rights of Women; With Strictures on Political and Moral subjects. By Mary Wolstonecraft. Vol. 1. 8vo. 6s. boards. Johnson.

A Vindication of the Revolution Society, against the Calumnies of Mr. Burke. By a Member of the Revolution Society. 1s. 6d. Ridgway.

Considerations on the Present and Future State of France. By M. de Calonne, Minister of State. Translated from the French. Thick vol. 8vo. 17s. boards. Evans.

An Appeal to the Public on the subjects of the Riots at Birmingham. To which are added, Strictures on a Pamphlet entitled, Thoughts on the late Riots at Birmingham. By Joseph Priestley, LL.D.F.R.S. &c. 8vo. 3s. 6d. sewed. Johnson.

EDUCATION.

A particular Attention to the Instruction of the young, recommended in a Discourse delivered at the Gravel Pit Meeting in Hackney, December 4, on entering the Pastoral Office to the Congregation of Protestant Dissenters assembling in that place. By Joseph Priestley, LL.D.F.R.S. 1s. Johnson.

Elements

Elements of Morality; To which is prefixed an Introduction addreſſed to Parents. Tranſlated from the German of the Rev. C. G. Salzmaun. By Mary Wolſtonecraft. 3 vols. 10s. 6d. bound. Johnſon.

Plans of Education, By Clara Reeve. 3s. Hookham, &c.

HISTORY.

An Hiſtory of the Chriſtian Church. By G. Gregory, D.D. F.A.S. Two vols. 8s. boards. Kearſley.

An Hiſtorical Sketch of the French Revolution to the Commencement of 1792. 8vo. 7s. boards. Debrett.

The Parian Chronicle of the Arundelian Marbles, with a Diſſertation on its Authenticity. 5s. boards. Walter.

BIOGRAPHY.

Anecdotes of the Right Hon. William Pitt, Earl of Chatham, and the Principal Events of his time. With his Speeches in Parliament. 2 vols. 4to. 1l. 1s. boards. Jordan.

The Memoirs of Mrs. Billington, &c. 8vo. 3s. 6d. Ridgway.

Intereſting Anecdotes of Henry IV. of France. Tranſlated from the French. 2 vols. ſmall 8vo. 6s. boards. Debrett.

MEDICINE *and* CHEMISTRY.

An Analyſis of the Medicinal Waters of Tunbridge Wells. Royal 8vo. 1s. Murray.

Medical Commentaries for the Year 1791. By A. Duncan, M.D. F.R. and A.S. Ed. 8vo. 6s. boards. Hill, Edinburgh; Robinſons, London.

An Eſſay Philoſophical and Medical, concerning Modern Clothing. By Walter Vaughan, M.D. 3s. boards. Robinſons.

Crell's

Crell's Chemical Journal. vol. 2d. Baldwin.

POETRY *and* DRAMATIC.

Abelard to Eloifa, a Poem. By Mr. Jerningham. 1s. 6d. Robfon, &c.

Poems, By F. Sayers, M.D. 8vo. 4s. fewed. Johnfon.

An Epiftle to W. Wilberforce, Efq. 6s. fewed. Darton and Harvey, &c.

Poetic Laurels for Characters of Diftinguifhed Merit. By Maria and Harriet Falconer. 4to. 5s. Owen.

The Fugitive, a Comedy. By W. Roberts, Efq. Barrifter at Law.

NOVELS, &c.

The Female Werter, a Novel. Tranflated from the French. 2 vols. 12mo. 5s. fewed. Robinfon.

Memoirs of a Baronefs. By the Author of the Conquefts of the Heart, and the Victim of Fancy. 2 vols. 5s. fewed. Robinfons.

Curiofities of Literature, confifting of Anecdotes, Characters, Sketches, and Obfervations, Literary, Critical, and Hiftorical. 8vo. 6s. boards. Murray.

CORRESPONDENCE.

A Friend to Truth is received, and will be inferted in the next Number.

It is requefted that all communications for this Work be fent (Poft paid) directed to the Editor of the Chriftian Mifcellany, at Mr. Stalker's, No. 4, Stationers' Court, Ludgate-Street, London.

The Lift of Publications in this Number is unavoidably very incomplete. It is fubmitted to the confideration of the friends of the Work, whether its pages might not be more ufefully filled by additional mifcellaneous papers, or by the extenfion of the Review.

THE

Chriſtian Miſcellany,

For FEBRUARY, 1792.

ARTICLE I.

On the Evidence of the Truth of Chriſtianity.

WHEN any propoſition, which is not ſelf-evident, is offered to us as a truth, it is not unreaſonable to expect arguments or facts to demonſtrate it to be true ; or, if it be on a ſubject which does not admit of demonſtration, to render it ſo highly probable as to claim our rational belief. As many things are firmly credited by us which can never be ſtrictly demonſtrated to be true, but of which it would be abſurd to doubt; as our opinions and our conduct are daily influenced, with the utmoſt propriety, by a belief in ſuch things ; and as no one could ſcarcely act at all without a reliance on this belief; it is plain from abundant and univerſal experience, that nature intended us to reſt with confidence, both as to opinion and practice, on arguments or facts which only prove very great probability. If, therefore, with reſpect to their faith in chriſtianity, men were willing to be determined by the ſame kind of reaſoning which is ſufficient to convince them on other occasions, it would be difficult to assign a cause for the reluctance which some have shewn to receive it.

In the following essay, I shall endeavour to give the outlines of the evidence of christianity, in the manner in which it appears to me most convincing; appealing to our common mode of reasoning and consequent belief on similar occasions.

Were a person, perfectly unprejudiced, to be presented with the New Testament for perusal, as a work consisting of the writings of different men, with their names prefixed to these writings, no suspicion could arise in his mind, that they were not the real productions of these men, any more than that Cicero was not the author of the Orations attributed to him, or that Pliny did not write the Epistles to which his name is annexed. And in reading the work itself, the language, the style, the matter, the simplicity of the narration, and the frequent occurrence of the names of the authors in their compositions, would sufficiently convince him (as on other occasions) that the different parts of the collection before him were really written by those to whom they are attributed, and were perfectly suitable to the character, and situation of the authors, and to the age in which they lived.

But even if this decisive internal evidence were not deemed sufficient, if other proofs were to be demanded of the genuineness and antiquity of the books of the New Testament, we should be at no loss for such proofs. Both their genuineness and antiquity are clearly established by the *testimony of authors* who lived in the same period with the writers themselves, or who were their immediate successors. These authors, at a very early date, indubitably

indubitably quote paffages from the New Teftament in the fame manner as Ariftotle and Lon-
ginus quote Homer and the Tragedians, or as
Cicero quotes Ennius; that is, apparently from
memory, without having the books before them,
but certainly from the books themfelves. And in
the beginning of the fecond century, the quotations
(as is reafonably to be expected) are found ftill
more frequent and more full. If this did not appear fatisfactory, (as in any other cafe it evidently
would) it can be fhewn, that, in a few years after
the publication of the New Teftament, large bodies
of men received it as the guide of their belief.*

E 2 —It

* Whoever will read Dr. Lardner's account of, and extracts from, the Fathers, from Barnabas to Irenæus, will
find the moft unqueftionable external evidence of the genuinenefs of the books of the New Teftament. *All* thefe fathers,
from the year 70, or fooner, (for fome place Clement at 61,)
to the year 178, clearly quote from, (ufing the expreffion *as
it is written,* and other marks of quotation,) and allude to,
various parts of the New Teftament. Their quotations and
allufions, which are very abundant and very copious, agree
accurately, the former as to words, and the latter as to
meaning, with that copy of the New Teftament which we
now poffefs. In the writings of thefe fathers alfo is to be
found the moft decifive teftimony, that the Gofpels were
really written by thofe to whom they are attributed, the
apoftles, Matthew and John, and the companions of
apoftles, Mark and Luke: and likewife that the Acts,
Epiftles, and Revelation, are genuine productions; the
former, of Luke, and the reft, of the authors whofe names
they bear. In the time of Juftin Martyr, about 133, (if not
before,) the New Teftament was read and expounded to the
churches. The refurrection and the other miracles were
firmly credited in the times of thefe fathers: fome of whom
were acquainted with the apoftles themfelves, and, of courfe,
were the beft judges poffible of the genuinenefs of the books
of the New Teftament. Their evidence may be confidered
as that of the great body of chriftians of their time. *Heathen*
authors, alfo, of early date, refer to various parts of the
New Teftament, and to miracles as being recorded in it.
[See Lardner's Credibility, vol. ii.]

—It appears then, that *the genuinenefs and antiquity of the books of the New Teftament are as well, or rather better, attefted than the genuinenefs and antiquity of any profane author whatfoever.*

I conceive alfo that no one would for a moment deny, that an unprejudiced reader would give the fame credit,* at leaft, to the events, recorded in the New Teftament, which are not miraculous, as he would to the natural events recorded by Thucidides, by Julius Cæfar, or by Salluft; as being related either by eye-witneffes, or by thofe who were intimately connected with eye-witneffes, and who themfelves bore a part in fome of the tranfactions which they defcribe. The events in Judæa, narrated by fuch men, have the fame claim to belief, as thofe recorded to have happened in Greece. The voyage of Paul bears the fame marks of natural relation as the journies of Cæfar. The fimple reprefentation of affairs in the New Teftament, the various particulars of cuftoms, manners, times, perfons, converfations and places, the mention of circumftances apparently difadvantageous to the writers, or to thofe connected with
them,

* It might juftly be faid, *more* credit: for we find in the New Teftament the relations of four different authors of the hiftory of their own times; and thefe relations agree in fuch a manner as to reflect the ftrongeft authenticity upon each other, and, at the fame time, to prove that the authors *did not copy* from the work of any of them. We find alfo their accounts corroborated by the Epiftles of their cotemporaries. Now, can any thing be conceived more miraculous, than that four men fhould feparately compofe a hiftory entirely from their own imagination, without any foundation in truth, and that the hiftories of thefe four fhould accidentally agree with each other in a variety of important particulars? and, befides this, that the authors of the fame time fhould confirm, by their letters, the inventions of thefe four men? Yet fuch muft be the belief of thofe who difpute the truth of the evangelifts' narrations.

them, the difcourfes and character of Chrift, and the defign of his miffion as ftated by the evangelifts, are moft abundant and convincing proofs, that the authors did not fabricate the work in their own imagination.*

Neither is external evidence deficient on this head. The fuffering of Jefus Chrift under Pontius Pilate is recorded by Tacitus. The exiftence of the princes and governors mentioned in the **New Teftament**, the Roman and Jewifh cuftoms, the treatment of the Jews by the Romans, the exact time faid to have been fpent in the building of the temple, the famine and banifhment of the chriftians under Claudius, and other particulars in the New Teftament, are confirmed by the cleareft teftimony of heathen writers†. *The New Teftament, therefore, poffeffes all the marks of truth which any hiftory can poffefs.*

Nor can it be urged, that, on account of the fupernatural events recorded in the New Teftament, the whole is to be regarded as untrue. This is not our ufual way of judging. Our belief in the natural circumftances cannot reafonably be fhaken by the miraculous. For although in Livy and Tacitus we meet with the relation of fupernatural events, we do not therefore believe that their hiftories were forged or invented; nor do the prodigies, recorded in them, weaken our belief in the natural occurrences in the flighteft degree.

It cannot, again, be reafonably afferted, that it is probable, that the miracles in the New Teftament are interpolated inventions, and the reft true. We never decide in this manner with refpect to profane authors. We do not believe that the prodigies, related in Livy, were introduced by another hand. We

* Lardner's Pofthumous Sermons on the Internal Evidence of Chriftianity,
† Lardner's Credibility, vol. i.

We do not believe, that the ftory of Vefpafian and the figns at the deftruction of Jerufalem were interpolations into Tacitus. Befides this, the ftyle in which the miracles are written, the belief of the early fathers in them, and their being quoted by heathen writers of early date, as being in the Teftament, put this matter in the cleareft light.

No one can infift upon any alterations which may have been made in the New Teftament during the period through which it has exifted, as being fufficient to invalidate its authenticity. Thefe muft have been fewer than in profane authors; in which they are univerfally judged of little, or rather of no, importance. I fay *fewer*: for the New Teftament was more likely to be carefully preferved than any heathen author; and it would alfo be deemed an impiety to alter it.

As it has been proved, then, that the New Teftament is genuine, and that it has the fame marks, or rather more, of a true relation, than any heathen hiftory however credible; as its precepts, the precepts of forbearance, charity, peace and benevolence, are confeffedly fuperior to the pureft canons of philofophy; and as its promifes are agreeable to our nobleft wifhes; it is plain, that the only difficulty, attending its reception, muft arife from a reluctance to believe in the *miraculous* parts of it. This objection we fhall next proceed to confider.

(*To be continued.*)

ART. II. *View of the Perfecutions which have been endured by confcientious perfons of different perfuafions.*

(continued from page 22.)

Though the acts and fayings of the martyrs were carefully recorded, few of them are come down to our

our times. Many accounts of their lives and actions are but a feries of fables; fo that, upon the whole, this part of ecclefiaftical hiftory, for want of ancient authentic monuments, is extremely imperfect, and neceffarily attended with much obfcurity. The principal ancient church hiftorian, whofe works have been tranfmitted to our hands, is Eufebius, who flourifhed in the former part of the 4th century. This writer is very careful in citing his authorities for the facts he mentions; fo that it is clear he frequently fpeaks upon fome better foundation than vague report, and bold conjecture. From his hiftory we learn that the chriftians met with very injurious and cruel treatment under the reign of Marcus Antoninus the philofopher. In confequence of the imperial edicts, the judges and magiftrates received the accufations which the vileft of interefted informers brought againft the followers of Jefus. Thefe were put to the moft cruel tortures, and were abandoned to meet death in the moft barbarous forms, notwithftanding their perfect innocence, and their perfevering and folemn denial of the horrid crimes laid to their charge. The imperial edicts were fo pofitive and exprefs againft inflicting punifhment upon fuch of the chriftians as were guilty of no crime, that the corrupt judges, who, through motives of intereft or popularity, defired their deftruction, were obliged to fuborn falfe accufers, that might charge them with actions, which would bring them within the reach of the laws. Among the victims to popular fury, were many men of piety and eminence; as Polycarp, bifhop of Smyrna, and Juftin Martyr. (Mofheim.) Irenæus, who, when a young man, had a perfonal interview with Polycarp, fpeaks of him as a perfon that had been converfant with many who had feen Chrift, and as

having

having received inſtruction immediately from the apoſtles. He lived to a good old age, and at length finiſhed his courſe in his maſter's ſervice. Euſebius has given us a particular account of his martyrdom; copied from a letter which was written from the church to which Polycarp miniſtered, to the brethren of Pontus. Previouſly to their ſpeaking particularly concerning Polycarp, they call the attention of their fellow chriſtians to the firmneſs and patience of other worthy men.

They make particular mention of Germanicus, who, animated by the principles of the goſpel, valiantly overcame that fear of death which is naturally incident to frail mortals. It was in vain that the proconſul exhorted him to make a recantation. It was in vain that he reminded him of his tender age, and conjured him not to throw away the flower of his days. Germanicus was firm and immoveable, and ſacrificed his life to the cauſe of Chriſt. At the ſame time a multitude of faithful believers ended their lives in the midſt of cruel tortures. Polycarp, the epiſtle aſſures us, was unſhaken by the perſecution in which his fellow diſciples were involved, and with unruffled tranquillity of mind would have awaited, in the city, the fate to which he ſeemed to be deſtined. By the intreaties of his friends, however, he was prevailed upon to retire, for a ſeaſon, to the country. But he was purſued to the place of his retirement. The perſons who were ſent to apprehend him, found him in an upper chamber, from which he might have eſcaped, but he ſaid; " the " will of the Lord be done." A life ſo nearly ſpent, as his, (he poſſibly thought) was ſcarcely deſerving great anxiety and trouble; and could not be more uſefully ended, than in bearing his dying and public teſtimony to the truth of the religion of

Jeſus,

Jefus. It is faid, that he came down ftairs, and converfed with the officers with the greateft eafe and compofure of mind; and, having ordered provifions to be fet before them, requefted the liberty of fpending an hour in prayer before their departure. Having finifhed his devotions, they conducted him to the city, where he was met by one of the rulers, who, taking him into his chariot, urged him not to be too refolutely bent againft making fuch trifling conceffions as would fatisfy the people. " Can it be any harm" (faid he) " to fay, My lord Cæfar; to facrifice, and to be faved ?" But, perceiving that he was immoveable, the ruler had recourfe to more fevere expreffions; and even went fo far as to thruft him out of the chariot. Polycarp, however, walked with undaunted boldnefs to the theatre; where he appeared in the prefence of a tumultuous and inflamed rabble.

The proconful demanded of him, if he were Polycarp; and, upon being informed that he was, advifed him to have pity on his venerable years, to fwear by the fortune of Cæfar,—and to reproach Chrift. " Fourfcore and fix years" (anfwered Polycarp) " have I been his fervant; neither hath he once offended me. How, then, can I revile my king, and my faviour ?" He then unequivocally declared himfelf to be a chriftian; and added, that, if the proconful wifhed to be acquainted with the chriftian doctrine, he needed but appoint the day for receiving the information. " Perfuade this people," replied the proconful. " With thee I have conferred" (faid Polycarp) " for it is a dictate in our religion to render to princes and potentates the honour which is due unto them. But as for this furious multitude, it would be to little purpofe that I fhould open my mind to them."

F

them." " The wild beaſts are ready to devour thee," (cried the proconſul) " unleſs thou repent." " Bring them forth ;" (anſwered the chriſtian conſeſſor) " for with us it is determined never to be led by repentance from better to worſe. On the contrary, we eſteem it commendable to turn from what is evil to that which is good and juſt." Again the proconſul ſaid, " Since thou doſt not mind the beaſts, I will order thee to be conſumed by fire, unleſs thou repent." " Thou threateneſt the fire of an hour ;" (replied Polycarp) " fire which is quickly quenched ;—but thou art ignorant of the everlaſting fire of the great judgment day. But wherefore this delay ? Inflict what kind of death thou pleaſeſt." Such things as theſe he ſpoke with ſo much compoſure and cheerful firmneſs, as to amaze even the proconſul himſelf. The beadle was then commanded to cry aloud, in the theatre, thrice, " Polycarp confeſſeth himſelf to be a chriſtian."

Upon this the furious multitide ſhouted, with the utmoſt rage, " This is that teacher of Aſia, the father of the chriſtians, the overthrower of our gods, who hath perſuaded a great number, that our deities are not to be adored." They then deſired that a lion might be let looſe to devour him ; but this requeſt being denied, the multitude of jews and heathens, reſolutely bent upon his deſtruction, quickly raiſed a pile of wood, and began to nail him to the ſtake. " Stop; (ſaid the venerable confeſſor) that Being, who giveth me reſolution to endure the tortures of the flames, will alſo give me power to be ſteady to the ſtake, without any proviſion on your part." Having thus ſaid, he addreſſed himſelf to the Father of mercies, in ſtrains of gratitude, for having allotted him

him a place among the martyrs for the caufe of Chrift. His prayer being finifhed, they lighted the faggots; but, finding that he was not fo quickly confumed as they expected, a perfon was ordered to pierce him with a fword, which ended his labours and his torments.

Many other chriftians fuffered the fame cruel but honourable fate; among whom was one named Pionius, a man famous for the honeft boldnefs of his fpeech, for an Apology in favour of the faith, for his excellent fermons, for his comforting perfuafions addreffed to fuch as fainted in the hour of perfecution, and for the fortitude with which he endured his laft, dying tortures. [Eufebius ap. Fox's Acts and Monuments, Vol. I. and Lardner's Works, vol. vii. p. 412, &c.]

Having thus given an account of fome glorious fufferers in the caufe of truth, we may remark, that the difciples of Jefus were not the *firft* who perfecuted on account of religion. Chriftians, it is true, have fhamefully difgraced their religion by their conduct; but they were not the original authors of perfecution. They learnt the practice from the jews and heathens. It is a practice which we have feen countenanced and fanctioned by the wifeft and the moft virtuous of the Roman Emperors. It is not, therefore, fo much to be wondered at, that, in after ages, it was adopted by the difciples of Jefus. We find that, in numberlefs inftances, men are governed more by generally prevailing ideas, and the common practices of the world, than by principles and precepts peculiar to the religion they profefs. We know not how we might have acted in their circumftances; probably we fhould have acted juft as they did. Inftead, therefore, of hating the men, we fhould hate the *principles* of perfecution, and take every poffible means to fecure ourfelves from be-

F 2

having

having as they did, fhould we ever be placed in a fimilar fituation. We fhould be particularly cautious not to fuffer a review of fufferings which our forefathers endured in confequence of jewifh and heathen bigotry and intolerance, to occafion the leaft ill-will towards the jews of the prefent day. They are not chargeable with the fins of their forefathers; and their prefent depreffed and humiliating condition fhould excite our pity.

At the fame time, we cannot be too folicitous to cultivate that attachment to the truth, that virtuous independence of mind, that collected firmnefs in what is right, and that fpirit of habitual devotion, which were the foundation of the truly noble and chriftian conduct difplayed by our elder brethren in the gofpel.

ART. III. *Remarks on the Sermons of Dr. Charters.*

IT is obferved in Fitzofborne's letters, "that " eloquence has by no means made equal advances " in our country with her fifter arts;" and the ingenious writer expreffes his furprize on this account, confidering " that we have a profeffion fet " apart for the purpofe of perfuafion, and which " affords the moft animating and interefting topics " of rhetoric." That this obfervation is no longer applicable to the prefent times, and that pulpit eloquence has of late been highly improved, may be fhewn in a variety of inftances. My illuftrations, however, at prefent fhall be taken from the Sermons of Dr. Charters.

The great principle that feems to reign in thefe Sermons, is the *folemnity* or *dignity* of fincere and of rational *piety*. This is the prevailing fpirit; and appears to dictate the fentiments, the ornaments

ments, (for some ornament is not inconsistent with this principle) the method and expression, in almost every discourse. It is a grave, serious and manly spirit, deeply impressed with a sense of awful truths and sublime objects. It is a pensive spirit, deeply sensible of the weakness of our nature, the instability of our enjoyments, the trials and dangers of our present state. But still it is a vigorous and even a lofty spirit. Endowed with superior powers, it is not depressed by the sense of infirmity. Capable of apprehending great objects, or of entertaining large desires, it is not humbled with conscious abasement. Extending its views to such enjoyment as no mortal change can affect, it is not cast down by the uncertainty of human happiness. Neither anxious nor desponding, it displays an earnest, solemn and deep-toned eloquence. It remonstrates and reproves, but does not upbraid. It alarms, but does not terrify. It soothes and comforts, but does not transport. Nor is it so solicitous to melt the heart with transient emotion, or ravish the fancy with fugitive rapture; as to impress the whole heart and soul with an awful sense of the situation of the human mind, immortal, accountable, animated with high desires, endowed with mighty powers, beset with danger, and in a state of probation. The thoughts suggested by the contemplation of human misery and affliction, though not plaintive, nor of that deeply pathetic kind which convulses the heart, and gives relief by gushing tears, are yet tinged with an amiable tenderness that makes the heart heave, the eye swim with a complacent tenderness, which, while it suffers, smiles.

Are not the sentiments, in the following passages, illustrative of these remarks?—" When the shadow " of death is changed into the morning, the heart

" feels

" feels joy unutterable, afcends in holy gratitude,
" and communicates with the fountain of joy."—
" The death of a parent is often the firft fad
" ftroke. The bright fcene vanifhes. Pleafure
" is fhut out. Your firft forrow is a facred feafon;
" facred to affectionate remembrance, to devout
" refignation, to the faith of immortality. Sober
" thoughts revolve on the part you have to act.
" In returning to the world, you feel yourfelf a
" ftranger, and caft your cares on God, and think
" of heaven as your father's houfe."—" It is
" fometimes difficult to fulfil the demands of juf-
" tice. Then a chriftian redoubles induftry, de-
" nies himfelf, accepts alms, does every thing hard
" and humbling, rather than be unjuft. It is not
" his leaft confolation, that the time is fhort."
Addifon fays of Virgil in his Georgics, " that he
" delivers the meaneft of his precepts with a kind
" of grandeur; he breaks the clods, and toffes the
" dung about, with an air of gracefulnefs." In
the foregoing paffage, we have a mendicant taking
alms with the majefty of a faint; we recollect the
dignity of Epictetus in bondage.—To thefe examples of elevated and affecting fentiment, I fhall
add the following. It is alfo a ftriking example
of our author's defcriptive talents. " Some have
" hours of deep and awful melancholy. Darknefs
" overfpreads the foul. All earthly enjoyments
" lofe their relifh. The ordinary cares of life are
" a burden. Even friends difpleafe. There is
" an appetite for retirement, for ' the lodging place
" of a wayfaring man in the wildernefs'; to fit
" alone, and liften to the howling winds, and fee
" the leaves falling, and mufe on the end of man.
" With difficulty we are dragged to the duties of
" life, and ' fulfil, as an hireling, our day.'—The
" foul is ftruggling through the mift of human
things

" things, to know their emptinefs, to know itfelf,
" to know its large capacity for happinefs, which
" God alone can fill."

The rational and exacted devotion which charac-
terizes thefe fermons, is, indeed, perfectly confiftent
with glowing emotions and an active imagination.
The figures and imagery, therefore, which the
ardent and fanciful mood brings along with it, are
not only admitted, but properly introduced. The
metaphor, for inftance, in the following paffage, is
happily applied. It fuggefts agreeable objects, it is
ingenioufly but judicioufly extended, and, in all its
circumftances, well preferved. " Cultivate the
" fruits of the fpirit, faith, hope, and love. Thefe
" flourifh in the winter of life; they are rooted in
" the foul; and the decay of thefe bodies, and the
" diffolution of this world, cannot deftroy them.
" They fhall foon be tranfplanted into the garden
" of God, and watered with the river of pleafure,
" and fpring up into eternal life. Every root of
" bitternefs fhall be plucked up, and no enemy
" fhall fow his tares any more." The metaphor
is indeed obvious; nay more it is not original; ftill
farther, the preacher, in the laft claufe, fuggefts to
us whence it is taken. But till he does fo, we are
not aware of it; the allufion comes out unexpectedly. He thus makes an obvious image excite
furprize, and arrays a well known object with the
grace of novelty.——The following paffage gives an
excellent example of the interefting effect and
happy application of queftion and anfwer. " To
" have the fympathy of one who is liable to the
" fame infirmity, who has fuffered the fame dif-
" trefs, who is interefted in our welfare, who is able
" in due time to work deliverance; this is ftrong
" confolation, and this confolation flows from
" Chrift, made in all things like his brethren.
" Are

" Are they poor and deſtitute in the world? He had
" not where to lay his head. Are they unkindly
" treated by their friends? He came to his own,
" and his own received him not. Is their good name
" unjuſtly taken away? He was made of no repu-
" tation. Is their good, evil ſpoken of, and re-
" quited with perſecution? He was deſpiſed, and
" rejected, and numbered with tranſgreſſors, &c.

The method, obſerved in theſe diſcourſes, has an
appearance of ſingularity. They have not the for-
mal introduction or regular peroration, required
by rhetorical critics; nor are the diviſions, in many
of them, very obviouſly or directly announced.
This apparent ſingularity, however, ſeems to depend on the ſame principle that dictates the ſentiment, and directs the embelliſhment. It is conſiſtent with the ſerious ſolemnity of rational and
ſincere devotion. In ſuch a ſtate of mind, the
preacher reaſonably believes that his audience, deſirous of improvement, are diſpoſed to give due
attention. He may, therefore, hold it ſufficient,
unleſs ſome previous difficulty require explanation,
merely to announce his ſubject. He may think long
introductions, unleſs they are neceſſary, inexpedient.
—He may think the ſame remarks applicable to the
coneluſions; and that diſcourſes, intended to inſtruct, and incite men, by rational conſiderations,
to the performance of religious and moral duties,
ſhould conclude with their ſubject, nor tire the
hearer with repetition. Still, however, the abrupt-
neſs manifeſt in theſe diſcourſes, though conſiſtent
with, or flowing from, the prevailing principle, is
unuſual; nor need the preacher be ſurprized, if
readers, accuſtomed to another method, ſhould wiſh
that he had lifted them up and let them down, more
gradually. At the ſame time, readers of true taſte
will remark, in ſome inſtances, the happy effect
even

even of this abruption. In cafes where the laft objects, prefented to our thoughts, are awful or interefting, when the mind is thrown into a fort of
extacy, and is inclined to purfue its own affocia-
tions; the filence of an abrupt conclufion is often
folemn, if not fublime. Take the following example. "We are ftrangers who have fojourned
"in a foreign land, and have the near profpect of
"returning home. The hour of departure rifes
"on the foul; for we are going to a land peopled
"with our fathers and our kindred and the friends
"of our youth. The heart fwells at times with
"the fadly pleafing remembrance of the dead."——
"Awake and fing ye that fleep in the duft. Your
"dew is as the dew of herbs." "At times we
"overpafs, by faith, the bounds of mortality, and
"penetrate within the veil. Our fpirits mingle
"with theirs."——A fimilar account may be given
of the preacher's mode of laying down the parts
into which his fermons are divided. An attentive
reader will obferve in them a regular, and very
often, as in the firft and fecond difcourfes, a fine
progrefs of thought; but the tranfitions are not
always very formally or directly announced. The
preacher, deeply impreffed with the importance of
his doctrine, and fenfible, at the fame time, that it
is not abftrufe or difficult, was, perhaps, of opinion
that his arrangement was abundantly clear. It is
indeed very frequently announced, but not in the
ufual manner; nor always in the ufual place.
Sometimes it is delivered indirectly, eafily, or
without feeming intention; and is fometimes fuggefted as a recapitulation at the end. In all thefe
methods there is a pleafing variety, which, to an
attentive reader, makes ample atonement for the
fingularity. Befides, the abruption and departure
from cuftomary form have a tendency to excite at-

G   tention.

tention.—The brevity of expreſſion, remarkable in theſe diſcourſes, has alſo a ſimilar effect. The author's periods, if they may be ſo termed, have often the air of abſtract and ſententious maxims. Hence ſome of the critics who have made obſervations on theſe diſcourſes, attentive to the form and ſize of the ſentences, rather than to the thoughts they convey, have conſidered them as containing heads for ſermons, rather than as diſplaying a full diſcuſſion of particular ſubjects. An attentive reader, however, will eaſily perceive that, in general, every ſubject is treated as diffuſively as needful, and that all the ſentences are intimately, though not, perhaps, on all occaſions, very obviouſly connected. In their moſt incoherent appearances, they exhibit, both in the choice of words, and ſtructure of parts, uncommon beauty and propriety of expreſſion.— Upon the whole, theſe ſermons are not to be read in a deſultory, curſory manner. They ſeem to have been written under a deep ſenſe of the ſolemn and awful views they diſplay. They require, and are entitled to, a ſerious peruſal.

PHILOTHEON.

ART. IV. *A Parable againſt Perſecution, in Imitation of Scripture Language.* *

AND it came to paſs, after theſe things, that Abraham ſat in the door of his tent, about the going down of the ſun.

And

* I have taken this piece (ſays the Editor of Franklin's Works) from the *Sketches of the History of Man*, written by lord Kaims, and ſhall preface it with his lordſhip's own words.

‘ The following *Parable againſt Perſecution* was communi‘cated to me by Dr. Franklin of Philadelphia, a man who
‘ makes

And behold a man bent with age, coming from the way of the wildernefs, leaning on a ftaff.

And Abraham arofe, and met him, and faid unto him, Turn in I pray thee, and wafh thy feet, and tarry all night; and thou fhalt arife early in the morning, and go on thy way.

And the man faid, Nay; for I will abide under this tree.

But Abraham preffed him greatly: fo he turned, and they went into the tent; and Abraham baked unleavened bread, and they did eat.

And when Abraham faw that the man bleffed not God, he faid unto him, Wherefore doft thou not worfhip the moft high God, Creator of heaven and earth?

And the man anfwered and faid, I do not worfhip thy God, neither do I call upon his name; for I have made to myfelf a god, which abideth always in my houfe, and provideth me with all things.

And Abraham's zeal was kindled againft the man, and he arofe, and fell upon him, and drove him forth with blows into the wildernefs.

G 2　　　　　　　　　　　　　　　And

' makes a great figure in the learned world; and who would
' make a ftill greater figure for benevolence and candour,
' were virtue as much regarded in this declining age as
' knowledge.
' The hiftorical ftyle of the Old Teftament is here finely
' imitated; and the moral muft ftrike every one who is net
' funk in ftupidity and fuperftition. Were it really a chap-
' ter of Genefis, one is apt to think that perfecution would
' never have fhewn a bare face among jews or chriftians.
' But alas! that is a vain thought. Such a paffage, in the
' Old Teftament, would avail as little againft the rancorous
' paffions of men, as the following paffages in the New
' Teftament, though perfecution cannot be condemned in
' terms more explicit. " Him that is weak in the faith,
" receive you, but not to doubtful difputations. For, &c."

And God called unto Abraham, saying, Abraham, where is the stranger?

And Abraham answered and said, Lord, he would not worship thee, neither would he call upon thy name; therefore have I driven him out from before my face into the wilderness.

And God said, have I borne with him these hundred and ninety and eight years, and nourished him, and clothed him, notwithstanding his rebellion against me; and couldst not thou, who art thyself a sinner, bear with him one night?

ART. V. *Plan for promoting Religious Knowledge.*

TO THE EDITOR OF THE CHRISTIAN MISCELLANY.

SIR,

A small number of gentlemen residing at some distance from each other in the country, but near enough for occasional meetings, propose to form themselves into a society for diffusing rational principles of religion. They have conceived a plan of their own for this purpose; but, before they resolve to adopt it, I apprehend it might be useful to them to have before them the sentiments of some of your correspondents, through the channel of the Christian Miscellany, upon the best means of accomplishing the object they have in view: whether it may best be done by the distribution of books, by supporting ministers of rational sentiments in religion, with societies which are too small or too poor to give them an adequate support themselves; by providing education for young persons of good talents and unexceptionable moral character, in order that they may be qualified to preach; or in what other way the interests of virtue and unadulterated christianity, chriftianity may be moft effectually promoted. If any gentleman, who has thefe interefts at heart, will fketch out fuch a fcheme as is practicable, adapted to the views of fuch a Society, and to the prefent fituation of things, he may fuggeft fomething which has efcaped the attention of thofe immediately concerned, and contribute effentially towards perfecting a valuable defign.

I am,

SIR, &c.

A FRIEND TO TRUTH.

ART. VI. *The Negro.*

——" Alas! I am very faint and very feeble," faid a voice which mifery feemed to have rendered almoft inarticulate. They were the words of a poor Negro, who, oppreffed by the heat of the fun, (for the day was hot and fultry) in a languid pofture was enjoying a fhort refpite from his labours. Curfe on European avarice that deals in cargoes of wretchednefs, and thrives by the traffic of defpair! I exclaimed the very moment my imagination caught the picture. Perhaps, faid I, this child of forrow has been torn from a father,—a mother. Nature muft have pleaded very loudly againft his captivity; for I thought I could perceive the tears of affection ftanding in his eyes. Or, perhaps, he has loved—one who returned his vows with an equal paffion, and for whom his heart beat high with rapture. Perhaps, he has looked forward, with eager expectation, to the days he feemed deftined to pafs with the companion of his youth; and now —— I thought on thee, Eliza, the partner

partner of my life, and I endeavoured to divert my thoughts from the gloomy road they were purfuing;—but in vain. My captive fpoke ftill louder.

"I once was happy," faid he. "When I lived "beyond thefe great waters, I heard not the yells "of defpair; the gale rung not with the fhrieks of "the wretched. Our hut was in a cool valley, "beneath the fhade of the lofty palm-trees. My "labours then were fweet; for I feared neither "ftripes nor mafter. My work in the fields pro- "vided my father with food, and he repaid with "fmiles the toil of his fon. All was joy, all was "pleafure. Strong and cheerful, I hailed the "breezes of the morning; at noon I bathed in "the ftream, and in the evening joined the happy "dance in the meadow. But now" - - - - - Wretched captive!

"I loved, alas! the beauteous Yoncha. She "was the theme of every fong, the envy of fur- "rounding virgins. For her love I fought, and "made two heroes bow at my feet. The maid "of my heart trembled for my fafety, and hailed "my victory with the fmiles of rapture. I "brought her the cluftered bananas. From my "hand, fhe faid, they were more lufcious. For "her I climbed the airy cocoa-tree, and threw "into her lap the milky fruit. In the chafe, fhe "nerved my arm with ftrength, and infpired my "breaft with courage. Then I fmiled on dan- "ger; I heeded not death. I attacked the indig- "nant foe in his den. Though his eyes gliftened "with anger, I pierced him, and he bled for "Yoncha. I carried home the fpoils of the "battle, and placed them in her bower. But now, "alas! fhe bleeds for her loft warrior. She hears "not his groans. He pines in flavery; he lingers "for

" for the ftroke of death. Ah me! the deep
" ocean divides us.—Methinks the breezes that
" play on the furface of the waters, might waft
" her a figh, or a prayer. I have often afked
" them, but they feem not to regard me."

Wretched captive!

" We were dancing on the green in the evening,
" and we dreaded not the hour of danger. But
" the tall fhip anchored in the ftream, and trea-
" chery lurked for our captivity. In vain we
" wept. The whites heed not the fighs of the
" negro. They knew not the treafure I have left
" behind me. She may yet be fafe!—I recal the
" fcenes of pleafure I partook with her, and me-
" mory adds new horrors to defpair."

Wretched captive!

" I have toiled till my hand is feeble. I muft,
" therefore, expect more lafhes. The white men
" are very powerful; for their Gods are ftronger
" than ours. They are not appeafed by the fighs
" of the negro. Our labours are bitter; but they
" furnifh a rich fweet for our mafters."—

And are thy fighs, wretched negro! thus ferved
up as a repaft to our luxury? Shall we not reject the drug thy forrows have prepared? Shall we
drown thy cries in the roar of the caroufal, while thy
tears are mantling in the bowl, and mixing it with
the gall of human anguifh?—No!—Be affured,
injured captives! your fighs have been wafted to
a corner of the globe where Humanity feldom
cries in vain. She has pleaded the caufe of mil-
lions, and the caftles of defpotifm have funk before
her. Why fhould we join in this facred triumph,
and our colonies refound with the yells of mifery,
and the pangs of infulted nature?

Gracious God! thy ways are infcrutable; but
thou haft furely fixed this to be the period of their
servitude:

fervitude : and, though thou haft divided us from thefe our fable brethren by a wide ocean, and mark-ed them with the livery of a fiercer climate, thou now requireft of us to reftore them the ravifhed *charter* of their *natures*, and erect on their coaft the white ftandard of *liberty* and *happinefs* !

ART. VII. *Anfwers to the Objections againft ab-ftaining from Weft Indian Productions.*

TO THE EDITOR OF THE CHRISTIAN MISCELLANY.

S I R,

You cannot but be acquainted with the practice which prevails fo much in many parts of England of abftaining from Weft Indian productions; and I conceive you will not be unwilling to infert in your Mifcellany the following replies to the objec-tions that have been ftarted againft a practice which certainly originated from the moft humane prin-ciples, and the tendency of which cannot but be beneficial.

The firft objection which I have heard is, that " it is not likely to be of any fervice." To this it may be replied, that the practice appears rapidly fpreading through England; that in Germany and France it has alfo been begun. Is it reafonable, then, to fuppofe that the Englifh, the Germans and the French are the only people who feel for the fufferings of others? But even if the practice was not efficacious, ftill every one, who abftains from Weft Indian productions, has the fatisfaction of knowing that he does not, by confuming, in effect partake of the crimes attending the pro-curing of thefe productions.

A fecond

A fecond objection is, that "thofe who abftain wifh to injure the revenue." Is this at all probable? Are not men of all parties to be found in their number? Did they not confume fugar, before they were aware that they were doing wrong? Would they not again confume fugar, if they could procure it without injuftice?

A third objection is, that " an immediate abolition of flavery would produce the worft of confequences." But who contends for an *immediate* abolition? An immediate ftop to the *importation* of flaves would compel planters to ufe them well for their own fakes.

It has been faid, with a fneer, that " œconomy has much to do in this bufinefs." Is œconomy lefs praife-worthy, becaufe it is the affociate of humanity? And, fifthly, " a parade of benevolence" has been urged againft the refrainers from fugar and rum. It is not much to any man's difcredit to wifh to be firft in doing good; but, in the prefent cafe, it will be found that thofe who have refrained from fugar, for fome time experienced the ridicule, rather than the applaufe of their neighbours.

I am, Sir,
Your obedient, humble fervant,
K. S.

TO THE EDITOR OF THE CHRISTIAN MISCELLANY.

S I R,

I SHALL efteem myfelf obliged to you, if you will infert the inclofed in your ufeful publication. It is copied from the common-place book of a friend lately dead; who, there is reafon to think, never intended it for the public eye.

I am, Sir, &c.
A. Z.

H ART. VIII.

ART. VIII. *A Fragment.*

—HE gives his mite to the relief of poverty. Joy enlivens his countenance, and pleasure sparkles in his eye. He can lay his hand upon his heart, and say,—" I have done a good thing." But who can do justice to his feelings ?—none but those whose lips the God of Israel hath touched with sacred fire! none but those whose pens are guided by the inspiration of the Almighty! And though at this moment my heart expands with the delightful sensation, I am totally unable to express it.—Most devoutly do I thank thee, O Lord, that thou hast given me feeling. The sensation, indeed, is sometimes painful; but the intellectual pain far excells the most delightful sensual pleasure.—Ye kings and princes of the earth ! possess in peace your envied grandeur. Let the epicure gratify his palate; let the miser hoard his gold in peace. Dear Sensibility ! do thou but spread thy benign influence over my soul, and I am sure I shall be happy.

He held out his hat. " Pity me," says he, but turned away his face, to hide his blushing countenance, and the tear which stole down his cheek. I saw it though ; and that little tear, with a force as powerful as the inundations of the Nile, broke through all the bounds of cautious prudence. Had the wealth of the Indies been in my pocket, I could not but have given it. I gave all I had.— He cast his glistening eyes upon me.—" You have saved a family. May God bless you !"—With my then sensations, I could have been happy through eternity. At that instant, I could have wished all the wheels of nature to have stopped.

POETRY.

POETRY.

Art. IX. *Ode to Fancy.*

When the fun has left the fky,
And grey clouds through the Welkin fly,
When evening breezes fan the vale,
And waft thy fong, fweet nightingale!
With varied fteps will Fancy rove
Through the folitary grove.
Oft will fhe wildly ftretch her hand,
Waving round her ebon wand:
While to the ravifhed eye appears
The progeny of other years;
Secrets wrefted from old time,
Or the long defcending line
Of kings and patriots, who fhall ftand
The joy and glory of the land.

But fay, where does the Enchantrefs dwell?
In the deep, romantic cell,
Where creeping mofs adorns the ground,
Whilft the gay cowflip buds around,
And fpreading woodbine greens its fide;
Near which a murm'ring, filver tide
Gently rolls its little ftore
O'er the pebble-ftudded floor?
Or on yon mountains airy brow,
Whence the wide expanfe below,
The grazing herd, the bufy man,
The wood, the meadow, fhe may fcan;
See where the circling hills arife,
Mark the green main, the diftant fkies?

Or where yon* Caftle's mofs-crown'd head
Rifes majeftic o'er the mead?

The

* Kenilworth Caftle, in Warwickfhire.

The tott'ring arch, the mould'ring ſtone
Mark the abode of grandeur gone;
The ivy ſpreads her ſable pall
O'er the once ornamented wall;
Whilſt ſolemn echoes long repeat
The hollow ſound of moving feet,
And ravens, ſtarting from the tow'r,
Hoarſe notes upon the dull air pour.
There is the wild enchantreſs found,
Scatt'ring all her ſpells around,
Recalling now the long paſt age,
Diſplaying now the future page.
The direful ravages of time
Start from her touch in youthful prime,
She clothes the furrow'd hill with wood,
O'er the green meadow pours a flood,
The Caſtle, on its verdant ſide,
Lifts high its head in ancient pride.
The rocky wall, the bow-looped tow'r,
The grim abode of Norman pow'r,
Strike the pale Saxon's haggard eye,
As, ſhudd'ring, ſad, he paſſes by;
Ere, riſing from her ſleep of years,
Scepter'd Magnificence appears,
Or Leiceſter guides her willing feet,
And bids her deck his proud retreat,

And, lo! amidſt a glittering train,
The great Eliza treads the plain;
While Jove forſakes his native ſkies,
And joins the northern deities,
Old Thor and Woden, newly dreſt,
Their rough forms hid in Grecian veſt,
They fade; and now, in many a band,
Soldiers on the ramparts ſtand.
Now peſtilence, with mortal breath,
Rolls on the gathering cloud of death.

The

The tow'ring fabric shakes, it falls;
Desolate its lofty walls.
The chryftal ftream is rolled away.
The falling wood admits the day.

    Yet though thy pomp, thy pride be o'er,
Though the palace shine no more,
Though the pompous court be fled;
Still with joy thefe paths I tread.
The ruin'd wall, the hollow tree,
Have charms for Fancy, and for me.
She gaily paints the varying fcene,
Shewing what thofe once have been.
But I, midft all thy ruins, find
Fit folace for the penfive mind;
That fame, that honours give not breath,
Nor crowns fecure the head from death,
Whilft thou, from every mould'ring wall,
Crieft that e'en their works fhall fall.

    I walk beneath thy folemn fhade,
Haunt for contemplation made,
See, perchance, the glorious fun
Ten, or twenty fummers run;
And then, fubmiffive to my lot,
Am loft in filence and forgot.
Oh! may contentment blefs my days!
I afk not, fame! thy with'ring bays.
And love! whence deareft bleffings flow,
Thy brighteft day has clouds of woe.
Yet may the tender, penfive, mufe
Her foothings o'er my foul diffufe,
And, wafted fwift on Fancy's wing,
Nature's varying beauties fing;
Lead my wild heart to nature's God,
Teach me to fear, to love his rod;
Teach me with eafe to yield my breath,
And fmooth with down the bed of death.

                     ART. X.

Art. X. *A Poem on Female Seduction.*

" Mr. Day retained, during all the periods of his life, as might be expected from his character, a strong detestation of female seduction. Happening once to see some verses written by a young lady on a recent event of this nature, which was succeeded by a fatal catastrophe, (the unhappy young woman who had been the victim of the perfidy of her lover, overpowered by her sensibility of shame, having died of a broken heart,) he addressed the fair poetess with whose sentiments he sympathized, in the following lines."

To the Authoress of " Verses to be inscribed on Delia's tomb."

Sweet Poetess! whose gentle numbers flow
With all the artless energy of woe,
The choicest wreath, Oh lovely maid! be thine,
Which pity offers at the muse's shrine.
Were there a strain of power to soothe the care
Of bitt'rest anguish, and assuage despair,
Thy gen'rous verse might ev'ry bosom cheer,
And wipe from ev'ry eye the falling tear.
But there are transports of the secret soul,
Which not the muse's sacred charms controul:
When ruin'd innocence, condemn'd to bleed,
Mourns the rememb'rance of the fatal deed;
While stern contempt attends, and public hate,
And shame remorseless points the dart of fate.
Yet shall thy votive wreath unfading bloom,
A grateful off'ring to thy Delia's tomb.
There, while celestial mercy beams confest,
And soothes the mourner to eternal rest,
Be fancy's mildest, softest visions seen,
And forms aerial glitter o'er the green!
Such forms as oft, by bow'rs and haunted streams,
Descend mysterious on the poet's dreams.

There

There, borne by hov'ring zephyrs through the air,
Returning springs shall wave her dewy hair;
While Flora, miftrefs of the milder year,
Marks ev'ry flow'r fhe fcatters with a tear.
There, when the gloom of midnight ftills the plains,
The facred guardians of immortal ftrains
To ev'ry blaft fhall bid their treffes flow,
And pour the fweet, majeftic founds of woe.
Lives there a virgin in the fecret fhade,
Not yet to fhame by perjur'd man betray'd ?
This facred fpot inftructed let her tread,
And bend in filent anguifh o'er the dead.
She once, like thee, to hope's gay vifions born,
Shone like the luftre of the dewy morn.
One hour of guilt, one fatal hour, is o'er:
Lo! youth, and hope, and beauty, are no more.
Go, now in mirth the fleeting hours employ,
Go, fnatch the flow'rs of tranfitory joy.
Let feaft and revelry prolong the night,
The lyre tranfport thee, and the dance delight.
Yet be one paufe of fad reflection given
To the low voice of Delia and of heaven!
That voice which rifes from the dreary tomb,
And calls thee to its folitary doom,
Dims ev'ry taper, palls the mantling wine,
And blafts the wreath which love and pleafure twine.
And thou, oh youth ! whom meditation leads
With penfive ftep along thefe glift'ning meads,
If yet thy bofom, unfeduc'd and pure,
Ne'er worfhipp'd fortune's fhrine or pleafure's lure;
If, at the tale of innocence oppreft,
Strong indignation ftruggle in thy breaft;
If in thy conftant foul foft pity glow,
And foes to virtue be thy only foe ;—
Approach this fpot, and mark with pitying eyes,
How low the young, the fair, the gentle lies.

Be

Be the ftern virtue of thy foul refign'd,
Let guifhing tears atteft thy yielding mind.
Swear by the dread avengers of the tomb,
By all thy hopes, by death's tremendous gloom,
That ne'er, by thee deceiv'd, the tender maid
Shall mourn her eafy confidence betray'd ;
Nor weep in fecret thy triumphant art,
With bitter anguifh rankling in her heart.
So may each blefling, which impartial fate
Show'rs on the good, but fnatches from the great,
Adorn thy favour'd courfe with rays divine ;
And heav'n's beft gift—a virtuous love, be thine.

KEIR'S LIFE OF DAY.

ART. XI. *Mr. Grigg's Epitaph on his Mother.*

IN labours confftant as the rifing day,
Hardly fhe liv'd, but in an honeft way.
Crown'd was her table with no fumptuous fare ;
But fweet each meal, for fweet content was there.
Her's, what's fo rarely found, that pious part
To live on little with a thankful heart.
Still thankful, e'en when life's beft blefling fled,
And princely dainties had been bitter bread.
Through nine long years by fore affliction tried,
Patience grew perfect, and the fufferer died ;
Died, favour'd with expiring Stephen's view.
Who would not thus bid this vain world adieu ?
She left her neighbours, relatives, the poor,
No legacies of gold ;—fhe left them more :
Left them a pearl not empires can fupply ;—
A fair *example* how to live and die.

THE

THE REVIEW.

Art. 1. *The Sufficiency of Revelation.* A Sermon, by William Turner, jun. 8vo. pp. 35. 6d. Humble, Newcaftle; Longman and Johnfon, London. 1791.

The propofitions which Mr. Turner endeavours to eftablifh in this Sermon, are, firft, that God has given to the Chriftian Revelation, characters of truth fufficient to convince every reafonable perfon who will give himfelf the trouble of examining them; and, fecondly, that he has enforced the precepts which it contains, by thofe motives which are moft proper to incline us to comply with them. The difcourfe is written in a plain and familiar manner. The views of chriftianity, which it exhibits, are juft and important; and its evident tendency is to fatisfy the underftanding, and imprefs the heart, of the fincere inquirer after truth.

Art. 2. *The Spirit of Perfecutors exemplified; and the Conduct to be obferved towards their Defcendants.* A Sermon, delivered at George's Meeting-Houfe, Exeter, Nov. 5, 1791. To which are prefixed, Some Obfervations upon the Caufes of the late Riots at Birmingham. By T. Kenrick. 8vo pp. 30. pref. 16. 1s. Johnfon. 1792.

In the preface to this Difcourfe, the author informs us that his ʻ defign in writing it was, to point out a few examples of the dreadful evils which have been produced in the chriftian world by the

intolerant

intolerant spirit of the church of Rome, and to shew how inconsistent both the practice and the principles of persecution are with the genius of christianity.' In the execution of this design, he has given, in a very spirited and able manner, an account of many of those sad effects of a persecuting disposition which the history of that church records.

Speaking of the dreadful evils which arose from the introduction of the Inquisition into the Netherlands, by Philip the second, he observes, that ' no merit, however distinguished, can wash away the stain of *heresy* in the apprehension of the persecutor. Piety, sincerity, fortitude, generosity, are all lost in this dreadful crime. The truth of this observation is illustrated by the following circumstance, which took place during these persecutions.

" Richard Willemson, an anabaptist, being pursued, in the depth of winter, by an officer of justice, ran away upon the ice, which not being very thick, it was with difficulty that he got over it; but it broke under his pursuer. Willemson, perceiving the danger his enemy was in, ran back, helped him out of the water, and saved his life at the hazard of his own. The officer, struck with his generosity, would willingly have let him go, but was prevented by the Burgomaster, who came up that instant; so that the officer, fearing left his gratitude should endanger his own life, carried the poor man to prison, and he was afterwards burnt alive. His torments were inexpressible; the inhabitants of Leerdam (at some distance from Asperen, the place of execution,) hearing him cry out above seventy times, O Lord! O my God!"

In inquiring what conduct we ought to observe towards the Roman Catholics of the present day, the author is actuated by the liberal and benevolent

spirit

spirit of the gospel of Christ. He proves the
injustice and impolicy of punishing the descendants
for the sins of their ancestors; justly observing,
that ' every one is answerable for his own offences
alone, and not for the offences of those over whom
he has no influence.'

Art. 3. *An Appeal to the Public, on the Subject of
the Riots in Birmingham.* To which are added,
Strictures on a Pamphlet, entitled ' Thoughts
on the late Riot at Birmingham.' By Joseph
Priestley, LL. D.F.R.S. &c. 8vo. pp. 181. pref.
39. 3s. sewed. Johnson. 1791.

On a subject so interesting as that to which this
work relates, the public will naturally feel a curiosity to know what account has been given by the
principal sufferer in the unhappy riots at Birmingham, and what ideas he entertains with respect
to ' their causes and probable consequences.'

In perusing this volume, the friends and the
enemies of Dr. Priestley will meet with, not only
much to interest their feelings, but much to enlarge the heart and inform the understanding. The
promoters of the late outrages will appear in their
true colours. The heart of sensibility and worth
will give to genius and to virtue its willing tribute
of sympathy and praise.

In a publication of this nature, to select is difficult. It will be sufficient to say of this work, that
it is written with temper and moderation. The
Narrative which it contains, is interesting and sa-
tisfactory; the *Reflections* are striking and important.—The volume concludes with an *Appendix*,
containing various papers which to many will be
highly acceptable.

ART. 4. *A particular Attention to the Instruction of the young recommended*, in a discourse delivered at the Gravel-Pit Meeting, in Hackney, Dec. 4. 1791. on entering on the Office of Pastor to the Congregation of Protestant Dissenters, assembling in that place. By Joseph Priestley, LL. D. F. R. S. &c. 8vo. pp. 40. 1s. Johnson. 1791.

To those who esteem the religious instruction of the young an object of great importance, this Discourse, and the Preface which accompanies it, will be particularly valuable. The writer's aim is to explain his views with respect to some of the great objects of the christian ministry. The methods of instruction, which he recommends, are not, he observes, ' mere projects, the success of which might be doubtful; but what he has employed to the greatest advantage in former situations of some continuance.'

' It will be my ambition, not only that you be well instructed in the doctrines of christianity, and exhorted to the duties of it, but that you distinguish yourselves among christian churches by your superior excellence in these respects. What I would principally recommend for this purpose is, to divide the younger part of the congregation into two or three classes, according to their age, and the degree of their knowledge, and to instruct them separately, when no other persons, strangers or parents, are present.

' The proper object of these lectures is to communicate, in the most familiar and effectual manner, the elements of religious knowledge ; in other words, to make young persons thoroughly to understand the reasons why they are christians, why they are protestants, and why they are protestant dissenters.

diffenters. It is also to teach them what pure chriftianity is, and what are the corruptions and abufes that have been introduced into it. And thefe important articles of inftruction cannot be given in detail, fo as to imprefs the mind properly, in mifcellaneous difcourfes, which thofe from the pulpit always, and, in a manner, neceffarily are, but only in a regular fyftem, in which the eafieft principles are explained in the firft place, and articles of greater difficulty in their proper connection afterwards.'

Thefe are the great outlines of a plan which feems eminently calculated to promote the religious inftruction of the young, and the confequent improvement of mankind at large: a plan, which, with fome variations, chriftian minifters, of all perfuations, might adopt; and many parts of which might very eafily and very ufefully be executed by parents and mafters of families themfelves.

The *particulars* of this ufeful fcheme are very fully explained in the preface.

Dr. Prieftley next proceeds to mention his intention of making the *expofition* of the fcriptures a part of his public fervices; and concludes with replying to fome objections which might be made to the plan of inftruction he had recommended. Under this head, the following liberal obfervations prefent themfelves to our notice.

' Since every perfon who ever called himfelf a chriftian, holds this great article of chriftian faith,' (the doctrine of a refurrection from the dead) ' I receive him as a brother, in whatever light he may confider me; believing that if we equally cultivate the fpirit, and equally attend to the duties, of chriftianity, our common faviour, and that God, whofe fervant our faviour was, will regard us with equal favour.

' I call

' I call myfelf an unitarian, hitherto more ufually called a focinian, but I do not believe I fhall have any advantage hereafter over the arian, or the trinitarian, who fhall equally feel and act as becomes a chriftian. Members of the church of England, and alfo of that of Rome, holding, as I do, the great doctrine abovementioned, as taught by Chrift, I confider as brother chriftians, though they may not acknowledge me in that light. I proteft againft the corruptions and abufes which I believe thofe churches have introduced into chriftianity, and have fupported in it; conceiving that the belief, and, in fome degree, even the moral influence of chriftianity, is obftructed by that means. But if they be fincere in their belief, I have no prejudice againft their perfons. I am willing to believe that they honeftly follow the light that God has given them, which is all I can pretend to do; and if I imagine that I *know* more than they, I certainly ought to *do* more, diftinguifhing myfelf by my zeal in the caufe of the gofpel, in proportion as I conceive that I hold it in greater purity.

' Our greateft duties relate not to fpeculation, but to practice. We are all to be *hearers* of the word; but the great article of all is to be *doers* of the work affigned us by God to do. When our lord fhall return, and take an account of his fervants, the enquiry that he will make will not be what we thought concerning his perfon, or any other fubject of fpeculation, but whether we fhall have obeyed his commands, and efpecially whether we fhall have fulfilled the great duty of chriftian love, which includes that of candour, and forbearance towards our erring brethren.'

Art. 5.

Art. 5. *Addreſs to the Engliſh Nation.* Tranſlated from the French of J. P. Rabaut de St.
Etienne. 8vo. pp. 23. 1s. Johnſon. 1791.

The writer of this ſenſible and benevolent
Addreſs calls upon us, in the name of humanity
and ſound policy, to unite with his countrymen in
renouncing ' that ſyſtematic rapine called con-
queſt,' in reſpecting the rights of nations, and in
endeavouring to bring back upon earth that peace
of which caprice and tyranny have ſo long deprived
it. Whatever be the effect of this well-tried truth,
that *war is the bane of nations,* France has obtained
immortal honour by being the firſt to proclaim it.

Art. 6. *Elements of Morality,* for the Uſe of
Children; with an introductory Addreſs to
Parents. Tranſlated from the German of the
Rev. C. G. Salzmann. Illuſtrated with fifty
Copper-plates. 3 vols. 12mo. pp. 200 in each.
9s. ſewed. Johnſon. 1791.

This is an uſeful entertaining work, containing
natural familiar incidents, and calculated to render
youth virtuous and happy. Mrs. Wollſtonecraft
informs us, that ' beſide making it an Engliſh
ſtory, ſhe has made ſome additions, and altered
many parts of it, not only to give it the ſpirit of
an original, but to avoid introducing any German
cuſtoms or local opinions.' ' Inexpreſſibly great
(ſays the author in his Introductory Addreſs) will
be my reward, if this work proves half as uſeful as
I intended it to be;—if it prevent, or root out of
our little poſterity thoſe prejudices which prey,
like poiſonous inſects, on human happineſs,—if it
excite in them a love for virtue, and a deteſtation
for every thing mean and vicious,—if it twiſt the

relaxed

relaxed band between parents and children, and give the former a taſte for the ſweeteſt of all enjoyments which God has ſent us—a taſte for domeſtic pleaſures. Thoſe which are ſought for from home, are, in general, coſtly, producing trouble and wearineſs of mind, and weakneſs and pain of body. On the contrary, the felicity which is enjoyed in the boſom of our families, is always within our reach, and healthful both to the mind and body. Without domeſtic happineſs, no other joys are able to procure us laſting ſatisfaction, or tranquility; but when this is ſecure, all others pleaſe.'

This Addreſs, though not wholly unexceptionable, contains many hints of good advice to parents reſpecting the education of their children.

CORRESPONDENCE.

*** In conſequence of the almoſt unanimous opinion of the friends of this work, the Editor has been induced to diſcontinue the inſertion of a Monthly Liſt of Publications. He hopes that this conſideration, and the additional articles which appear in this Number, will be thought to afford a ſufficient apology for the alteration.

The favour of 'I. X.' is received. As it arrived ſo late in the month, the Editor can in this place only ſay, that a letter is left for him at the Publiſher's; which will, if he pleaſes, be forwarded according to his direction.

It is requeſted that all communications for this Work be ſent (poſt paid) directed to the Editor of the Chriſtian Miſcellany, at Mr. Stalker's, No. 4, Stationers' Court, Ludgate-Street, London.

E R R A T A.

In the laſt Number, page 37, line 14, for *Sufferings,* read *Sufficiency.*

In this Number, page 55, line 4, for *exacted* read *exalted.*

THE
Chriſtian Miſcellany,

For MARCH, 1792.

ART. I. *On the Evidence of the Truth of Chriſtianity.*

(Continued from page 46.)

HAVING, in a former paper, eſtabliſhed the *general* credibility of the New Teſtament, let us now proceed to conſider the objection which ariſes from the *miraculous* parts of it.

And here I would firſt obſerve, that miracles appear perfectly conſonant to a divine revelation; and therefore that they are found in the New Teſtament in thoſe circumſtances, in which of all others it is moſt probable they ſhould have been performed: and alſo, that a want of miracles would probably have been accounted, by the very perſons who object to them, and certainly by others, a want of a material part of the evidence of a divine revelation. This again increaſes the probability that they actually took place.

I believe no one has ever yet denied, that a miracle *may* be wrought. Indeed, as the original formation of the earth and of its inhabitants, and many other appearances which we daily ſee, muſt have been at firſt miraculous; we have proof poſitive, that a miracle may be wrought, and has been wrought. But it has been ſaid, that a miracle, if wrought, can never be ſufficiently evidenced to

K   produce

produce rational belief. For a miracle is a variation from the laws of nature; that is, from our experience; and our belief in testimony is built on experience. Therefore we may as well suppose, that our experience should be contradicted in the latter case, as in the former.

It is not difficult to answer this objection. Let any one fix upon three persons with whom he has been long acquainted, and who are all men of strict integrity and of good common understanding: let these three agree in the relation of a fact totally contrary to experience and the common laws of nature: let them seriously affirm that they were eye-witnesses to this fact; and let the fact be of a kind, which it should be rather detrimental to their own interest, and that of those connected with them, to relate, or, at least, which they have no temptation to tell, if not true. I say, in this case, would the friend of these men believe their relation? No doubt; if he believed on reasonable grounds. For it would most undoubtedly be a greater miracle, that their testimony should not be true, that such men should deceive without a motive, or that *all the three* should instantaneously have their faculties so changed as to be deceived themselves, than that any *single* supernatural event should come to pass. A supernatural event, that is, an event contrary to common experience, certainly *may* happen; but that honest men should deceive knowingly, cannot happen; it is impossible, it is a plain contradiction in terms. No man can deceive without a motive, and an honest man not at all. If the friend of these men, therefore, does not rely upon their testimony, does not believe the event they relate, he must believe that the senses, or perception, or minds and character, of the three were instantly changed by miraculous means; that is, in other words, he must

believe

believe *three* miracles inſtead of *one*. As it is plain, therefore, in this caſe, that the friend of theſe men *muſt* believe in ſomething totally contrary to experience, he would ſurely determine more reaſonably in believing *one* ſupernatural event rather than *three*, in believing what is *leſs* rather than what is *more* contrary to experience. *Therefore, there may be ſufficient evidence to induce the rational belief of a miracle. For it would be more miraculous that the teſtimony of ſuch men ſhould be falſe, than that a ſupernatural event ſhould happen.*—This being premiſed, it remains to inquire, Whether the qualities which are to be expected in thoſe, whoſe evidence may be conſidered as deciſive in miraculous events, are to be found in the perſons who bear teſtimony to the miracles recorded in the goſpel.

The qualities which we ſhould reaſonably expect in witneſſes, and the only ones which we can deſire, are *honeſty* and *common ſenſe*, or the free uſe of their faculties. In a court of judicature, two witneſſes, in whom only the latter of theſe is evidently proved, are judged ſufficient to decide on the life of a man. If, therefore, beſides the *competency* of witneſſes to judge, we can prove their honeſty alſo, we have all that we can expect in a human being, and all that we can have.—To apply this to the authors of the New Teſtament.

In the former part of this eſſay I have ſhewn, that there is every reaſon, at leaſt, which determines us on other occaſions, to believe that the apoſtles wrote the books attributed to them; and that the ſame perſons who wrote the natural, wrote alſo the miraculous, events. The apoſtles, therefore, and their companions, Mark and Luke, are the perſons whoſe credibility is to be examined by the above-mentioned ſtandard.

Were they honeſt? To this it may be replied,

is

is it poffible to receive from any perfon a more de-cided, unequivocal proof of honefty, than his per-fifting in a relation which expofes him infallibly to danger and to great inconvenience, without the moft diftant profpect of worldly advantage; and which inconvenience he not only expofes himfelf to, by a bare teftimony when called upon, but which he alfo willingly encounters, by a laborious fpreading of his belief? Now, even if it could be proved (as fome have afferted,) that the apoftles and their companions did not really fuffer much during their miffion, (though there are convincing proofs to the contrary,)* ftill it muft be admitted that they had every thing to fear; that they readily offered themfelves to receive the hatred which had raged againft their mafter; and that they had little reafon to expect mild treatment from thofe who had crucified him. Befides this, Jefus Chrift him-felf forewarned them of the reception which they would meet with in the world. Yet thefe men perfevered in their courfe. Can there be any doubt, then, of their honefty?

With refpect to their *competency as witneffes,* it may be obferved, that Matthew and John were themfelves eye-witneffes; that Mark and Luke certainly both wrote from the relations of eye-witneffes, or from what they had themfelves feen; and that the authors of the Epiftles were themfelves eye-witneffes, or in-timately connected with thofe who were: that the miracles which are recorded in the gofpel are of a kind which could not be counterfeited; and that the mere ufe of their fenfes was all which it was neceffary for the witneffes to poffefs, to preclude any poffibility of their being deceived: that every one of them was competent to judge, whether a paralytic man was inftantly cured, or not; whether

five

* See Lardner's Lives of the Apoftles.

five thoufand people were actually fed and fatisfied, or not; whether Jefus Chrift appeared to them after his death, or not; and whether they themfelves, and others, fpoke in tongues they had never learned, or whether they did not: and fo of the other miracles. We infer, then, that the writers of the New Teftament were no lefs competent to judge, than honeft in their relation; and, of courfe, if we do not believe their relation, muft we not infallibly believe, either that honeft men deceived us knowingly, (which is impoffible,)* or that the faculties and minds of all thefe people were changed very frequently by miraculous interpofitions? But this is no lefs miraculous than any facts which they have related. It is alfo increafing prodigioufly the number of the miracles, and thofe very miracles would alfo be proofs of a divine revelation.

Such is the evidence of the apoftles and their companions, even when ftanding by itfelf. But a very ftrong argument in its favour (granting what has been already proved, that the New Tefta-

K 3   ment

---

* It will not be improper to notice an obfervation which may here be urged, that it is not altogether impoffible for an honeft man to deceive knowingly, when the motive which influences him is the good of another, which is to be effected by this deception. Whether any one who does this is ftrictly honeft, is a nice point of morality, which it is not neceffary now to enquire into. It is fufficient to obferve, that I have avoided the poffibility of it in the cafe which I put of the three men (in page 82), and that the characters of the apoftles cannot be defended as honeft on this ground, for it is evident that they did not infift upon obedience to the Mofaic inftitution, which, being Jews, they clearly believed to be of divine reign, and the obfervance of which, except they firmly believed in the divine miffion of Chrift, muft have appeared to them to have been, *above all things*, important.—Their teaching chriftianity was alfo clearly difadvantageous, in a *temporal* view to their followers; who were all expofed to perfecution on account of their converfion,

ment was really written by thofe whofe names it bears,) is to be drawn *from the accomplifhment of prophecies.* If any fingle miraculous interpofition (fuch as prophecy,) can be proved, the belief in other miracles is rendered eafier. Now we find a variety of prophetic paffages in the Old Teftament fulfilled by Chrift, and all centering, as it were, in his character. We have alfo the moft pofitive proof of the exact fulfilment of the prophecy refpecting the deftruction of Jerufalem,* of the rife of Antichrift, and of the fufferings of the early chriftians. To the accomplifhment of a remarkable prophecy in the Old Teftament, (the genuinenefs of which is, in fact, eftablifhed by the New,) the difperfion, but prefervation of the Jews as a diftinct nation, we are ourfelves eye-witneffes.

Now what farther evidence of miracles can be reafonably expected? and can there poffibly be ftronger evidence without *prefent* miracles?

Perhaps fome one may be here difpofed to inquire, why the Chriftians fhould receive, as authentic, the miracles recorded in the New Teftament, and reject thofe of hiftorians who bear a high character for veracity? It was the opinion of the great Hartley,† that it was impoffible to prove all pagan miracles to be falfe. But I conceive that they are ufually regarded as fabulous for the following

* Tacitus, who has recorded the deftruction of Jerufalem, relates prodigies which happened at the demolition of the temple very different from the common prodigies of heathen hiftorians; and fuch as the prophecy of Chrift would give reafon to expect. His evidence, therefore, as well as that of Jofephus, and alfo of Pliny and others, to the perfecution of the Chriftians, may be confidered as the evidence of unbelievers to the truth of the miraculous parts of the New Teftament.

† Evidence of Chriftianity in Vol. 2. of his Obfervations on Man.

lowing reafons : viz. that the hiftorians, relating them, do not declare that they were eye-witneffes, nor did they hear them from eye-witneffes; that they often give reafon to think, that they did not themfelves believe them ; that they often record them as common, vulgar reports only; that they evidently infert them, in fome cafes, through flattery; that their miracles have no important tendency; that the relation of them was not attended with any inconvenience to the authors, but the omiffion of them might. It may hence be inferred, that the heathen hiftorians had not the qualities required in credible witneffes with refpect to the miraculous facts which they relate.

From the foregoing remarks, then, it follows, that if we allow the fame weight to the arguments for chriftianity as we do to fimilar arguments on other occafions, they lead us to conclude, that the New Teftament is a genuine production of thofe to whom it is attributed ; that the facts, both natural and miraculous, recorded therein, can be proved by teftimony; that the teftimony of the apoftles has all the marks of truth which we can expect or require in any teftimony ; and that their evidence is ftill farther corroborated by the unqueftionable proofs of the fulfilment of remarkable prophecies in the Old and New Teftaments, fome of which proofs remain even in the prefent day.

F. S.

ART. II. *Obfervations on Luke's Account of what paffed between our lord and thofe who were crucified with him.* [See Luke xxiii. 39—43.]

THERE is fome little variation in the accounts which the evangelifts give us of the conduct of the two malefactors who were crucified with Jefus.

Matthew

Matthew and Mark speak of them both as joining in the insulting language of his persecutors. The former says "the thieves also, who were crucified with him, cast the same in his teeth." Mark says, "and they that were crucified with him reviled him." But Luke speaks of one only as behaving in this manner, and represents the other as reproving him for it. It is by no means improbable, that Luke had an opportunity, in this case, of being better informed than the other two writers. Matthew, it is to be observed, was one of our master's earliest followers,—was one of the twelve apostles,—and consequently well known to be a disciple by many of the jews. It is not likely, therefore, that he was a near spectator of what passed at the crucifixion. Mark, it is probable, drew up his history with the assistance of those who both enjoyed the same opportunities, and were exposed to the same disadvantages, as Matthew himself. Luke, on the contrary, who does not appear to have been a regular attendant upon our lord, would not be so generally marked out as a disciple of Jesus; and, consequently, not being afraid to mix with those who stood nearest to him during his crucifixion, would enjoy the best means of being accurately informed of what took place in that awful scene. That this was the case, is evident from the very circumstantial manner in which he has related the transaction. It cannot be wondered at, then, that the evangelists do not exactly agree in their accounts. But so far is this disagreement from invalidating their testimony, that it renders the leading facts of their histories still more credible; as it proves that they did not write in concert, and consequently that the general agreement subsisting in their several accounts, is owing, not to artful contrivance, but to the truth of the facts which they have related.

Having

Having made these general observations, I propose confining myself to Luke's account of the transaction.

I am induced to treat upon this portion of scripture by the apprehension that there is too common a propensity among men to draw unwarrantable and dangerous conclusions from our lord's declaration to his penitent fellow-sufferer; " verily I say unto thee, to-day shalt thou be with me in paradise." Mistaking the grounds of this declaration, mistaking, perhaps, the character of the man to whom it was addressed, and the nature of the expectation which it was designed to raise, many a deluded sinner, buoyed up with empty hopes, has flattered himself that he ought not to despair of receiving that mercy which was extended to the thief upon the cross. Happy, thrice happy shall I be, if, by demonstrating that the scriptures afford no foundation for believing that salvation can be purchased by what is termed a death-bed repentance, I should be the instrument of rousing one sinner to a proper sense of duty, and of causing him to " seek the Lord while he may be found, to call upon him while he is near." There is no man, it is to be presumed, who has any regard to his own salvation, that will not feel himself disposed to attend to such a subject with seriousness. There is no sinner, I trust, who will not attend to it with solicitude.

The passage which is now to be considered is the principal passage, I conceive, which hath ever been pressed into the service of the doctrine that maintains the efficacy of a death-bed repentance. But if this passage be carefully attended to, no man in his senses will derive encouragement from it to " continue in sin," upon the vain hope that, when he is about to leave the world, " grace will abound towards him."

Whatever

Whatever were the character of the person to whom our lord replied, " to-day, I fay unto thee, thou fhalt be with me in paradife," there is a very material difference between his cafe and that of a modern finner in a chriftian country. The thief upon the crofs had received advantages for leading a life of virtue, but fmall, compared with thofe of men who have always enjoyed the light of the gofpel. If he had repented of his fins as foon as he became acquainted with the doctrine of Jefus, it was far furpaffing thofe who have heard of his religion from their infancy, but never paid any practical regard to it, till upon the verge of eternity.

For any thing that appears to the contrary, the penitent thief might have committed the deed, for which he fuffered the vengeance of the law, a confiderable time before his execution : his confinement might have been a long one : he might have heard of Jefus at the beginning of it ; in confequence of which, he might have become a believer in him, and have acted from that time agreeably to the precepts of chriftianity. At leaft, all this ought to be fuppofed, rather than admit a fact which fanctions conclufions full of abfurdity and mifchief.

If, then, there be any finner who has felt himfelf difpofed to derive encouragement from our lord's declaration to the thief upon the crofs, let him confider that he has enjoyed means of improvement of which the thief had no knowledge till late in life ; that he has rejected many calls to holinefs with which the thief was never favoured ; that he knows concerning himfelf, that he has never repented, whereas he does not know but that the thief did repent as foon as he heard the doctrine of " repentance for the remiffion of fins." Vain, therefore, are thofe hopes of falvation which are built upon the acceptance of the penitent thief, even though it be admitted that

the

the perfon fo called had been a man of profligate character. But this, I would now obferve, is by no means a clear cafe. It is very probable that the men who, in our tranflation of Matt. and Mark, are called *thieves*, and in that of Luke, *malefactors*, were not houfe-breakers, or, what we call, high-way men, who rob and plunder all perfons for the fake of the profit; but, on the contrary, were of that fort of Jews, who took up arms upon a principle of religion, maintaining that God was the only go- vernor of the Ifraelites, that the Romans were not to be fubmitted to, and that their levies of tribute- money upon the Jews were an oppreffion. Of this defcription of men was Judas of Galilee, who is mentioned in the fcripture; and though he and his party were foon fuppreffed, their principles had taken deep root in the country; and whenever the Roman governors acted in an arbitrary and oppref- five manner, as they often did, the people always fhewed a difpofition to rebel. It confirms the opi- nion that the perfons who were crucified with Jefus were of this clafs of Jews, that Jofephus the Jewifh hiftorian, calls thefe revolters by the fame name as the evangelifts give to our lord's fellow-fufferers. But the circumftance which appears to me to be little fhort of demonftrating that they were fuffering for conduct originating in a miftaken opinion of the rights of their nation, is that the malefactor who railed at Jefus, faid " if thou be the Chrift, fave thyfelf and *us*." Now furely no *thief*, in thofe circumftances, could ever entertain the moft diftant idea that the meffiah, the annointed of the Lord, would exert his miraculous power to refcue from the hands of juftice an houfe-breaker or an high- wayman: whereas an enemy to the Roman govern- ment, fuffering, as he would believe, in the caufe

of

of liberty and his country, would naturally expect some favour from that meſſiah whom he conſidered as raiſed up on purpoſe to avenge upon the Romans the injuries of the perſecuted Iſraelites ; and had he believed Jeſus to be the Chriſt, would have ſeriouſly made that requeſt, which, whilſt viewing him as an impoſtor, he made only in ridicule. But, as many perſons of the beſt character and intentions muſt have embraced, and acted upon the principles I have ſtated, it is very probable that one of our lord's fellow-ſufferers was of that number; and being a man whoſe conduct aroſe from conviction, he would, upon cool reflection, be grieved at any improprieties of behaviour into which he might have been hurried by the heat of party, and be diſpoſed to ſay that he ſuffered juſtly, receiving the due reward of his deeds. At the ſame time, convinced of the purity of his principles, he would hope for acceptance with God; and if he believed Jeſus to be really that meſſiah whom he had been expecting, the ſcourge of the Romans, the deliverer of his country, would raiſe an hopeful look, and ſay " lord ! remember me when thou comeſt into thy kingdom." Jeſus diſcerning in him ſome promiſing diſpoſitions, and convinced that the conduct, for which he was ſuffering, was to be aſcribed rather to the erroneouſneſs of his principles than to the depravity of his heart, would be diſpoſed to encourage his hope of obtaining the favour of that Being who can penetrate into the ſouls of men, and with whom many will find mercy who have become obnoxious to the judgment of earthly tribunals.

Let the ſinner, then, ſeriouſly weigh theſe conſiderations and impartially ſay whether he can derive any encouragement to continue in his ſins, from the caſe of the penitent malefactor. The man who fuffered with our lord, fuffered, probably, for doing what he thought he was bound to do, by love to his country, by a regard to his religion, by a reverence for his God. But can the finner plead this? Can he plead that he is led into his iniquities by fuch principles as thefe? Does he cheat or rob his neighbour, for the good of his country? Does he indulge himfelf in gaming and intemperance for the honour of his religion? Does he lie and fwear, out of reverence to his maker? Alas! he knows that he does all thefe things, in *oppofition* to every principle of benevolence or of piety. And does he not know that the " wrath of God is revealed from heaven againft all ungodlinefs and unrighteoufnefs of men, who hold the truth in unrighteoufnefs?"

I cannot difmifs the confideration of our lord's declaration to his fellow-fufferer, without obferving that it has been doubted whether it really contains any promife of future happinefs. It cannot be fuppofed that the perfon upon the crofs had a more juft idea of the nature of our mafter's kingdom than his difciples themfelves. Now they, it is evident, imagined to the laft, that he would appear in the character of a temporal prince; and when he was apprehended by the jews, concluding that there was an end to their profpects, " they forfook him and fled." The criminal, it is probable, confidering Jefus as the meffiah, believed that God would interpofe in fome extraordinary manner to fave him from death, and to inveft him with that power by which he would be able to deliver others. Upon this prefumption, he fays, " lord! remember me when thou comeft into thy kingdom." To this requeft, our mafter anfwers, that whatever expectations he might form of his future power and reign, they fhould both of them this very day, be in paradife, the abode of the departed,

parted, and be joined to the dead of former ages : for paradise, was, according to the opinion of the Jews, one part of the habitation of the dead, assigned to righteous and good men. Our lord, therefore, either supposes him, notwithstanding the judgment of the law, to be a good man, and on this account tells him he should soon be in the number of the pious dead, or else he gives the appellation of paradise to the whole state or place where the dead are supposed to dwell. (See Alexander's Paraphrase on 1 Cor. xv. p. 42.)

Having now taken a full view of this most interesting passage of scripture, I may confidently appeal to any man, whether it can administer any solid comfort to the wilful sinner on the bed of death. No one, I am persuaded, whose judgement is not carried away captive by his vices, can imagine that the declaration of our master affords the least encouragement to those unhappy men who go on, day after day, filling up the measure of their iniquities.

Let it not be said that the man who is brought to reflection by the approach of death, though he look back with no comfort upon his past life, may still look forward with some hope to the mercy of God. Where do the scriptures convey such a notion? No where. The mercy of God is magnified, in *calling* us to holiness, in *aiding* us by the most encouraging prospects, in forgiving the penitent and *reformed*; but never in accepting those who have given no proofs of their repentance, but that sorrow which the approach of the messenger of death inspires. Let it not be said that Christ, by his death, hath purchased the favour of God for those who have led a sinful life. The bible says nothing of the kind; and if there be a destructive heresy, it is this. Jesus died to "redeem us from all iniquity," "to make

us

us the righteoufnefs of God," " leaving us an example that we fhould follow his fteps." He died to *engage* us to be holy, not to procure us an inheritance among the faints of light, whether we are holy or not.

To be plain upon this fubjeɛt, and God knows that it is my duty, and the duty of us all to be plain upon it, I am verily perfuaded, that it is abfolutely impoffible for the confirmed finner, whatever be his feelings in his laft moments, to enter into that reft which remaineth for the people of God. He poffeffes thofe qualities which he cannot get rid of at once, and he is deftitute of thofe virtues without which there can be no heaven. Let him look back upon his paft life, and confider how long it is that he hath been praɛtifing thofe fins, the confequences which now appear fo dreadful. Probably, it has been the greater part of his life. His bad difpofitions are, therefore, deeply rooted in him ; vice is become a fecond nature. Let him confider again, in what manner iniquity hath thus taken poffeffion of him. Was it all at once ? Was he at once fo ftrongly addiɛted to covetoufnefs, to intemperance, or to enmity ? Rather has he not found his evil propenfities *grow* upon him ? Did he not find that his fins fat lighter upon him at firft, than they have of late ? Was he not once confcious of a power to lay them afide at *pleafure?* And did he not go on in them, beguiled by this perfuafion, till they have abfolutely gained the maftery over him, fo that it is impoffible for him to difmifs them ?

And can fuch a man as this be fit to enter into the kingdom of heaven ; Can he now in a moment pluck up what hath taken fuch a root in his foul? Can he now overcome what he hath fo often ftruggled with to no purpofe ? Alas! the attempt is vain. His doom is fixed. " He that foweth to

the

the flesh, shall of the flesh reap corruption." Unhappy man! he is destitute of those qualifications which are absolutely necessary in the inhabitants of heaven. Could he be admitted into heaven, heaven would be to him a wilderness. He would be destitute of employment. He would find nothing suited to his taste. Suppose some great office were offered to any one, provided he would qualify himself by obtaining a thorough acquaintance with the learned languages, in which it would be necessary for him to be very well versed; and suppose he presented himself for admission, without having acquired the least knowledge of the kind; should we not call him a mad-man, and expect to see him rejected with disdain? But what infinitely greater madness is it to think of being admitted into the heavenly society of saints and angels, when destitute of those graces which are expected as indispensable qualifications? Indeed, if the circumstance of a death-bed repentance were a sufficient ground of hope, there would be scarcely any man excluded from the kingdom of God: whereas our lord assures us " that strait is the gate and narrow the way, and *few* there be that find it."

Lay these things to thy heart, sinner! No longer trifle with thy soul! thou art hastening to the tomb. Turn, turn from thy evil ways. "Now is the accepted time, now is the day of salvation. Seek the things which belong to thine everlasting peace, before they be for ever hid from thine eyes."

ART. III. *An Illustration of Psalm* lxxxiv 5. 6. 7.

In the dry countries of the east, wells of water are scarce and valuable. Many wells have been made for the pilgrims to Mecca, but afterward stopped

up

up by rain and great quantities of fand. Hence the 5th and 6th verfes may be thus tranflated. " Bleffed is the man whofe ftrength is in thee. The fteps, or paths which conduct to mount Sion, are in their heart, who, paffing through the valley of Baca, (of fhrubs or mulberry trees, a valley fo called from what grew there,) make a well for the refrefhment of thofe who afcend the mountain; but the rain filleth the pools. With this refrefhment they are ftrengthened, enabled to afcend the mountain. They go from ftrength to ftrength; they appear in Sion before God."

A learned foreigner makes the word, Baca, to fignify mourning. The careful traveller eafily finds a well, with which he quenches his thirft. The faints, even in their affliction, are attended with felicity. They are confcious of their own virtue, and are fenfible that they are protected by the gracious providence of God.

ART. IV. *The Duty of Sincerity and Perfeverance in the profeffion and communication of Religious Truth.*

TO THE EDITOR OF THE CHRISTIAN MISCELLANY.

SIR,

As the plan of your Mifcellany affords you " liberty to introduce extracts from interefting publications," I have tranfcribed the following paffage from the celebrated Archdeacon Blackburne's Difcourfes to the Clergy, in hopes you will give it a place among your other papers.

I. X.

There is nothing which more evidently proves the divine miffion of the apoftles, than the exact defcription they have given us of the laft days which

L   were

were immediately to precede the clofe and confummation of this worldly fyftem. As we approach nearer to thofe days, we perceive all thofe evil habits and difpofitions increafing among mankind, which the apoftles gave as the marks and tokens of " perilous times," and which were intended as warnings to thofe whofe province it fhould be to apply the correctives of the gofpel, to reform the principles and manners of that generation of men among whom their lot fhould fall. Thefe warnings we have in the 3d chapter of the Epiftle to Timothy, when the firft heat of perfecution was, probably, over, and when the freedom of the chriftians from the terrors of it had left them no enemies fo dangerous and formidable as their own irregular paffions; and they were given to Timothy, a preacher and minifter of the chriftian religion, to awaken his circumfpection, to direct him to the beft expedients of providing againft thofe evils which were moft likely to corrupt the integrity of his flock, and debafe the fpirit of their religion by impure mixtures, and fecular interefts, utterly inconfiftent with that purity of heart and innocence of life, which were the principal diftinctions of the chriftian brotherhood. From Timothy, thefe admonitions have defcended to us; and it is incumbent upon us to make that ufe of them, which a careful obfervation of perfons and facts within our refpective departments may enable us to do.

Our bufinefs, indeed, is chiefly with the particular congregations where our lot is fallen. To thefe we are more efpecially bound to fhew ourfelves " patterns of good works," and in our doctrine to fhew " uncorruptednefs, gravity, fincerity, found fpeech which cannot be condemned, that they (fays the apoftle) of the contrary part may be afhamed, having no evil to fay of you."·

It

It is eafy to fee that, under thefe general directions, many fpecific duties are comprifed. They have refpect to every fort, and every means of feduction, to which our refpective flocks may be expofed; whether from the profligate corrupters of our public manners, the ignorant zeal of enthufiaftic teachers, or the more refined fophiftry of thofe defigning emiffaries who would enflave their minds, by bringing them under fubjection to an idolatrous and tyrannical fuperftition. In a world that is fo much given to the ftudy of fecular wifdom, a religion, of fo great purity as the chriftian, would run the hazard of being totally neglected, if the *nominal* profeffion of it was not found neceffary for certain *political purpofes*; which, however, it could not be made to anfwer, if it were only to be profeffed in its native fimplicity : a confideration that has given birth to a thoufand formalites in the different eftablifhments of it, all of which may be practifed without producing the leaft emotion of that " power of godlinefs" upon the heart, which was felt by the firft converts upon the preaching of the apoftles.

And here it is, that is to fay, in our endeavours to revive this influence, that we muft expect our fincerity and perfeverance will be put to the utmoft teft. It is an undertaking next to defperate to attempt to bring back a carelefs, diffipated people to the pure and uncorrupted fountains of evangelical truth and piety, while fo many hypocrites and plaufible profeffors teach them to put fo high a value upon mere formalities.

But it is a work indifpenfably annexed to our callings, and, therefore, to be undertaken at all events. It is our efpecial commiffion to enforce the *power* of godlinefs; and wherever this is our aim, as it is always our duty, it will be of very little confequence

to

to our final account, what becomes of those *forms* of it, by whatever precedents or examples they are recommended, which derive not their authority from the word of God.

The two following articles, though similar in their object, have been thought proper for insertion, both as the plan which they recommend is of great importance, and as they may prove mutually useful in the execution of it.

ART. V. *A Plan for the Promotion of Religious Knowledge.*

TO THE EDITOR OF THE CHRISTIAN MISCELLANY.

SIR,

I applaud the zeal which has induced a number of gentlemen to associate themselves together, for the purpose of diffusing the knowledge of what they deem pure christianity; which I learn from the 5th article of your Miscellany for February. It discovers a warmth of piety and benevolence which reminds me of the spirit of the first reformers from popery, and carries back my thoughts to a still higher period, the first planting of the christian religion. I shall esteem myself happy, if any thing which I can suggest, may contribute, in any degree, to promote so excellent a design. I shall, therefore, proceed to lay my sentiments before you freely, upon that plan which appears to me best adapted to answer their purpose; that the person who subscribes himself a *Friend to Truth*, and whom I suppose to be one of their number, may communicate them to his friends, if he think them deserving of so much notice.

Three methods of promoting this design are mentioned in the article to which I have referred;
the

the diſtribution of books, the ſupport of ſettled miniſters, and providing academical education for young men. Each of theſe methods is, no doubt, well calculated for diffuſing religious knowledge. But there appears to me ſomething omitted, which is likely to be more uſeful than any of the preceding articles, and might be very conveniently connected with ſuch a ſociety as your correſpondent ſays is about to be formed. The character of a great part of the common people in this kingdom muſt ſtrike every attentive obſerver as truly deplorable. It is a dreadful mixture of ignorance, ſuperſtition and vice, which proves the ſource of much wretchedneſs to the individuals themſelves, and of great danger to the community. For whenever their paſſions are inflamed by bigotry or a temporary ſcarcity of the neceſſaries of life, there is no act of violence or brutality which they are not prepared to commit. To give to perſons of this deſcription a knowledge of the chriſtian religion, certainly appears to be the moſt effectual method of humanizing and reforming them. Great ſums are annually expended for the ſupport of public inſtruction, both in the eſtabliſhed church and among the diſſenters; but this has done but little towards correcting the manners of the populace. It evidently labours under ſome eſſential defect, which renders it incapable of anſwering this purpoſe. What better method, then, can be adopted? How may the important work of a reformation be accompliſhed? Some perſons will, perhaps, anſwer, by diſtributing among them religious books. But are you ſure that they can read, or, at leaſt, with ſufficient eaſe to comprehend what is written? Beſides, who ſhall put proper books into their hands, or induce them, if that were done, to look into them? For it is well known that reading is a dull, unintereſting employment to

L 3

thoſe

those whose minds have not been much cultivated, over which they doze and soon fall asleep, or which they lay aside in disgust; unless they happen to possess understandings of more than ordinary vigour, or have their curiosity awakened by some powerful motives which cannot be supposed to exist here.

With respect to ministers already established with societies, they are certainly very useful within the sphere to which their labours extend, and to support them may be performing an essential service to the interests of piety and virtue. But it must not be expected that much can be done by them, in their present situation, towards instructing and reforming the great mass of the common people. Their mode of preaching, being adapted to the circumstances of well informed christians who have been brought up in the knowledge of christianity, is but ill suited to the understanding or feelings of the ignorant, who require something plainer and more familiar. Occupied in attending to the interests of the societies with which they are immediately connected, they have no time for addressing themselves to those whom I wish to see instructed, and who seldom come within the walls of any of the ordinary places of worship. Nor am I sure, if they were to adopt such modes of address as are necessary for enlightening the multitude, that their present friends would be perfectly satisfied with their conduct.

If, then, neither books, nor the stated preaching of ministers, will extend such a knowledge of religion to the common people as is necessary to make them virtuous and useful characters, I may be asked what other method I have to propose for this purpose. I answer, *itinerant preaching*. Be not startled, sir, at the proposal. It has hitherto been connected with much ignorance and enthusiasm; but it is capable of being associated with reason and
knowledge;

knowledge ; and, under such direction, I have no doubt of its producing the most salutary effects. By itinerant preachers I mean, ministers who do not settle with any particular society of christians, but travel about the country for the purpose of religious instruction ; which they are ready to deliver, not only on Sundays, but likewise on week days, and in any place where they are likely to be heard with most advantage.

The advantages of this plan of instruction will be, that the knowledge of the christian religion may be communicated, in an easy and intelligible manner, to the poor and ignorant, without disgusting persons of greater refinement, and that, coming from a living instructor, and being received by the hearer in the society of many others, it will be more deeply impressed upon the mind than in any other way. The preacher, being unconnected with any particular congregation, will feel himself at liberty to expose without reserve any corruptions which have been unhappily mixed with the christian religion. As proselytes are made, societies might be formed with a regular plan of discipline, which should have for its object, the keeping up of public worship in case of the want of a professed teacher, the instruction of children and other young persons, and the exclusion of all immoral characters. In this article of discipline almost all christian societies are, at present, defective. Having once grown into disuse, it is not easily revived in old societies, but might be adopted without difficulty in such as are newly formed.

Here, then, is an object worthy of the attention of those who wish to see a rational system of religion prevail in the world, and particularly of those who are associating themselves to promote it. Let them establish a fund for supporting well informed itine-

rant

rant preachers, who have imbibed rational principles of religion, in inftructing the common people in different parts of the kingdom. Let them hire rooms, for the ufe of public affemblies, in the principal towns and villages, and give to the focieties, which are formed by thefe means, fuch affiftance as they may want during their infant ftate. As they increafe in numbers, or in the wealth of the members which compofe them, they will be able to defray their own expences, and to fupport ftated minifters; or, at leaft, with a little foreign aid. By adopting fuch a plan as this, they will provide for the inftruction of a clafs of people, who are either totally ignorant of religion, or whofe minds have been poifoned with error and enthufiafm. They will lay the foundation of a new ftate of things, which will exhibit chriftianity in its pureft and beft form. The diftribution of well chofen religious books, may, undoubtedly, greatly forward this defign. But I apprehend it fhould not be attempted till curiofity has been a little awakened by public preaching. In order that this fociety may be fatisfied that their money is ufefully expended, regular accounts of the ftate of every congregation, in regard to numbers, difcipline and moral conduct, might be laid before them every year at their annual meetings; and, in the interval, the affairs of the body might be left to the management of a committee, who fhould have authority to chufe the preachers, to appoint their circuits, and to direct their proceedings in every refpect; the committee meeting once every quarter for this purpofe, or oftener, if neceffary.

With refpect to the qualifications requifite in the minifters who are to be employed in executing this plan, as well as with refpect to the means by which they are to be obtained, I may perhaps ftate my opinion more fully at fome future time. At prefent,

I fhall

I fhall only obferve that my views go no farther than an englifh education. A perfon who has good natural talents, who can fpeak and write his native language with propriety, and is well acquainted with the fcriptures, is, in my apprehenfion, if his moral character be unexceptionable, fufficiently qualified to become a public teacher of religion. Greater furniture may be defirable, but it is not neceffary.

To thofe who may entertain doubts of the fuccefs of fuch a fcheme as I have now propofed, I might mention that the chriftian religion was firft propagated in this manner: or, if the authority of this example fhould be denied me, as being inapplicable to the prefent cafe, I can appeal to one of more modern date, to which no one can reafonably object. Mr. Wefley and his followers have given us a ftriking inftance of the utility and fuccefs of a fimilar plan. With fcarce any other advantages than what their own zeal furnifhed, (Mr. Wefley himfelf excepted) they have eftablifhed focieties of their own perfuafion in every part of the kingdom, and formed a body of people, in a few years, amounting to near one hundred thoufand perfons. If, then, what we deem miftaken fentiments in religion, have been fo fuccefsfully propagated in this way, why fhould we doubt whether thofe which are true may not be diffeminated with, at leaft, equal fuccefs? If methodifm, notwithftanding all its errors and abfurdities, has been fo ufeful in civilizing and reclaiming the lower orders of mankind, how much more good might there not be expected to arife from a rational fyftem of religion inculcated upon the fame clafs of people? But I muft forbear to enlarge upon this fubject, left what I write fhould exceed the limits of your plan.

I am, Sir,

A FRIEND TO THE POOR.

ART. VI.

Art. VI. *Another Paper on the same subject.*

TO THE EDITOR OF THE CHRISTIAN MISCELLANY,

SIR,

It was with singular pleasure I observed in your last Number a design announced of a small number of gentlemen forming themselves into a society to promote *unadulterated*, which must necessarily be *rational*, christianity. As joined with them in object and aim, I presume to lay before them a plan, which I desire them not to reject from the appearance of something novel and eccentric in it, without due consideration of its *practicability* and *utility*.

Distributing books, supporting ministers already settled with small societies of rational christians, educating persons for the ministry, &c. must be doubtless fitted in some good degree to answer the valuable end. But, I conceive, there is a necessity of some measures being taken which shall draw the attention of the people in general to the pure doctrines of christianity, in a more direct and forcible manner than those before mentioned, which have been tried, and though not without success, yet without that extensive effect which might be expected. We have seen the effects which have been produced by methodistical preachers, chiefly in consequence of their preaching to different congregations, preaching in the fields and public places, delivering their discourses extempore, and with warmth and animation in their manner. What reason can be given against the supposition, that *rational* religion would be as generally received, at least that it would be far more attended to than it is, if propagated in something of a similar mode. Only let the preacher of rational religion avoid the buffoonery and stunning vociferation, the ridiculous attitudes, which characterize this sort of preachers, and imitate them in,

what

what he may confiftently, their preaching extempore or memoriter, their frequency in preaching and in public fituations.

Now is it not poffible for the propofed fociety to find two or three men of abilities fuited to the work, amongft the increafing number of enlightened chriftian minifters, particularly thofe who are young. Let thefe go out as miffionaries in the courfe of the fummer, the proper time for taking the field, and traverfe as much of the kingdom as they are able, preaching both on the Sundays and other days, *wherever* and *whenever* they can collect a number of auditors; at the fame time difperfing thofe tracts with which they may be furnifhed, calculated to forward the object of their preaching. Let them efpecially preach in all large towns, where there is the greateft probability of a number of people attending upon them, even though there fhould be minifters of the fame fentiments fettled there. Numbers will come and enquire what the new doctrine is, delivered under fuch novel circumftances, who would never give themfelves any concern with the fame doctrine, delivered in a regular way. Farther, let thefe miffionaries form focieties wherever they are able, on liberal principles, yet with due attention to difcipline; leaving them to be governed by thofe of the greateft piety and intelligence amongft their own members, themfelves paying occafional vifits, until they are fufficiently numerous to fupport a learned regular miniftry.

I cannot think the fociety will be able to direct their pecuniary affiftance better than in the execution of fuch a plan. What is wanting but fome pious, zealous men who will voluntarily offer themfelves to the fervice? And let me not fuppofe that an *enlightened underftanding* is fo inconfiftent with *extraordinary zeal*, as to forbid the hope that fuch

may

may come forward. I am, for my own part, clearly of opinion, that, according to the prefent ftate of religion among us in this kingdom, rational fentiments of religion, will never prevail among the bulk of the people, till fome meafures of this kind are adopted.

I am, SIR,

Your humble fervant,

EVANGELICUS.

ART. VII. *The Temple of Wealth. A Vifion.*

As I was one evening meditating on the great eagernefs of mortals to obtain wealth, I gradually fell into a gentle flumber. My imagination, being impreffed with the images which it had formed during the time of my reverie, inftantly fet to work, and I found myfelf at the bottom of a fteep and craggy mountain, on the top of which there appeared a Palace built of folid gold, and adorned with a variety of jewels, pearls, diamonds, and other precious ftones. The gates were of the moft tranfparent cryftal; and, in fhort, it was the moft fplendid ftructure that mortal eyes ever beheld. At the bottom of the mountain, I obferved an innumerable crowd of people, of various nations, ardently gazing at the lofty manfion, and attempting to climb up to it. Some fet out at firft with great alacrity, and, by the affiftance of a goddefs, called Fortune, made an amazing progrefs; but I took notice that the fickle being fuddenly deferted them, and they came down with much rapidity, mangled, torn and difappointed. I obferved alfo that thefe perfons were received at the bottom with a malignant joy by thofe who had made the like unfuccefsful attempt, or thofe who

had

had proceeded but a little way; becaufe, when the former had made a fuccefsful progrefs, they defpifed and triumphed over thofe whom they had left behind. Others I obferved afcending with confiderable fuccefs for a fhort time; but, when they came to a certain place, they were accofted by a youth in gay attire, and of a moft bewitching countenance, attended by two alluring females. The youth, who was called Prodigality, I faw put on the appearance of a very amiable perfonage named Good Humour, and affect the air of feftivity and joy to fuch an extreme, that I was induced to fufpect him an impoftor. I, therefore, watched him narrowly, and difcovered that, though he put on the appearance of mirth and joy, his bofom was continually torn by remorfe, confcioufnefs of guilt, and fear of punifh-ment; and that his body was wafting away by the private attacks of an hag, called Intemperance. The two females were Pleafure and Illicit Love. Thefe, by their enticements, gradually brought back the per-fons whom they met, to the place whence they fet out, and then left them with derifion and fcorn. Some, whom I obferved fet out, proceeded a very little way before they were met by a graceful per-fonage, who invited them into a building, wherein I faw depofited a vaft number of books in all arts and fciences, claffed in their feveral ranks, befides feveral valuable collections of natural curiofities, and of all the machines which have ever been invented for the improvement of the arts. Some few, I perceived, were fo taken up with ftudying the con-tents of this delightful repofitory, that they forgot the journey on which they fet out, and did not re-collect their firft defign, till they were too well pleafed with their prefent abode to quit it for an uncertainty. While I was gazing at this edifice, which was called the Temple of Science, a new tra-veller

veller at the foot of the hill attracted my attention. He set out with the utmost carefulness, and constantly examined the ground, before he made any considerable progress. He went on for some time in this cautious manner, till he came to a place where there were two roads which led to the top of the hill; the one guarded by Virtue, the other by Vice. These two roads were very contiguous to each other, and the boundary between them was so flight, that it was with difficulty discerned by those whose eyes were rendered dim by the mist of self-interest. The traveller hesitated a long time, which of the paths he should chuse; for that of Vice seemed much easier and shorter than that of Virtue, which appeared rough, steep, and difficult of access. Besides Vice, attended by Pleasure, solicited the traveller in specious terms to enter upon her path; and she would have prevailed, had it not been for the interposition of a grave personage called Conscience, at whose instigation he at length entered on the path of Virtue. However, as I said before, the roads being very contiguous, Vice and Pleasure went by the side of the road, as near the path of Virtue as they could, and, by their magical arts, gradually raised the mist of self interest before the eyes of the traveller. When first the mist appeared, he endeavoured to drive it away; but it gradually became thicker and thicker, till he could no longer distinguish the boundaries, and insensibly strayed into the path of Vice, who, by her allurements, prevented him from returning. He had not advanced far before he was met by Conscience in a rough unseemly garment, and armed with a monstrous whip of snakes. Her visage was tremendous, and her eyes flashed with fire, when, with a terrible voice, she asked him what he did there. The man was struck dumb, and Conscience with her whip

was

was preparing to drive him out of the deteftable path, when an evil genius, named Avarice, came and encouraged him to oppofe the punifher, and gave him fuch effectual affiftance that Confcience was at laft conquered. When fhe was gone, Avarice accompanied the man on his paffage in order to guard him againft any attack from the fame quarter. They had not travelled far in company before they were joined by a perfon of a moft malignant look, called Envy, who conftantly made a practice of pointing out to the traveller thofe who had afcended higher than he had, and thus difturbed his peace of mind. They foon met with another being alfo, named Rapine, a friend of Avarice, the twin brother of Violence. He was a greedy, infatiable wretch, who always went armed, after the manner of a Mogul Tartar. Rapine prefently began to teach the traveller to ftrip the widow, the orphan and the defencelefs, whenever they fell in his way; and to make inroads upon the property of every one whom he met. After a painful and tedious journey, our traveller came, attended with thefe companions, to the gates of the Palace. His heart now beat high with expectation, and he hoped to be admitted into the hall of audience, where ftood the throne of Plutus, from whence immenfe favours were diftributed to thofe who vifited his abode. The gates were opened, and he rufhed in with unfpeakable ardour and joy. But, lo! inftead of being admitted into the hall of audience, he was fhewn into a gloomy cloifter, where he was, indeed, prefented with immenfe treafures; but immediately on his being left by the officers who conducted him to this apartment, two ill-looking fellows, Care and Fear, feized him, and confined him to this gloomy cell. Confcience too broke in upon him, and began to lafh him with the utmoft violence. Thefe three
perfons

persons tormented him in so terrible a manner, that I was glad to leave him and turn away from the horrid sight.

Immediately I quitted the walls, and retreated, pitying the folly of the wretch whom I had just beheld. Just as I was arrived at the bottom of the mountain, I met another man coming along at a slow pace. His looks were composed, and he had an air of dignity and gentleness which charmed me. I was so delighted with his appearance, that I instantly determined to follow him, and, if possible, to keep him from falling into the errors of his predecessors. As he went along, he constantly made it a rule to assist other travellers who were in distress. If he found them fallen, he raised them up; if they were tottering, he gave his assistance, and confirmed their faltering steps. When he came to the two paths, he wisely chose the former, notwithstanding the solicitations of Pleasure, who, with gentle softness, endeavoured to entice him into the latter. No sooner was he entered into the right path, than he was accompanied by a heavenly form, called Wisdom. I also saw a female join him, of a most winning look and contented aspect. Upon enquiring who she was, I was much surprized to find that it was Conscience, the same being who had appeared in so horrible a form to the other traveller. Instead of terrifying him, she, by her encouragements, alleviated the toils of the way. I also observed this circumstance, that if ever this wise traveller happened to slip or stumble, he was instantly raised and supported by those for whom he had done the same kind offices. After a long journey, the fatigue of which, however, was alleviated by the agreeable company into which he had fallen, he at length arrived at the gates of the Palace. He was immediately admitted, and introduced by the officers into
the

the hall of audience. At the upper end of this hall was placed a magnificent throne, adorned with every ornament which the human mind can conceive. On this was feated Plutus, the God of wealth, arrayed in his robes and attended by his minifters of ftate. Upon our traveller's entering this fuperb hall, Wifdom gave teftimony to his good behaviour and fteadinefs on his journey, afferted that he had avoided all the allurements which had captivated the former travellers, and gave it as her opinion that he merited true wealth. Upon this, the God majeftically waved his wand; and a celeftial figure advanced flowly from an alcove behind the throne. Her face was flufhed with a healthy glow, and her eyes gliftened with a modeft fmile. The God ordered the traveller to approach. He obeyed with becoming reverence, and the God, taking the lovely figure by the hand, fpoke thus to the enchanted mortal. " In content is true wealth centered; take her and be happy." With this, he prefented the fair one to the delighted traveller, who led her to a fopha on one fide of the room, and immediately a band of invifible muficians fang the following air.

Happy man ! content poffeffing,
Thou enjoy'ft a perfect bleffing :
Sweet content's the greateft treafure ;
Sweet content's the trueft pleafure.

Here the noife of the voices awoke me, and put an end to my dream ; which, being rather extraordinary, I thought fit to communicate to the public.

M POETRY.

P O E T R Y.

ART. VIII. A Monody.

Oft' times, in beauty's praife, the lyre
   Has tun'd its foftest fong;
Oft has the poet feign'd the lover's fire,
   And, as his numbers gently flow'd along,
His fabled woes he would rehearfe,
And weep and figh, in cadence with the verfe.

Fancy has often drawn an angel's form,
   And feen the poet offer at her fhrine;
Fictitious paffion would his bofom warm,
   As wild imagination framed the line.
And fure, when friendfhip's gentle flame
   Firft was lighted in his breaft,
Oft did the mufe repeat the tender name,
   And all the joys it gave confefs'd.

But now no more the lays
Can found in beauty's praife;
   No more can fancy's airy vifions pleafe:
E'en friendfhip's fun a fhort eclipfe muft bear,
Till, freed from all this anxious care,
   The bofom's more at eafe.

For ah! difeafe, with noxious breath,
Scatters around the blafts of death;
And all the beauteous profpect fades.
   She, who alone my life could blefs,
Is finking to the fhades;
   And with her all my hopes of earthly happinefs.

All hail! ye circling woods!
   Here in this filent, this fequeftered feat
   Sure I may find a calm retreat,
And ftaunch thefe fwift defcending floods,
Which fhew an uncontrouled grief!

Ah

Ah no! for every tree
Recalls the thought of thee;
The weeping willow bows it head,
And seems to whisper, my Cleora's dead.
Here then is no relief.

Yon Naiad, leaning o'er her urn,
Teaches the gurgling rill to mourn.
Oh say, ye streams which gently flow along,
Has art enchain'd your winding way?
Has Sirius drank your chrystal wave?
Has ought remov'd the pebbly stones ye lave?
Not thus you murmur'd to Cleora's song,
Which, seated on your bank, she warbled gay.
The same the chrystal wave, the same the pebbly
    stone;
But I am not the same, for my Cleora's gone.

Dim is the eye, and dull the heart,
Which finds no beauty in these winding vales;
Yon grott, too simple for the hand of art,
Attracts us by its cooling gales.
Ah me! Those lines Cleora's pencil wrote——
Farewell, thou cooling grott!

The grott, the stream, the arching grove
Recall the image of my love.
Where can my wandering fancy rest?
Where? On the mansions of the blest.
The mental eye can pierce the gloom
Which superstition wraps around the tomb,
And see, beyond these clouded skies,
Realms of light and glory rise.
Eternal goodness fills th'extended scene;
Pours o'er the gazer's soul, and leaves his mind
    serene.

ART. IX. *Thoughts in a Garden. By Mr. Grigg.*

That just open'd flow'r, 'tis a fair one indeed:
A flower am I? or am I a weed?
No longer lies nature asleep in the root;
She blooms in yon bough, lo! she's setting the fruit.
O nature! defend it from cold chilling air.
If I am a branch, let me bloom, let me bear.
Too soon from the branch if the blossom should fall,
No fruit will succeed, the mere blossom is all.
Think, think, O my soul, what a lesson for thee;
The bough may bloom fair, yet quite barren the tree.
While planted I am in this garden below,
Some fruit, if but little, some fruit I must shew;
Lest he that has planted should say, with a frown,
The axe to the root, cut the cumberer down.
My season for bearing, not long can it last;
I know not how nearly that season is past.
Let it pass;—for earth is not my favourite clime,
Nor skilful the hand of the gardener, *time.*
Heaven, heaven is the clime, and once plant me but
    there,
O how will I bloom, and what fruit will I bear!
In the planter's own garden, beneath his own eye,
My leaf shall not wither, my fruit shall not die:
By the fountain of life I shall flourishing stand.
Kind planter! remove me with gentlest hand.

ART. X. *The Rose.*

The rose had been wash'd, just wash'd in a show'r,
    Which Mary to Anna convey'd;
The plentiful moisture encumber'd the flow'r,
    And weigh'd down its beautiful head.

The cup was all full and the leaves were all wet,
    And it seem'd, to a fanciful view,

To

To weep for the buds it had left with regret
  On the flourishing bush were it grew.

I haftily feiz'd it, unfit as it was
  For a nofegay, fo dripping and drown'd,
And fwinging it rudely, too rudely, alas!
  I fnap'd it, it fell to the ground.

And fuch, I exclaim'd, is the pitilefs part
  Some act by the delicate mind,
Regardlefs of wringing and breaking a heart
  Already to forrow refign'd.

This elegant rofe, had I fhaken it lefs,
  Might have bloom'd with its owner awhile;
And the tear that is wip'd with a little addrefs,
  May be follow'd, perhaps, by a fmile.

COWPER.

ART. XI. *April, a Sonnet.*

I.

Emblem of life, fee April comes,
  In varied vefture clad;
Now joy's bright gleam his face affumes,
  And looks with tranfport glad.
Anon his eye befpeaks diftrefs and woes,
And, fighing o'er the plain, he flowly goes.

II.

Now Taurus, on his flaming car,
  Sees golden Phœbus roll,
Pour " floods of glory" from afar,
  And gild the northern pole.
A blue ferene the heav'nly cope appears,
And all beneath the garb of beauty wears.

III.

Cloudlefs fee the morning rife,
  And every fcene look gay;

At

At noon through all the "founding fkies"
  The tempeſt wings its way.
The rolling clouds with dark'ning aſpect lour,
And ſwift and black deſcends the ſtreaming ſhow'r.

IV.

But 'midſt the gloom that ſwells the ſtorm,
  A thouſand bleſſings come,
The flowery tribes reſume their form,
  And ſcatter rich perfume.
So heav'n directs the changes of our lives,
And 'midſt diſtreſs the ſadden'd heart revives.

THE REVIEW.

Art. 1. *The Principles of Proteſtant Diſſenters*, ſtated
  in a Sermon preached at Fairford, Auguſt 28th,
  1791. By Joſiah Townſend. 8vo. pp. 26. 6d.
  Johnſon. 1791.

From the declaration of Chriſt before Pilate,
" My kingdom is not of this world," Mr. Townſend
obſerves " that the conſtitution of this kingdom is
ſo very different from that of the kingdoms of the
world, that, as it does not ſet itſelf in *oppoſition* to
them, as long as they keep within their proper
limits, ſo it does not ſeek *ſupport* from them, or
defend itſelf againſt its oppoſers *in their manner or
with their ſpirit.*" He then endeavours to ſhew
" that, as theſe remarks are applicable to the Chriſtian Religion in general, ſo they are particularly
applicable to that claſs of the profeſſors of it, which
in England is diſtinguiſhed by the name of Proteſtant Diſſenters."

  'The Chriſtian Religion does not call in, or deſire,
the aid of the civil magiſtrate for its propagation.
It relies on its own native excellence, and its own
  proper

proper evidence; and there is no doubt that, by means of thefe, it will in due time make its own way, and, with the divine bleffing, will become the religion of the world. And of this I am perfuaded, that no fincere difciple of Chrift will at all wifh for, or in the leaft value, a profeffor of chriftianity, who does not become fuch in confequence of rational conviction; or will at all defire that this moft excellent of all religions fhould be propagated by any other means than thofe of argument and perfuafion.

'Now this, my friends, is the very principle of the Diffenters. We defire not the aid of the civil magiftrate in making converts. We defire not, that our way of worfhip, or that any religious fentiments which any of us adopt, fhould be favoured by the civil magiftrate fo far as to give them afcendancy over all others. If we exprefs a difapprobation of the Ecclefiaftical Eftablifhment, it is not becaufe we wifh to be exalted on the ruins of it. We wifh, that all good fubjects may be alike countenanced and protected in the enjoyment of their religious fentiments and modes of worfhip; and that if any fupport be given by the magiftrate, as fuch, to the teachers of religion, (confidered as perfons who endeavour to contribute to the good order and happinefs of civil fociety) thofe of every denomination may be fupported and encouraged alike. We are not ambitious of power over others. The mere poffeffion, and much more the exercife, of this, would be an infringement of their religious rights. And we ourfelves might be corrupted by it.'

This difcourfe is well written, and cannot fail of producing fome good effect on the minds of thofe who read it. Evidently tending to remove prejudice, and to ftrengthen rational conviction, it is to be wifhed that it may obtain an extenfive circulation.

Art. 2.

Art. 2. *The Contraſt; or, the Hiſtory of James and Thomas, a Tale.* Written for the Uſe of Sunday Schools. 12mo. pp. 88. 6d. Scatcherd, &c.

Art. 3. *The Effects of Vanity; or, Mary Mean-well and Kitty Pertley, a Tale.* Written for the Uſe of Sunday Schools. 12mo. pp. 87. 6d. Darton and Harvey.

Theſe are two very inſtructive and entertaining books, adapted to the capacities of children, and likely to inſpire them with a love of learning, ' by ſhewing them the advantages to which it leads, and the evil tendency of idleneſs and ignorance.'

CORRESPONDENCE.

The letter ſigned, ' An Unitarian Chriſtian,' is received.— It is wiſhed that thoſe correſpondents whoſe eſſays are de-ſigned for the current Number, would tranſmit them as early in the month as poſſible.

The communication of ' P. Y.' is likewiſe juſt arrived.

It is requeſted that all communications for this Work be ſent (poſt paid) directed to the Editor of the Chriſtian Miſcellany, at Mr. Stalker's, No. 4. Stationers' Court, Ludgate-Street, London.

N. B. Publications, which are calculated to promote reli-gious knowledge, or the practice of virtue, are advertiſed on the cover of the CHRISTIAN MISCELLANY at conſiderably leſs than the uſual prices.

⁎ For the enlargement of this Work, ſee the fourth page of the blue cover.

THE

Chriſtian Miſcellany,

For APRIL, 1792.

═══════════

ART. I. *A View of the Perſecutions which have been endured by conſcientious perſons of different perſuaſions.*

No. II.

IN the beginning of the 3d century, the chriſtian church ſuffered calamities of various kinds throughout the provinces of the Roman empire. Many diſciples of Jeſus were put to death in conſequence of a law made by the emperor Severus. Among theſe were Perpetua and Felicitas, two famous African ladies; and other martyrs, of both ſexes, acquired an illuſtrious name by the magnanimity and tranquillity with which they endured the moſt cruel ſufferings. Upon the death of Severus, the chriſtians enjoyed a more proſperous ſtate; but upon the acceſſion of Maximin to the imperial throne, the face of affairs changed. During his reign they were treated with the utmoſt ſeverity. This ſtorm, however, was ſucceeded by a calm, in which the chriſtians enjoyed a happy tranquillity for many years. But the emperor Decius, in the year 249, raiſed a new tempeſt. He publiſhed the moſt terrible ediĉts, by which the prætors were ordered, upon pain of death, either to extirpate the whole body of chriſtians without exception, or to force them, by torments of various kinds, to return to the ancient worſhip. Hence, in all the provinces of the empire, multitudes of chriſtians were, during the ſpace of two years, put to death by the moſt horrid puniſhments.

The immediate ſucceſſors of Decius purſued his bloody meaſures, and kept alive the flame of perſecution. But the longeſt and moſt dreadful calamities which the chriſtians ſuffered, were in the reign of Diocletian, in the beginning of the 4th century. This emperor at firſt ſhewed no diſpoſition for exerciſing peculiar ſeverity towards the diſciples of Jeſus; but he was at length prevailed upon, by ſome of their inveterate enemies, to publiſh an order that their churches ſhould be demoliſhed, their books burnt, and the chriſtians themſelves deprived of their civil rights and privileges. This was followed by other edicts, much more ſanguinary: one ordering that the miniſters of the chriſtian church ſhould be caſt into priſon, and methods uſed to force them to ſacrifice to the heathen gods; and the other commiſſioning the magiſtrates to force all chriſtians, without diſtinction of rank or ſex, to ſacrifice to their deities, and authorizing them to employ all ſorts of torments in order to drive them to this act of apoſtacy. It muſt indeed be confeſſed that, under the latter emperors who perſecuted the chriſtians, the ſimplicity and purity of the chriſtian religion were greatly corrupted, and that ambition, pride and luxury had too generally prevailed both among the paſtors and the people. Cyprian, who lived under the Decian perſecution, writing concerning it to the preſbyters and deacons, ſays, " It muſt be owned and confeſſed that this outrageous and heavy calamity, which hath almoſt devoured our flock, and continues to devour it to this day, hath happened to us becauſe of our ſins, ſince we keep not the way of the Lord, nor obſerve his heavenly

commands

commands given to us for our falvation. Though our lord did the will of his heavenly Father, yet we do not do the will of the lord. Our principal ftudy is to get money and eftates. We follow after pride. We are at leifure for nothing but emulation and quarrelling; and have neglected the fimplicity of the faith. We have renounced the world in words only, and not in deed. Every one ftudies to pleafe himfelf, and to difpleafe others."

After Cyprian, Eufebius, the hiftorian, gives a fad account of the degeneracy of the chriftians about the time of the Dioclefian perfecution. He tells us that, " through too much liberty, they grew negligent and flothful, envying and reproaching one another, waging, as it were, civil wars between themfelves, bifhops quarreling with bifhops, and the people divided into parties; that hypocricy and deceit were grown to the higheft pitch of wickednefs; that they were become fo infenfible as not to think of appeafing the divine anger; that the bifhops themfelves had thrown off all care of religion, were perpetually contending with one another, and did nothing but threaten and envy and hate one another; were full of ambition, and tyrannically ufed their power."

Still, however, it may be right to make fome abatement in reading thefe defcriptions of the degeneracy of paft times. Good men are accuftomed to ufe too ftrong and glaring colours, in drawing pictures of the vice and profligacy of their own age. The multitude of fufferers in the caufe of truth, which then appeared, proved that religious principle had by no means forfaken the church of Chrift, and that the difciples of Jefus were not entirely devoted to worldly purfuits and enjoyments.----I fhall now felect fome few out of the numerous inftances of chriftian virtue which thofe times afforded.

The

The conduct of the celebrated Origen is particularly noticed by Eufebius. He informs us that, when the heat of perfecution was very vehement, and a great number of perfons were crowned with martyrdom, Origen, who was then a young man, indulged fo fervent a defire of fuffering in the caufe of Chrift, that he expofed himfelf to the greateft dangers, and unneceffarily threw himfelf in the way of his enemies; a conduct which does not feem confiftent with fober reafon, nor with the charge given by Jefus to his difciples, if perfecuted in one city to flee into another. The intreaties of a tender mother had no other effect upon him, than to make him more eager to end his life by martyrdom. His father being imprifoned on account of his religion, he wrote to him, exhorting him moft earneftly to be ftedfaft to the faith, and on no account to facrifice his principles, though urged to it by a regard to a numerous and deftitute family. Origen fignalized himfelf in a very great degree by the affectionate and unremitting attention he paid to all who were in a ftate of perfecution; not only vifiting fuch as were bound in chains, and confined in difmal dungeons, or fuch as were every moment expecting to receive the fentence of condemnation, but daring to exercife the duties of chriftian friendfhip and affection towards thofe upon whom judgment had been paffed, and boldly accompanying them to the place of execution. But notwithftanding the various dangers to which he was expofed, he was wonderfully preferved, and fpent a long life of indefatigable labours in the fervice of religion. Eufebius fpeaks of his enduring the moft dreadful fufferings in the Decian perfecution. But neither what he fuffered, nor what he was threatened with, moved him. He furvived this perfecution, was afterwards inftrumental in ftrengthening the brethren, and died at the age of feventy.

Eufebius

Eufebius has preferved a letter from Dionyfius bifhop of Alexandria, giving an account of the martyrdom of certain believers of Alexandria, during the Decian perfecution. This perfecution (fays he) was not begun in confequence of an imperial order, it having taken place a year before the emperor had iffued any edict againft the chriftians. There came into this city a certain foothfayer and inventor of mifchief, who inflamed the heathen multitude, and urged them to defend the religion of their anceftors. The magiftrates being enlifted in defence of the popular fuperftition, they began their perfecuting meafures by feizing a chriftian minifter, and finding that he fteadily adhered to the faith of Jefus, they beat him cruelly with clubs, and after making him fuffer farther effects of their rage, they led him forth to the fuburbs of the city, and ftoned him to death.

The next perfon whom they hurried into the temple of their idols, to try if fhe would pay religious homage to their gods, was a faithful woman, named Quinta. This being done, they bound her feet together, and after dragging her over the fharp pavement of their ftreets, after inhumanly fcourging her and beating her againft millftones, they took her to the place of execution. Thefe perfons having been fingled out as particular objects of their vengeance, they rufhed with one accord into the houfes of the chriftians, and, like a band of ruffian foldiers upon entering the city of an enemy, plundered them of every thing valuable ; whilft the fufferers were enabled to take joyfully the fpoiling of their goods, knowing in themfelves that in heaven they had a better and more enduring fubftance.

Upon the publication of the emperor's edict againft the difciples of Jefus, the flame of perfecution burft forth with additional fury ; and though fome trem-

bled

bled at beholding the dreadful devaſtation it occaſioned, though ſome even denied their lord, and
joined themſelves to the enemy; yet it was the
means of exhibiting many g'orious examples of
firmneſs, of patience and of fortitude. Beſides an
innumerable liſt whoſe names have not been tranſ-
mitted down to poſterity, there were Epimachus and
Alexander, who were fettered, tormented with ſharp
razors, and thrown into the fiery pile; there were
Ammonarion and Mercuria, two upright matrons,
who, being unmoved by the entreaties of the judge
or by the moſt exquiſite tortures, were publicly beheaded; there was Dioſcorus, a youth of fifteen,
upon whom neither the flatteries nor the threats of
the judge could produce any effect; there was the
venerable Julianus, who was ſo afflicted with natural
diſeaſes that, unable to move himſelf, he was borne
upon the ſhoulders of his friends, and thus hurried
by the populace into the devouring flames. (Euſebius,
B. 6. c. 41.)

But ſevere as was the perſecution under the emperor Decius, it was exceeded by that which raged
in the reign of Diocleſian. The accounts which we
have of this perſecution, are peculiarly worthy of
credit, becauſe it happened in the time of the hiſto-
rian from whom we derive our principal information
upon this ſubject. Euſebius ſpeaks in terms of the
warmeſt applauſe of ſome noble martyrs from the
emperor's houſehold, men who were held in the
higheſt eſtimation. By way of example, he mentions one nobleman who was brought forth at Nico-
media into a public aſſembly, and commanded to
ſacrifice. Upon his reſolutely refuſing to make this
idoiatrous compliance, it was ordered that he ſhould
be lifted on high, naked, and his body be ſcourged
till he ſaw fit to pay that religious homage which
was due to their gods. Finding this ineffectual to
move

move him from his conftancy, they poured upon his flefh, made raw by the whip, vinegar mixed with falt. But thefe torments proving too little to fhake his fortitude, they laid him upon a grate, and fufpended him over a flow fire prepared on purpofe, which confuming him by degrees, they perpetually tempted him to facrifice, by affording to him the profpect of a deliverance from his tortures. But notwithftanding every thing, he remained to the laft firm to the chriftian profeffion.—Such were the fufferings of this excellent nobleman, and yet the hiftorian informs us that thofe which fell to the lot of many other chriftians were by no means inferior to them. (Eufeb. B. 8. c. 6.)

" But the pains and tortures endured by the martyrs at Thebais exceed (fays he) all expreffion, for they were torn all over their bodies with fharp fhells till they expired. Women were tied by one of their feet, and drawn up on high into the air by certain machines, with their heads downwards; and their bodies being naked and wholly uncovered, they were made a fhameful as well as an inhuman fpectacle to all beholders. Others were bound to the boughs of trees and fo killed; for by certain engines they drew together the ftrongeft boughs, and having faftened the legs of the martyrs to each of them, they let the boughs return to their ufual fituation. Such things were done, not for a few days nor a fhort fpace of time, but for whole years together, when fometimes more than ten, at other times above twenty in number, were deftroyed. At fome times not lefs than thirty, at other times almoft fixty, and at other times an hundred men together, with many little children and women, were killed in one day; they having been condemned to various and interchangeable punifhments. We ourfelves alfo, when in that country, have feen many fuffer in one

day;

day; when fome were beheaded, others were confumed with fire: infomuch that the fwords of
of the executioners were blunted, and being ufelefs,
were broken to pieces, and the executioners being
tirec, they fucceeded one another by turns."

Is it poffible to read fuch accounts without feeling our hearts warmed with admiration of thofe excellent perfons who thus glorioufly facrificed their
lives in the caufe of religion? We have feen the
aged and the youthful, the fuccefsful courtier and
the tender female, choofing to undergo the moft
dreadful tortures, rather than renounce their faith,
and violate their confciences. They all uniformly
difdained a life which muft have been purchafed at
the expence of their fidelity to their mafter and to
their God.

Great as muft be our admiration of their principles and conduct, we may feel fome very ferious
and painful apprehenfions that, fhould we be called
to the fame fcene of duty, we fhould be unable to
acquit ourfelves with equal honour. But ftill there
is reafon to believe that the God of all grace would
enable us to difcharge our duty much better
than in the prefent ftate of things, we might be
ready to expect. We fhould, probably, difcover
various fources of comfort and various incentives to
fortitude of which we can now form but an imperfect conception; and it is an undoubted fact, that
thofe who have moft diftrufted themfelves, have, in
the day of trial, done the greateft credit to themfelves and to their religion.

ART,

ART. II. *An Essay on Catechising, introductory to a Course of Lectures on Mr. Holland's Catechism.*

TO THE EDITOR OF THE CHRISTIAN MISCELLANY.

SIR,

It has often been a question among the students of human nature, upon what principles it may be accounted for that the nation of the Jews, through such a multitude of ages, and in spite of so many vicissitudes and calamities, should have continued stedfast in the possession of their religion, and in the maintenance of their distinguishing customs and habits. The zeal and constancy with which, through honour and dishonour, through good report and bad report, in prosperity and adversity, in glory and in captivity, collected in a nation, and dispersed throughout the world, they kept, notwithstanding, the faith of their forefathers, has been one of the greatest paradoxes which those have met with who are fond of accounting for every thing by natural causes merely.

But though the mind can rest, on this great subject, in nothing short of the extraordinary interposition and superintendance of Almighty God, yet, as far as he acted herein by second causes, it is probable that that which had the greatest efficacy in maintaining them stedfast in the observance of the law of Moses, was the practice of early religious instruction, in conformity to the directions given in Deuteronomy, vi. 7. " Thou shalt teach them di-
" ligently unto thy children, and shalt talk of them
" when thou sittest in thy house, and when thou
" walkest by the way, and when thou liest down,
" and when thou risest up."

This custom of early religious instruction was adopted by the primitive christians, and was one great cause of the firmness and constancy with which they adhered to the truth, amidst the heat and number of the persecutions which were raised against them. When the christian world was overwhelmed in the ignorance and darkness which followed its subjection to the papal yoke, all care to teach their youth the principles of christianity, and to enable them " to give a reason of the hope that was in them," was entirely dropped. Indeed, mankind had then no principles to learn, their religion consisting in little else than fine shews and unmeaning ceremonies. But when the oppressions and absurdities of the church of Rome had forced a partial reformation, those who conducted it became sensible of the importance of imitating the primitive christians in their great care to instruct their offspring; and, for this purpose, they set up schools, published catechisms and summaries of doctrine, in which their youth were carefully taught the principles of christianity, according to the respective views of the respective parties, together with the grounds of the reformation, and were prepared for supporting, with firmness and ability, the cause in which their ancestors had so gloriously signalized themselves. In like manner the puritans, especially when forced to open separation by the act of uniformity, and exposed to all the hardships inflicted upon them during the arbitrary and persecuting reigns of the second Charles and James, took this method of careful religious instruction to account to their children for " the spoiling of their goods," and for the various marks of civil reprobation which, like another original sin, they inherited from their fathers. But when the danger of relapsing into popery was in a great measure got over, and a long toleration, or at least connivance, had cooled the zeal of the nonconformists, this careful instruction of the rising generation began to be again much neglected, till it has now grown almost entirely out of use. Some

people

people began to find out that it is an irkfome and tedious bufinefs, which muft needs give children a difguft to religion. They remembered, they faid, the tirefome ftrictnefs with which they were themfelves brought up, and they had heard of libertines and infidels who had declared they were made fo by means of it *; forgetting that they owed to this ftrictnefs the good principles which then influenced their conduct, and that many more infidels and libertines have become fuch through a total neglect of their religious education. The faulty method in which the little affiftances of catechifms, &c. have been drawn up, fo as each to become the vehicle of its author's particular fyftem of divinity, has prevented fome, who did not choofe to have their children fhackled in the trammels of any fyftem; while the fear of teaching their children too much, left they fhould open their eyes upon the abufes that ftill continue unreformed in proteftant churches, has probably prevented others. And it is not improbable that a general apprehenfion of the want of fome farther reformation will fhortly induce chriftian parents, efpecially among the diffenters, to return to their old method of giving their children an early fenfe of the importance of religion, and of their obligation to enquire after and ftudy it.

From the foregoing obfervations, it appears that the religious education of their children has been always carefully attended to in the moft diftinguifhed ages of the chriftian church; that it has been followed with folid and lafting proofs, by producing whole generations of eminently pious and excellent perfons; and that, whenever it has been neglected, the world has funk into a ftate of great darknefs and ignorance. And though a prefent view of knowledge

* Lord Bolingbroke charged his infidelity to the account of his tutor, Dr. Manton.

ledge exhibits it in a ftate of confiderable advance-ment, yet this having been the confequence of the care of our anceftors, and fo little care being taken of thofe who are to come after us, what are we to expect but as total an ignorance in the next genera-tion, as we fee indifference in this? And though at prefent we call this indifference, moderation, and flat-ter ourfelves that bigotry and intolerance can never again obtain rule in the world; yet, as ignorance we know is the mother of devotion, which, in that con-nection, is only another word for bigotry, I fee not why we ought not to be upon our guard againft a return of fpiritual bondage, and a tyranny equally hateful with the papal, though, perhaps, in different hands. The only way to prevent this muft be to enlighten, and confirm in proper principles and habits, the minds of the rifing generation, thofe candles of the Almighty, without which the world would be in darknefs.

It is very extraordinay, that while every other branch of knowledge is not to be acquired without much care and labour, the fcience of religion fhould be expected to unfold itfelf, and to take poffeffion of the mind, as it were, by infpiration. The moft trifling accomplifhments are made the objects of the parent's anxious folicitude. The arts of drefs, the graces of figure and motion, the cultivation of the mufical powers in the one fex,---the fciences of de-fence and exercife in the other,---employ the greateft part of the time of our fafhionable youth, to their utter ruin, as to the more ferious and refpectable employments of life. While thefe purfuits engage the gay and diffipated, great pains are taken with the reft to fit them for fome ufeful bufinefs or honourable profeffion. Language, the fciences, and the liberal arts, make up their daily ftudy. No pains are fpared to obtain the ableft mafters, no expence is deemed

extravagant

extravagant when neceſſary to ſecure them. All this is perfectly right. The importance of the objects fully ſanctions this ſolicitude; and ſucceſs, in any tolerable degree, will amply repay it. But all this is only for the preſent life, and when theſe accompliſhments have anſwered the end of ſecuring reſpect and comfort through the courſe of it, they muſt give place to other qualifications, in compariſon with which they are almoſt equally trifling with thoſe external accompliſhments, to the acquiſition of which they are themſelves too frequently ſacrificed. Religion and virtue alone, manifeſted in a well-principled mind, and an habitual practice of what is right and good, can then avail to ſecure our happineſs. Theſe will remain for ever; but without theſe, however great our attainments may have been in the ſciences and arts, or in conducting the buſineſs or amuſements of life, we ſhall make but a poor figure when we are called to that world where beauty and wit will be faded and gone, learning will have vaniſhed away, and all the arts of life be forgotten.

If, then, religion and virtue are of ſuch conſequence to man that, without them, his future eternal ſtate muſt be inevitably miſerable, but that due cultivation of them will amply repay him even in the preſent life, it is of the higheſt importance that he ſhould be early taught their principles, and be encouraged from his infancy to acquire their habits. For it is a neceſſary conſequence of the principle of aſſociation, that the mind, as it advances in years, ſhould become more callous perpetually to the reception of new ideas, it being already occupied with a ſufficient variety. It is, therefore, highly deſirable to have it impreſſed with thoſe which are of the greateſt importance, while it continues ſuſceptible and unoccupied. There muſt be as great a difference between the idea which a perſon entertains of God, who has

never

never thought of religion till he has come to years of maturity, and that of one who has been bred in an habitual reverence of a Supreme Being, as there can be between the views which that man muſt entertain of a father, who has never known a father of his own, or, which is the ſame thing, has had little connection with, or obligations to him, and thoſe of one brought up in a conſtant, uninterrupted intercourſe with him, and accuſtomed to be made the object of innumerable indearments and kind offices *.

And yet how careleſs in this great concern do we find the generality of parents, who ſeem to think they have diſcharged all their duty to their offspring when they have brought them to be baptized, or ſent them to be preſented by others ; and as ſoon as this cere-mony is any how huddled over, ſeem very willing to truſt Providence with the reſt ! As for inſtruction, whether public or private, they make themſelves ſufficiently eaſy about it ; and ſeem to conſider it as a buſineſs which may ſafely be deferred from year to year ; or, without any great danger, neglected al-together.

No wonder, if ſuch a conduct excites the ſcoffs and ridicule of the oppoſers of infant baptiſm. Surely, if there be any meaning at all in the ordinance, it is when conſidered as nothing but a part of the parent's own profeſſion of chriſtianity, and an acknowledge-ment of the obligation which, as a chriſtian, he is under to inſtruct his children and other dependants in the principles of the chriſtian religion. But it cannot operate as a charm, or have any immediate magical efficacy. If the *child* is to receive any ad-vantage from it, it can only be by impreſſing the *parent* with a more ſerious ſenſe of his obligation to diſcharge his duty to it, by giving it that religious

and

* Prieſtley on Education.

and chriftian education to which in that folemn manner he acknowledges it to have a right.

It is not my prefent defign to apply thefe obfervations to every branch of a parent's moral and religious
conduct towards his offspring *. My intention, in
what farther remains, is to plead for the revival of
the too much neglected, but excellent cuftom, of
catechetical inftruction; or the method of teaching
children the firft principles of virtue and religion in
the way of queftion and anfwer. This, I am fatisfied,
if properly conducted, would greatly tend to unfold,
enlarge, and improve the powers of their minds;
would remove their exceffive bafhfulnefs and ina-
bility to exprefs themfelves; would give them enlarged and worthy notions of religion, by fhewing
them that it confifts not in nice fpeculative diftinctions and trifling ceremonies, but in a few plain and
momentous points of doctrine, and perfect rules of
life; and, at the fame time, would be of great ufe
to parents themfelves, by obliging them to renew
their acquaintance, in the moft familiar manner, with
thofe great truths which, for want of fome fuch occafions of recollection, they are in danger of forgetting.

[To be concluded in the next Number.]

---

* This fubject has lately been treated, with great force
and energy, in three fermons on the Parental Duty, by the
Rev. Mr. Walker, of Nottingham. See Vol. ii. p. 229—287.

ART. III.

ART. III. An Attempt to Illuftrate Ecclef. xii. 1—7.

Remember now thy Creator in the days of thy youth, while the evil days come not, &c.

ON this curious, affecting, obfcure, and difficult paffage, much conjectural criticifm has, perhaps, to very little purpofe, been beftowed. After all the labour of learned and ingenious men, there is great reafon to doubt about the real meaning of its feveral parts. We are pleafed with the different ideas which have been fuggefted; but when the glow of imagination is fubfided, when the delight of novelty is removed, when the ardour of admiration is cooled, we begin to withdraw our affent, and to perceive that the fuppofition with which we were enraptured is little more than a fable or a dream. Hence in examining the writings of very ancient times, which contain allufions to cuftoms unknown, refer to events unrecorded, defcribe appearances peculiar to the countries, the climates, the feafons, or the periods, we fhould be very cautious of admitting any interpretation as certain which is only probable; as probable, which is only plaufible; as plaufible, which is only doubtful; as doubtful, which is only poffible. Such caution is efpecially requifite in confidering the allegories, parables, and fables which the holy fcriptures offer to our perufal. The manners and cuftoms of eaftern nations, in the days of antiquity, have been furrounded with a cloud of darknefs. This cloud is now partly diffipated. By the travels of many curious perfons into Afia and Africa, many difficulties in the Old and New Teftament have been cleared up in a very fatisfactory manner. The accounts of the modern ftates of the eaft have been
carefully

carefully compiled, and applied by an ingenious author * to the illuftration of many paffages in fcripture. With his affiftance, I fhall endeavour to give fuch an explanation of this curious paffage, as appears both more natural and more probable than others which have been given of it before. To thofe who are acquainted with any former interpretations, it muft furely be obvious that they are very fanciful and uncertain. What, for inftance, can be more fo, than to fuppofe that the light of the fun, the moon, and the ftars, fignify perfection, memory, knowledge, and all the various powers of the human mind; that the clouds and the rain are fymbols of care and anxiety; that the daughters of mufic are the ears; that the locuft is a diforder in the internal parts; that the filver cord is the fpinal marrow; that the golden bowl means the head; and that the pitcher and the fountain, the wheel and the ciftern, exprefs other parts of the animal fyftem. To get rid of thefe far-fetched and improbable notions, it has been propofed to refer the firft verfe only to old age, and the reft to peftilence. When God fends calamities of this kind upon the affrighted nations, the heavens are darkened, the men of valour are laid low in the duft, the fenfes decay, and the man is carried to his long home. But this interpretation, though in fome refpects plaufible, feems fcarcely admiffible, becaufe the preacher gives no notice of a plague, becaufe it leaves almoft equal room for the exercife of fancy, becaufe the defcription of fuch a difpenfation would add little force to the exhortation, " Remember thy Creator *in the days of thy youth*," and becaufe, if unconnected with this exhortation, it is mere idle mifplaced defcription.—Let us, then, advance to the more probable fuppofition before alluded to.

* Harmer.

O

It

It feems to have been ufual with Solomon to fingle out his fon as the object of his moral exhortations. But though, like other wife and philofophical fathers, he probably drew up his inftructions principally for the benefit of his offspring, yet, like them too, he hoped that his writings might be of further ufe to the general race of mankind. This confideration gives his precepts an additional value. For it cannot be fuppofed that an intelligent and kind parent would recommend any duty to his children, which he did not think would prove, in its practice, of real and lafting advantage. At the fame time, however, that they are capable of univerfal application, there is no doubt that they are efpecially addreffed to his own fon, the heir-apparent to the throne.

The royal fage, after long experience, was drawing nearer and nearer to the end of life. He had tafted pleafure, he had treafured up riches, he had collected maxims of wifdom; but he now perceived, that, in comparifon with virtue and piety, all was vanity and vexation of fpririt. Perhaps, the infirmities of old age were upon him; his eyes might be dim, and his natural force abated. In fuch circumftances, which are not wholly improbable, it may eafily be conceived that a man of his talents would draw a very natural, affecting and forcible picture of the decline of life, and might illuftrate the truth of his defcription from his own fituation. The young prince, comparing the portrait with the original, might fee that there was not a feature but what was copied from the life. And if any of the lines fhould now be found obfcure, it may fairly be fuppofed that they were drawn originally with fufficient diftinctnefs to be eafily known by the perfon for whofe fake they were more efpecially exhibited.

In fo ancient and allegorical a compofition, even with the aid of the beft interpretations, fome diffi-

culties

culties and inconfiftencies muft be expected. Though fome claufes may be ftill in the dark, yet if, with the help of our ingenious author, more light can be reflected upon it, we may be well fatisfied, and hope that, in fome future time, the meaning of every the fmalleft portion may be clearly afcertained.

" Remember thy Creator in the days of thy youth, while the evil days come not, nor the years draw nigh, when thou fhalt fay, I have no pleafure in them; while the fun and the light, and the moon and the ftars, be not darkened, and the clouds return not after the rain."

Thefe two verfes, in their literal fenfe, are applicable to the winter; in their figurative, to the approach of age. Old age has been fo frequently compared to winter, that " the winter of old age" is no very uncommon or improper expreffion. In the holy land, the winter is a very wet, gloomy and terrible feafon. The rain falls in torrents from the clouds, and the heavens are almoft continually obfcured. It is not, therefore, a matter of furprife that, in the times of the crufades, whole armies were deftroyed by the feverity of the weather. So great a bleffing was the return of fpring deemed in the eaft, that in former days the ancients had a joyful proceffion at the end of the winter, and reprefented the departure of this feafon by a bald old man. As, then, in thefe countries it was incumbent upon the inhabitants, before the rainy period arrived, to collect their grain from the fields, and to lay up their ftock of provifions for the enfuing winter, fo Solomon advifes his fon to " to remembe his Creator in the days of his youth," before the winter of old age, coming upon him, fhould put it out of his power to difcharge his duty to God.

O 2

" In

" In the day when the keepers of the houfe fhall tremble, and the men of might fhall bow themfelves."

Man is here compared to a houfe; not to the cottage of a fwain, but the large and magnificent palace of a powerful and opulent monarch of the eaft. This comparifon the wife king derived from his own fituation and abode, attended by fervants and furrounded by guards. David, it feems, had thirty guards of his perfon, and had, every night, centinels at the door of his palace. As thefe fervants would tremble, as thefe guards would bow themfelves, if a more powerful band fhould arrive to oppofe them, fo will their youthful lord at length be enfeebled and fear; fo, at the approach of the king of terrors, age is feized with paralytic tremblings, and the body ftoops and bends down to the ground.

" The grinders" or grinding women, " fhall ceafe, becaufe they are few;" or, becaufe they do little, or have little to do.

When the aged fovereign is finking into years, his fenfes gradually decay. His tafte, in particular, is blunted; and he cannot defire or relifh that vaft variety of food which was formerly brought to his table. As nicety of tafte is continually decreafing, fo fewer preparations will be neceffary; and the women who were once ufed to grind rice*, and other food, for his meals, may now in a great meafure defift from their labour.

" Thofe who look out of the windows," or rather, the women who look out of the windows, " *fhall be darkened.*"

* It is aftonifhing in how many different methods rice is dreffed for an eaftern entertainment. Chardin, a celebrated traveller, was once treated with fixty different difhes of rice of different colours and tafte, mixed with fugar, cinnamon, pomegranate juice, and various other ingredients.

It

It is well known that in the eaft the great keep large feraglios of women, and that on this account jealoufy is, in thofe regions, a thriving plant. This principle leads to the clofe confinement of the fair fex, who have ufually a retired part of the palace allotted to them, and whofe apartments, except on particular occafions, generally have their windows fhut to the ftreet.

In all ages and countries, old men feldom get that portion of fleep which they enjoyed in their youth. Hence, Solomon reprefents the venerable monarch as rifing at the voice of the bird, or the crowing of the cock, before his fervants are ready to wait upon him.

It appears to have been the cuftom, in eaftern countries, for a band of mufic to entertain the monarch as he was rifing from his bed, to ufher in the morn, and to welcome him to the enfuing day. But the preacher defcribes the venerable royal per-fonage as leaving his bed for want of fleep, and thus preventing the ufual employments of the muficians. " He fhall rife up at the cock-crowing, and the daughters of mufic," or the bands of muficians, which confifted of men and women, " fhall be brought low."

The two next claufes are perfectly literal and true. " Then fhall they be afraid of that which is high, and fears fhall be in the way." The fteps of the aged are uncertain, their knees tottering through in-firmity; and their pace is unfteady to a proverb. Hence are they naturally afraid of climbing high places, and feldom undertake any travelling expedi-tions, through the apprehenfion of accidents in the way. In the hilly country of Judea there are paths in which a fingle falfe ftep would be fatal. Like the roads over the Alps or the Pyrenees, they are fo narrow that the traveller who miffes the proper

O 3

ground

ground may be thrown over a precipice, and be dashed to pieces. In such situations, any one has reason to tremble; but a monarch enfeebled by age, enervated by pleasure and luxury, cannot without horror even think of such dangerous paths, and would deem it certain destruction to venture upon them.

The meaning of the three next clauses, " The almond-tree shall flourish, the grasshopper shall be a burden, and desire shall fail," is particularly uncertain. Some say that the first should be translated, " The almond tree *shall be loathed*; the aged sovereign shall lose his sense of smelling, and shall despise the fragrance of the sweetest flowers, of the most odoriferous plants. Mr. Harmer's explanation, though, highly fanciful, is, at the same time, singularly curious and beautiful. The blossoms of the almond, tree are of the colour of snow, while so mixed with purple as very much to resemble the few white hairs sprinkled over the almost bald head of an old man. In the east, the hair of young men is generally black, so that a grey headed old man among the youths, or an aged sovereign among his subjects, would look like the blooming almond tree among other vegetables. As the almond tree flourishes in winter, so a venerable old man seems again to revive, to be the counsellor and instructor of youth, who gather around him to receive the lessons of aged and experienced wisdom. According to this idea, the proper translation of the passage would be, " He shall flourish an almond tree," or as the almond tree.

From a comparison of other parts of scripture it is generally allowed that the word translated, grasshopper, should be rendered, locust. The " locust shall be a burden." Admitting that the locusts frequently commit such ravages that they may be aptly stiled a burden, yet in the present passage there

seems

feems a difficulty in making any proper application, or difcovering any probable refemblance. There are, however, paffages in the prophets in which the fields and vineyards are called fields and vine-yards of defire. * As, then, the locuft ftrips the trees of their vegetation, and fucks up their juices, infomuch that "defire faileth," the defire of green fields and vineyards, fo doth old age dry up the juices of youth, and diminifh defire. As the hufbandman fighs over his ravaged plains, his defolate fields laid wafte by the locuft, fo doth the aged monarch lament the lofs of his ftrength, his tafte, his relifh for pleafure; he remembers the joys which are paffed away, and is grieved that they are now no more. When his fenfes are loft, when his appetites are blunted, when his ftrength is wafted away, he has no farther enjoyment of life, and is foon obliged to yield to the ftroke of death. Then do "the mourners go about the ftreets, and man goeth to his long home."

Thus have we attended the venerable king through the feveral ftages of infirmity to the period of inter-ment. It is natural to fuppofe that we are now to obferve the fucceeding period, the fpace between his interment, and the diffolution of his frame.

This is, perhaps, obfcurely intimated in the be-ginning of the fixth verfe. "While the filver cord," or bandage, "be not diffolved, or the gol-den bowl," or diadem, "be not broken." The word tranflated, bowl, fignifies fomething rolled, fo that without any great force it may be rendered fomething rolled round the the head, as a crown or diadem. Funerals in the eaft, efpecially among the great, the noble, and the royal, have ever been condufted with great pomp and folemnity. The body has been embalmed, and every neceffary pre-

O 4   caution

* If. xxxii. 12. Amos v. 11.

caution taken to preferve it from a ftate of putre-faction. Jofephus tells us that the body of Herod was carried forth, laid upon a couch of gold, adorned with precious ftones of great value and of different kinds. The mattrafs was purple, and the corpfe was wrapped up in veftments of the like colour, adorned with a diadem. When the fepulchre of a prince of Tartary was opened, by an order of the Ruffian court, the body was found wrapped in fheets of gold, and in a mantle bordered with precious ftones. The body and its veftments all crumbled into duft. To fuch appearances it is fuppofed that Solomon refers. Though interred with all the pomp of eaftern royal magnificence, the prince is now defcribed as in a ftate of complete diffolution. At fuch a time, it may eafily be conceived that the place of interment would run into decay, and that the whole fcene would exhibit a ftriking picture of frail mortality. It was, and is cuftomary, it feems, in eaftern nations, to plant flowers in the repofitories of the dead. Several of the jewifh princes and nobles, we are told, were buried in gardens. And Jofeph of Arimathæa had prepared for him a tomb in a garden, in which our lord was laid. Thefe gardens, in fo dry and hot a country as, in the fummer, Judea ufually is, would frequently want watering. Whilft the dead continued in any tolerable prefervation, the ground around them would probably be kept in good order. But when corruption preyed upon the corpfe, the burial place would be neglected, and the inftruments of watering, the pitcher at the fountain, and the wheel at the ciftern, or draw-well, would be broken. " Then fhall the duft return to the earth as it was, and the fpirit," or life, " to God, who gave it."

With whatever advantages or difadvantages this explanation may be attended, it muft be acknowledged

ledged to be plain, to be free from all remote analogies of phyfic and anatomy, to arife from the appearances and cuftoms of eaftern countries, from the palace of an oriental monarch, from the manner of preferving the dead, from the places in which they are interred, and from the various ornaments and decorations common in the ufual receptacles of mortality.

The picture in this view is, doubtlefs, fingularly affecting. It is well calculated to influence a young prince not to fet his heart upon the grandeur and magnificence of a throne, upon the pleafures of regal dignity and power, to turn afide his eyes from the glitter of a crown, to warn him that thefe gay fplendid fcenes will foon vanifh from his fight, and to engage him to apply his attention to higher and nobler objects, to be the father of his fubjects and the friend of his God.

Nor is the paffage unufeful to perfons in an inferior condition. It is of great fervice for them to contraft their own fituation with that of their fuperiors. It confoles them in their moft abject ftate to perceive that wealth and grandeur, dignity and power, unattended with virtue and piety, cannot give peace of mind, or afford any genuine, lafting fatisfaction. The vanity, the mifery of the great may teach us the infufficiency of earthly enjoyments, and the fuperior value, dignity, and happinefs of moral and intellectual attainments. If thefe fcenes fhould not convince us that mankind are more on a level than they appear, the infirmities of old age, and the total diffolution which will at length come upon all the children of men, may well fatisfy us that there is little diftinction among us. " The wife man dieth as the fool." At the hour of death, the rich and the great are ftripped of their grandeur and wealth, and are in nothing different from the

poor

poor, the needy, and the mean. The monarch and his fubjects are then on an equality. Their magnificence, their poverty, their power, their flavery, are all buried in the duft. The grave is the common houfe of all the living. The proud and the humble fhall at laft dwell in the fame apartment, in company with corruption and worms.

> The boaft of heraldry, the pomp of power,
> And all that beauty, all that wealth e'er gave,
> Await alike the inevitable hour.——
> The paths of glory lead but to the grave.

BATAVUS·

Art· IV. *An Argument in favour of Perfonal Remembrance in a future ftate.*

In what manner is the love of virtue formed and improved in the mind of man? By frequent experience of its pleafures, honours and advantages, the mind receives fo lively and durable an impreffion of them, that, whenever the idea of a virtuous action prefents itfelf, it appears furrounded with pleafures, honours and advantages of all kinds. Hence, the idea of a virtuous action becomes in the higheft degree pleafing, and every occafion of performing it is fought for with the greateft eagernefs. By a fimilar procefs the hatred of vice is formed. In confequence of frequently experiencing or remarking the pains, loffes, difgraces and forebodings of future mifery which accompany it, the mind receives fo piercing a conviction and retains fo conftant a remembrance of them, that, whenever the idea of a vicious action prefents itfelf, it appears furrounded with all that is melancholy and difaftrous. Hence, the idea of a vicious action becomes hateful, and all temptations to the commiffion of it are

avoided

avoided with the utmoft folicitude and circum-fpection.

Now can it be doubted, whether the love of virtue and the hatred of vice, which are thus formed in the prefent, will continue to actuate the foul in a future ftate? Why elfe are we appointed to pafs through this world, but that we may acquire and con-firm fuch principles of action as will be conducive to our perfection and happinefs hereafter? And the love of virtue and hatred of vice are undoubtedly principles which muft contribute to our perfection and happinefs in every poffible fituation, and during our progrefs through eternity.

Confider, then, in what we have juft found the love of virtue to confift. Does it not confift in the com-bined impreffion of its various happy effects? And the hatred of vice in the combined impreffion of the infinite diafters and miferies which attend it? Sup-pofe now, at death, all capacity of retaining the vari-ous impreffions received during life to be deftroyed. Would not this amount to a deftruction of the whole medium by which the prefent ftate can act upon the future? In this cafe, every acquired or improved fentiment and difpofition would vanifh as if it had never exifted; the fruits of all our experience would be entirely loft; and the mind would be a blank, without ideas and without habits. Confequently, neither the love of virtue nor the hatred of vice could remain. Since, therefore, it is not to be doubted that we were fent into this world, chiefly, that we might acquire thefe principles from experience, and that we are deftined to exercife them more exten-fively hereafter, what conclufion can we draw, but that the powers of recollection are not to be deftroyed by death, that the impreffions received in the prefent ftate will doubtlefs remain in the future one, will probably even be ftamped deeper? If fo, with what

inconceivable

inconceivable fenfations of delight, may we hope to recognize, in a happier world, thofe who were moft dear to us in this!

D. S. N.

Art. V. *Remarks on the Duration of Future Punifhment.*

Mr. Wakefield, in his tranflation of Mathew, has, under c. xxv. 46, given an excellent fummary of the arguments againft the eternity of hell-torments; as being incompatible with the attributes of the Deity, whofe mercy, and not whofe vengeance, is faid to endure for ever; as what cannot be equitably inflicted for a few years of guilt; as making the faviour of the world the caufe of endlefs mifery to a majority of the human race, whereas, without him, they would only have been annihilated, &c. His own opinion he ftates to be, that fince the world is to be deftroyed by fire (2 Pet. iii. 10.) this univerfal conflagation will roufe all mankind from the fleep of death, that the righteous will then be received into the happinefs of heaven, and the wicked entirely confumed in the fame fire which will deftroy the material world; which fire, as it will not be extinguifhed till all things are annihilated, is denominated in the N. T. *unquenchable* fire; and, becaufe it will *irrecoverably* confume the wicked, they are faid, with perfect propriety, to be punifhed with *everlafting* fire.——This hypothefis he thinks is countenanced by the expreffions of being " *flain* before his face," (Luke xix. 27.) of " eternal deftruction," (2 Theff. i. 9.) of " the fecond death," &c. &c.

With refpect to the hypothefis of the *final happinefs* of the wicked, he thinks it *unreafonable*, becaufe the fuperadded fenfe of happinefs, arifing from the comparifon of their former and prefent ftate, will make them more happy than the uniformly righte-

ous;

ous; and *unfcriptural*, becaufe then, in no inftance would it have been better for any man not to have been born, a cafe which the N. T. not only fuppofes, but exemplifies.

Now, I confefs, I cannot fee why the fchemes of ultimate happinefs and everlafting punifhment are at all incompatible; or why either of them is contrary to reafon or the fcriptures. The true doctrine of morality and of the gofpel appears to be this, that every vicious action carries along with it its own neceffary and inevitable punifhment; and alfo that this punifhment will be *for ever* felt, inafmuch as it operates as a clog upon farther improvement. Every wicked action lets a man fo much lower in the fcale of perfection; or, which is the fame thing, prevents his rifing fo high as he would have rifen, if he had been well employed during the time that he was doing wrong. Therefore, as a conftant courfe of good actions is perpetually carrying a man forward nearer and nearer to perfection, fo a mixture of evil actions, in proportion to their frequency and enormity, retards his progrefs towards perfection. And fuppofing the wicked man, at any period of his exiftence, to get clear from the influence of vice, and, by a thorough reformation, to reftore himfelf to a *capacity* of happinefs, he muft ftill feel the effect of his former crimes in his inferiority of excellence, and confequently of happinefs. So that the uniformly good man will *for ever* keep the ftart, in excellence and happinefs, of even the reformed wicked man; and every wicked action of every wicked man may properly be faid to be everlaftingly punifhed, inafmuch as its bad confequences will be for ever felt, in the everlafting diminution of his capacity of happinefs.

This view of the future confequences of wicked actions feems moft agreeable to the moral per-

fections

fections of God, to juft notions of morality, and to the declarations of the fcriptures; and at the fame time to be of the beft practical tendency: fince it fets in the ftrongeft light the fuperiority of an uniform courfe of virtuous conduct to any the flighteft deviation, however attended it may afterwards be with the fincereft repentance and reformation.

As to the notion of ultimate happinefs being *unfcriptural*, " becaufe then it could not have been better for any man not to have been born," it feems very frivolous; both becaufe Mr. Wakefield's own explanation, (" that it is a *proverbial* fentence, meaning, in general, calamitous confequences; and that it is common for unhappy people to wifh themfelves not to have been born") fets it afide, and becaufe Job (c. iii. 3—22.) makes ufe of much ftronger expreffions than our lord does refpecting Judas, and yet was himfelf reftored to happinefs even in this world.

The above thought, as far as I know, is quite my own; at leaft I have not got it from books. I have never read either Chauncy or Petitpierre; though I believe the curious criticifms of the former are well adapted to convince the diligent fearcher after truth, and the lively declamation of the latter calculated to make a deep impreffion upon the benevolent heart. Dr. Hartley's two chapters upon this fubject I have always thought excellent; and I have lately been much pleafed with an inference ingenioufly drawn by Mr. Walker of Nottingham, from the anxiety of the rich man for the reformation of his brethren; though, I confefs, I do not like to eftablifh doctrines upon the incidental circumftances of parabolical relations; efpecially of one which has in this way been made the chief foundation of the doctrine of an intermediate ftate, and which might alfo be preffed fo far as to prove, in direct
contradiction

contradiction to Mr. Walker's inference, an abfolute and everlafting divifion between the righteous
and the wicked.

WAKEFELDIENSIS.

ART. VII. *Obfervations on the Letters figned, a
" Friend to the Poor," and " Evangelicus."*

TO THE EDITOR OF THE CHRISTIAN MISCELLANY.

SIR,

As my laft communication arrived too late for
publication in your Mifcellany for March, I will
folicit your prefent indulgence in the infertion of a
few remarks upon the letters figned, a Friend to the
poor and Evangelicus. The good intention difplayed encourages me to hope, that their authors will
excufe the liberty I have taken. I would not be
underftood to oppofe one of the propofitions they
have advanced. My defign is only to fuggeft a few
reafons for doubting the expediency and efficacy of
the plan they propofe, becaufe of the particular
circumftances in which unitarians ftand, and becaufe
of the nature of that fociety of benevolent gentlemen,
for whofe benefit the difcuffion was principally undertaken. Methodifm fprang out of the eftablifhed
church. During its firft appearance, its adherents
were ftudious to avoid the odium which the terms
heretic or fchifmatic would have occafioned. This
circumftance did not a little contribute to its
fpread. But the reverfe of all this muft be the cafe
with thofe who engage in the diffufion of rational
fentiments of religion. Exclufive of having fepe-
rated from the pale of the church, arians and fo-
cinians are fubject to other inconveniences. Againft
them prejudice, combined with intereft, hath occafioned

fioned the belief, in a large number of the lower claffes, that their intention is to fubvert chriftianity. This erroneous opinion will not be removed by itinerant, but by fixed teachers. The former will, from their very fituation, only, or principally, make choice of practical fubjects; the latter may and ought to intermix thefe with difcourfes on the evidences of revelation and the particular doctrines it contains. Another circumftance which greatly facilitated the progrefs of methodifm, and which will not be enjoyed by the itinerant preachers which the writers before-mentioned recommend, is, the ufe of the phrafeology of fcripture in the very meaning which a wrong tranflation or eftablifhed opinion may fanction. This the enlightened chriftian and the honeft man will cautioufly avoid. He will give to every paffage of holy writ its true fignification, whether it oppofes or countenances what our forefathers have inculcated. Add to thefe difficulties the immenfity of the fum requifite for fupporting fuch a number of teachers as might introduce the variety for which the Friend to the poor pleads. It is unneceffary to point out the fmallnefs of the number of places in which, could proper inftructors be found, an opportunity for their exertions would be furnifhed. Give me where I may ftand, and I will move the world, was the affertion of a philofopher of old. Where may I ftand to produce the greateft benefit, fhould be the inquiry of the friend of piety. An inveftigation of the ftate of the different fects in this country may contribute to the folution of the queftion, as far as it refpects the fubject before us. The harmony which fubfifts amongft the different denominations of proteftant diffenters may not only teach their common oppreffor an important leffon, but may alfo fomewhat direct the conduct of thofe who are folicitous to promote the beft interefts of their-brethren.

The

The candour and efteem they now manifeft towards each other encourages the hope, that ere long thefe will be fucceeded by an unity of faith in the bands of knowledge and of love. But there is another, a moft numerous, body, whofe peculiar fituation demands fingular attention; the methodifts. Though their knowledge be not extenfive, their difpofition to attend upon public fervices is well known. From habit many of them are admirably fitted to conduct the religious exercifes of a chriftian fociety. Mr. Weftley feemed fully convinced that after his death his followers would divide, and the exifting bond of union be deftroyed. Fact has already fubftantiated the juftice of the opinion. The difciples of Baron Swedenborgh have found many advocates amongft the methodifts, and fome focieties have difcovered an inclination to enjoy the inftructions of a fixed minifter. Do not thefe circumftances evince the propriety of paying a peculiar attention to thofe methods by which their inveftigation of religious truths may be moft powerfully excited? If they be fo well qualified to undertake the office of itinerant preachers, fhould not endeavours be firft applied to convince them of error, and to lead them to the attainment of true knowledge? They difcover a readinefs to attend upon the public worfhip of other focieties, if it does not interfere with their own. Ought not, therefore, an opportunity to be eagerly improved in every place in which it can properly be granted? Will not that be moft effectually attained by fupporting a fixed minifter in thofe places where a defire is already fhewn to form an unitarian fociety, but in which pecuniary circumftances prevent the attempt? I moft highly approve of the obfervations which Evangelicus and the Friend to the poor have made concerning the difcipline of every new-formed fociety. May I be permitted to add to them the propriety of explaining

P

and

and paraphrafing the fcriptures. The utility of that plan will be queftioned by thofe only to whom it is not known. The poor may be greatly benefited, if due attention be paid to catechifing of fervants and children. I have already intruded fo much upon your patience that I muft conclude with expreffing the fincere wifh for fuccefs in your undertaking of

Your humble fervant,

P. Y.

ART. VII. *An Abftract of a Treatife on the union of the ecclefiaftical and civil powers, by John Milton.*

' They who govern fhould difcern between temporals and fpirituals, or they, who difcern, fhould govern.' Then would they difcover, ' that any law againft confcience is alike in force againft any confcience.' It is not poffible, it is not right, it is not politic to ftop the progrefs and fpread of thought and enquiry. Perfecution, reftraint, religious tefts and penal ftatutes in matters of religion are only proofs of power on one fide, and of weaknefs on the other. They alfo lead to the fufpicion, that in fuch inftances right and might are two oppofites. Surely truth and religion are fufficient for their own fupport. Let not the fentimentt of Gamaliel be forgotten ; " whatever is of man will come to nothing, but whatever is of God cannot be overthrown." But who fhall be the judge of religious controverfy ? " The bible, the bible," faid Chillingworth, " fhould be the only religion of chriftians." He found church againft church, council againft council, fynod againft fynod, and, therefore, concluded that the fcriptures were the only proper rules of faith and obedience. Hence, they who have protefted againft any other, and have difclaimed mere human authority in matters of religion, have juftly been called proteftants.

ants. They have been charged with the crime of blafphemy, with the guilt of herefy. But the world has been too long deluded with hard and learned terms. Blafphemy is but evil fpeaking, which cannot be imputed to thofe who diligently and impartially fearch the fcriptures, whatever their fentiments may be. The word, herefy, fignifies nothing more than a fect, which, according to its principles and motives, is good, bad or indifferent. Schifm means divifion, and may imply diffention, with which the honeft and candid can never be chargeable.

Hence, Milton concludes them heretics, fchifmatics, papifts, in the worft fenfe of the words, who believe againft the fcriptures, and who count all heretics but themfelves. Proteftants, he fays, rather than papifts, have to anfwer for perfecution and intolerance, and for refufing to grant univerfal freedom in religious matters. A church which affumes or profeffes infallibility, has a better colour of reafon for infifting upon conformity and uniformity than one which allows itfelf to be fallible. The worft feature in popery is, that it is a roman principality. Though it be regarded as a catholic herefy againft the fcriptures, it is to be fufpected only whilft the pope has temporal dominion, and is mainly wrong for its connection of temporals and fpirituals. They who force religion, therefore, are popifh in the moft popifh point. The civil power has no right to meddle with confcience, nor can it with any effect. Evangelical religion confifts of faith and charity, belief and practice. But thefe require free powers. Hence the kingdom of Chrift is not to be governed by outward force, efpecially fince, as he himfelf faid, it is not of this world.

It may inded be urged, that among the jews there was a union of the ecclefiaftical and civil powers. But

the

the law and the gofpel were totally different. The law was a ftate, a temporal, religion ; but the gofpel, which indeed hath a tendency to abolifh the ceremonial part of the law, concerns the heart and mind only. Befides, the jews profeffed to have the affiftance of divine infpiration, to which chriftians fince the days of the apoftles, at leaft in temporal and civil matters, cannot pretend. Certainly it hath never given them temporal or civil power over the confciences of the children of men. Nor fhould it be forgotten that the jewifh kings only put in force the laws of the nation againft idolatry; laws authorized by God himfelf, becaufe idolatry was the caufe or confequence of wickednefs and impiety. God, indeed, compels and draws by his fpirit, by his providence, or by the fpirit of truth and holinefs. Chriftians fhould be a willing people ; yet in whatever way the civil power is exerted in matters of religion, it violates chriftian liberty. If the ends of religion be alfo confidered, that it is intended to promote the glory of God and fpiritual good, it may eafily be concluded that it is likely to be moft effectual when it is left to itfelf, unaided by the civil power.

ART. VIII.

ART. VIII. *A Chapter of Modern Apocrypha.*

N. B. This was written in the year 1773, immediately after the defeat of the second application of the proteftant diffenting minifters for relief from the obligation to fubfcribe the doctrinal articles of the church of England. On both occafions, it paffed the houfe of Commons; but being vehemently oppofed by the bifhops, to whom lord Chatham addreffed his memorable fpeech *, it was thrown out in the houfe of lords. A partial relief was granted in 1779, but fuch as few diffenters can avail themfelves of. Perhaps, its perufal may not be unfeafonable in 1792, after the third application of the diffenting laity for a removal of their civil difqualifications, has been rejected in fo high a tone.---It was remarkable that, on the application in 1773, it was oppofed by thirteen diffenting diffenting minifters of calviniftical fentiments, upon the ground that fubfcription was a barrier againft that heterodoxy which they did the honour to reprefent as the natural offspring of free enquiry.

Thefe are introduced under the character of the Little Sifter, who loved not the light, xix. 16. ---It is but juftice to add, that moft of them were afterwards heartily afhamed of their conduct.

The Vifion of Anna, the Daughter of Haikin.

1. Now it came to pafs in the month Nifan, that I was weary with much watching, and I fell into a deep fleep;

2. And

* See Dr. Price's Sermon on the Love of our Country.

2. And I saw in the visions of the night which came unto me upon my bed, I looked, and behold, a woman clothed in fine linen and gold and purple and silver; and she stood by the king of the isles of the weft, near unto him, even at his right hand;

3. And her countenance shined with the oil of gladness; the husbandman brought her of the fruits of the earth; and corn and wine and oil were poured out before her; the nobles bowed themselves in her presence, and her sons sat upon thrones among the princes of the land.

4. Then I lifted up mine eyes, and behold, another woman sitting in the wilderness; her loins were girded with sackcloth, and there was dust upon her head; she did eat of the wild fruits of the forest, and was wet with the dews of heaven; and the rich ones and the great ones of the earth laughed her to scorn, and moved the finger at her*; yea she was an outcast among her own people.

5. Yet for all these things was she not ashamed, neither was her countenance cast down. So she prophecied in the wilderness.

6. Now I saw, as she prophecied, that she was in bonds, and the bondage was very grievous upon her; it entered into her flesh and into her soul, and she was vexed.

7. So she cried and said unto the woman that was clothed in fine linen and purple, Behold now, I pray thee, loose these bonds, for they are too heavy upon me,

---

* "Like new settlers, he finds it necessary to clear the "ground before him, and is even obliged to root up a preju- "dice, before he can plant affection. All that distinguishes "him from other men to common observation, operates in his "disfavour. His very advocates, while they plead his cause, "are ready to blush for their client; and, in justice to their "own characters, think it necessary to disclaim all knowledge "of his obscure tenets." Mrs. Barbauld's Address. p. 7.

me, even as a yoke of iron; and there is no caufe why I fhould be holden of them. *

8. Neverthelefs the woman would not; but fhe fet her foot upon her neck; and there was a fword

P 4   in

* 1. If the diffenting teachers have not fubfcribed the 35 Articles and a half, or by the Act 1779, made the declaration therein prefcribed, (to which diffenters in general equally object, and, therefore, very few of them have made; not becaufe it contains any thing in their opinion falfe, but becaufe they conceive that the fubfcribing to any religious teft at all is acknowledging the right of the civil magiftrate to prefcribe to and controul the peaceable member of fociety in matters of confcience and religion) he continues liable to all the old laws againft nonconformifts; particularly he muft not come within five miles of a corporate town, or of any town or place where he has ever preached, under the penalty of 40l.; he fhall be incapable of teaching a fchool; and fhall be liable to a penalty of 100l. for not ufing the common prayer book according to the act of uniformity. 2. If any perfon fhall deny any of the three perfons in the trinity to be feparately and diftinctly God, or fhall fay that there are more Gods than one, he fhall be incapable of holding any office, or of being a truftee, guardian, executor, legatee, or purchafer of land, and fhall fuffer three years imprifonment. 3. If any perfon fhall fpeak in derogation of the book of common prayer, he fhall forfeit, for the firft offence, one hundred marks, for the fecond, four hundred; and for the third, fhall forfeit all his goods and chattels, and be imprifoned for life. Such is the *fword* that ftill remains *in the hand of the woman clothed in fine linen*. And her *fifter in the wildernefs* muft continue to truft to the fpirit of the times alone *for the woman's hand being holden that fhe fhould not flay her.*—Laftly, if any man, not having taken the facrament at church, be elected into any corporate office, his election is void, and if he accept of any office or place of truft, he forfeits 500l. and incurs all the difabilities mentioned at No. 2. To this condition the diffenters object, not merely becaufe they fcruple to pay divine honours to bread and wine, or to countenance the worfhip of Jefus Chrift, as a being equal to God, even the Father, but becaufe they abhor the idea of debafing the memorials of their abfent lord into a qualification for a petty office; and for this, at leaft, unblameable fcrupulofity, they fuffer the abridgement of their civil rights. Such is the *compleat toleration* they enjoy, and fuch the moft " *tolerant and enlightened church in chriftendom.*"

in her hand, and fhe held it over her neck, as though fhe would flay her.

9. Then the woman that was girded with fack-cloth, faid unto her, What meaneth this fword? Haft thou indeed fet thy face againft me to flay me? feeing the Lord made us both.

10. And fhe faid; That be far from me that I fhould lift up my hand againft thee to do thee any harm. I am meek and delight in peace; and have not dipped my hands in blood; the Lord judge between me and thee, if I do aught againft thee; therefore, fear not, but truft in me. Howbeit, fhe removed not the fword.

11. Then the other faid, nay, but I will truft in the Lord my God.

12. And fhe cried again yet more earneftly, faying,

13. Haft thou forgotten the days of thine adverfity and of thy tribulation, when thou waft held in captivity by the harlot that fitteth upon feven hills, when fhe broke down the gates of thy temples, and burned thy fons and thy daughters with fire within thy borders, and bruifed thy foul?

14. Then thou criedft unto the Lord in thy affliction, and he broke the bonds of thy captivity, and fet thy feet in a large place, and now thou liveft delicately.

15. Now, therefore, keep that thou haft; delight thyfelf in the bravery of thy ornaments which are upon thee, thy fine linen, and change of raiment, and bells which make a tinkling as thou goeft, and inftruments of mufic within thy courts.

16. I will not eat of thy bread, nor drink of thy cup; I defire not the flefh of thy fatlings, nor any of thy pleafant things *, only loofe my bonds that my foul may live.

17. Now

---

* The Author feems not to have forgotten this paffage when writing her Addrefs to the Oppofers of the Repeal of the Corporation

17. Now there was with her in the wildernefs a Little Sifter, tender eyed; she loved not the light, and she was alfo under the yoke; and she lift up her voice and cried, faying; It is good for us to be in bondage, my fifter; they are bracelets upon thine arm, and the cords are cords of filk; they are not a yoke iron, and my foul delighteth in them.

18. And the other faid unto her, my fifter, if thou wilt be bound, be bound for thyfelf, and if thy chains are chains of filver, keep them on ftill; but as for me and my children, hinder not that we be fet free.

19. And I faw many of the elders, and of the wife men, and of the chief rulers not a few that harkened unto the woman, and fpake boldly for her; howbeit, the voice of her that lived delicately prevailed.

20. So the bonds were not ftricken off, and the fword was upon her neck; only the woman's hands were holden that she should not flay her. And she turned, and looked unto the Lord, and cried, and faid, Lord, How long?

poration and Teft Acts. See p. 8. " After all, what is it we " have afked? To fhare in the rich benefices of the church? " No; let her keep her golden prebends, her fcarfs, her lawns, " and her mitres. Let her dignitaries be ftill affociated to the " honours of legiflation; and in our courts of executive juf- " tice, let her inquifitorial tribunals continue to thwart the " fpirit of a free conftitution. Let her ftill gather into barns, " though she neither fows nor reaps. We defire not to fhare " in her good things. We know it is the children's bread, " which muft not be given to dogs. But having thefe good " things, we could have wifhed to hear her fay with Efau, " I " have enough, my brother." " We could wifh to be con- " fidered as children of the ftate, though we are not fo of the " church. We claim no fhare in the dowry of her who is not " our mother; but we think it hard to be deprived of the in- " heritance of our father."

POETRY.

POETRY.

ART. IX. *Verses addressed to Clarinda, by a Quaker.*

Clarinda ! to my verse attend,
   And mark the truths I teach ;
Nor wonder if you find your friend
   In a grave hour should preach.

Beauty's the flow'r of blooming spring,
   The blushing rose of May ;
Which, clad in gay attire, but shines
   The triumph of a day.

Unfading Virtue feels no blast
   From time's destructive rage ;
But flourishes, improv'd by years,
   And blooms in wintry age.

Be this alone your noble aim,
   In virtue to excell.
This is the first of human arts,
   The art of doing well.

Seek not, with anxious, fond desire,
   The haunts of public sport,
The gaming rout, the crowded play,
   Or gayly glitt'ring court.

Nor altogether shun such scenes,
   As idle, empty joys ;
For social virtue still demands
   Her share of social joys.

Life is a tragi-comic play,
   Which asks our double skill ;
And she, who knows not to be gay,
   Performs her part but ill.

O may you learn, at others good
   With social joy to glow !
O may you learn, at others pain
   To melt in social woe !

Unless,

Unlefs, by focial paffions warm'd,
 You bear a mind humane,
Faith's but a raphfody of words,
 And pray'rs are pour'd in vain.

Our mutual failings, cares and wants
 For mutual mercy call :
Mercy we claim from all mankind;
 And mercy's due to all.

Then never, with afperfing tongue,
 Rejoice that others fail;
Or be the firft, at fcandal's court,
 To bear the welcome tale.

With chearful, thankful heart, enjoy
 The bleffings heav'n has fent;
Nor droop beneath the ills of life:
 They're leffen'd by content.

ART. X. *Ode to Health.*

 Health, lovelieft nymph!
When fpring with dewy fingers paints the lawn,
 And wakes the fleeping flow'r,
Oft let me meet thee where the wand'ring path
 Strays o'er the foutbern hill.

When fummer's flaming car has parch'd the fod,
 I woo thee, where yon filvery ftream
  Invites to plough its wave;
  And oft when blufhing morn,
  And oft when meekeft eve,
 Exalts her fhadowy car.

 Oh health, capricious maid!
Say on what mountain's brow thou fit'ft enfhrin'd.
 Where ruddy exercife and rofy mirth
  Weave the light dance?
  Shall autumn lure thee,
With all his varied tints and golden ears?

Winter!

Winter! in vain thy ftorms
Shall ftrive to rend her robe.
I fee her gliding on thy rougheft blaft,
With magic circlings fkim the lake,
Or feize the polifh'd bow
And chafe thy fhiv'ring fons.

THE REVIEW.

Art. 1. *The Book of Nature:* A Sermon preached in a Country Parifh. 12mo. pp. 40. 6d. Dilly 1791.

Among the many publications which are daily iffuing from the prefs, few will be found that are better calculated for the inftruction of young perfons than the *Book of Nature.* From an attention to the various objects which furround us, the reader's heart is animated with gratitude to the great Creator. This little work is, indeed, truly pleafing and ufeful. Like Mrs. Barbauld's *Hymns in profe for children,* it will be read with pleafure by thofe whofe minds are moft refined and improved. An extract from it will to many be a fufficient recommendation; and it may be added that it might be ufed with peculiar benefit in Sunday fchools.

'But, if we have great reafon to praife God becaufe he has commanded the earth largely to fupply us with the neceffaries of life for our comfortable fubfiftence, we have likewife reafon to praife him for an abundance of delicacies which the earth alfo produces; amongft which *Flowers* feem particularly formed to pleafe and delight mankind. No eyes, but thofe of man, feem to enjoy their beauties. Brutes never appear to receive pleafure when they behold them, nor do they ftop to confider them with
attention;

attention; they confound them with the common grafs of the field, trample upon the moft beautiful, and are not at all fenfible of this ornament of the earth. Men, on the contrary, amidft a variety of riches, diftinguifh the flowers with peculiar pleafure; we are, as it were, invited to approach them, and, whenever we gather them, they prefent us with new perfections, in proportion as we view them with more attention.

'Each part of nature unfolds them to our view in their turn. They rear their heads on the tops of lofty trees; they are fcattered through the herbage that creeps along the ground; they adorn the mountains, vallies, and meadows; are gathered from the fkirts of woods, and make their appearance even in deferts. The earth is a garden covered with their bloom. Man fees himfelf encompaffed with a multitude of beautiful objects, that are offered to his view with an intention to cheer him in his labours, by prefenting him with pleafures that amufe him without corrupting his heart. And, as the providence of God hath kindly appointed many flowers to fucceed each other in regular order, fo thofe that bloom at the fame time have a pleafing variety of forms, which prove the invention of their author, together with his defign kindly to multiply the ornaments of our habitation.

'But flowers are not only intended to adorn the earth; the greateft part of them, in order to render our entertainment more agreeable, fweeten and perfume the air all around them; and it is remarkable that they fend forth their fweeteft fmells in the morning and evening: the morning, when walking is moft healthy; and the evening, when men repair to them for recreation after their labours. God hath been pleafed to gratify mankind with flowers upon the moft eafy terms; and indeed the value of the gift

gift would have been leffened, if they could only have been obtained by labour and toil. But the care of flowers is only an amufing employment to man, requiring nothing more than a moderate induftry; which, inftead of proving a fatigue, is rather a recreation after his daily labour, and is entirely the work of his own choice.

' Flowers alfo, in fome meafure, fupply the abfence of company, when we are alone. Melancholy difpofitions are brightened into gaiety and joy by flowers; fadnefs vanifhes at the fight of them, and it feems hardly poffible to be diffatisfied amongft them.

' They alfo furnifh us with inftruction, and conduct us by pleafing fteps to the knowledge of their maker. If we confider that they put on their beautiful raiment, and perfume the air to entertain our fancy, to pleafe our fenfes, and multiply our innocent pleafures; we cannot fail to acknowledge with great thankfulnefs the goodnefs of God, who has thus adorned the earth for our better entertainment and refrefhment in our journey through life. Let us not then be afhamed to go to this *School of Nature*, and learn inftruction from the flowers of the field: They will teach us very ufeful leffons, and even improve us in our Chriftian duties.

' From them we may learn how lovely and good He muft be who is the author of fo many charms in fuch a vaft variety of objects, on which he continually beftows the fame beauties which they poffeffed when they firft appeared on the face of the earth: from them we may learn what we all fhould remember, but are all too apt to forget; that " all flefh is grafs, " and all the goodlinefs thereof as the flower of the " field;" which " in the morning flourifheth and " groweth up, and in the evening is cut down, and withereth."

withereth." And when, after the winter has fhut up the paffages of life in flowers, and ftripped them of all their beauties, we behold them rife again at the return of fpring, and a new creation, as it were, open upon us; may we not then learn that life will rife out of corruption, that we fhall fpring from the grave, like feed buried in the ground, and be clothed with raiment more glorious than that of the flowers?

' Such knowledge as this lies open to the way-faring man; it grows in every field, and meets us in all our paths; and it is the moft important knowledge that the wifeft of men can purfue or obtain; it will make us " wife unto falvation."

Art. 2. *Short Addreffes to the Children of Sunday Schools*, on particular Texts of Scripture. 12mo. pp. 143. 1s. 6d. half-bound. Rivingtons. 1791.

Of thefe *Addreffes*, which are fixteen in number, the greater part are founded on particular paffages of fcripture, and the remainder are fuited to Chriftmas-day, Good Friday, &c. Some of the author's fentiments may be deemed exceptionable; but this work will probably be thought by all who confult it well calculated for anfwering the benevolent purpofes for which it is defigned. A fhort example of the familiar manner in which it is written, muft fuffice.

' I fhall endeavour to convince you, that it is your duty to treat all the brute creation with humanity, that is, with tendernefs. Now by the brute creatures you are to underftand every creature that has life, though no reafon or fpeech to complain, nor the power of protecting itfelf from the injuries which may be done to it.

' In the Bible you are told that God made the world, and all that is therein. This alone fhould be fufficient to make you treat all creatures with tender-nefs.

nefs, and avoid doing them any injury; for you have only to afk yourfelf this queftion. By whom are thefe defencelefs animals made? The anfwer will be, by Almighty God. This reflection then would prevent your being guilty of any act of cruelty to them; for as they are the work of a great, good, and merciful God, to injure them, or deface his work, muft doubtlefs be criminal. How thankful fhould you be to God for hindering many animals from injuring you, which they certainly could and would do, if their Creator had not implanted in them a fear of man. He has given you reafon to know what is right and what is wrong, and that reafon forbids you to injure thofe helplefs and innocent creatures that are in your power. It is an act of cruelty and injuftice in children to deprive them of life. Since the Almighty Creator of us and them has permitted us to kill many of them for our food, proper perfons may kill them for that purpofe; but they fhould do it in fuch a manner as to give them as little pain as poffible.'

CORRESPONDENCE.

' An Unitarian Chriftian' may reft affured, that the Society, to which he alludes, will not confine its exertions to the diffufion of rational fentiments of religion, but extend them to the promotion of univerfal virtue. The latter object, as well as the former, is mentioned by the writer of the letter figned, *A Friend to Truth*; and if the great end of that Society was not *to do good*, in the nobleft fenfe of the words, its proceedings would fcarcely be entitled to the attention of the public.

It is requefted that all communications for this Work be fent (poft paid) directed to the Editor of the Chriftian Mifcellany, at Mr. Stalker's, No. 4. Stationers' Court, Ludgate-Street, London.

It is wifhed that thofe correfpondents whofe effays are defigned for the current Number, would tranfmit them as early in the month as poffible.

THE

Chriſtian Miſcellany,

For MAY, 1792.

ART. I. *Remarks on certain Objections to miracles, in a Novel, entitled, The Hiſtory of Charles Went-worth.*

AN anonymous writer in the preſent day hath choſen the form of a novel to convey ſome of his doubts reſpecting revelation. He is not, per-haps, to be blamed either for his doubts or for his manner of communicating them. They, who can-not believe, muſt doubt, and none can believe, till they have obtained ſufficient evidence. Nor has the author in queſtion uſed the weapons of banter-ing ridicule. He has expreſſed himſelf in a candid and ſerious manner. Yet, poſſibly, but few of the profeſſed advocates for revelation are likely to ſee the arguments aimed againſt it in ſuch a perform-ance. As, however, many may read that part of the novel which contains ſuch ſentiments, and may not be prepared to anſwer them, this eſſay is deſigned for thoſe who are diſpoſed to conſider and to weigh both ſides of the queſtion.

The author of the novel has not been conſiſtent in firſt acknowledging what are called the orthodox doctrines of chriſtianity not to be a part of revela-tion, and then urging them againſt it. The moſt formidable part of his argument is his objection to miracles. Theſe he defines to be violations of the laws of nature, and deſcribes as contrary to the

Q experience

experience of mankind, at least for many centuries past. As the evidence for miracles must spring entirely from human testimony, he declares it to be more extraordinary that miracles should be true than that human testimony should be false. He insinuates that the evidence for some heathen and popish miracles may be as strong as that for the miracles of Jesus Christ, and that the one, as well as the other, ought to be allowed to be impositions on the credulity of the children of men.

According to such an insinuation, they must be the offspring of knavery; and yet he never imputes them to any thing but ignorance and superstition. There is nothing new in this author's objections. They may be found still more plausibly, yet, perhaps, not so openly, urged in Hume's essay on miracles; an essay which has been repeatedly answered by the friends of revelation. But a new champion on one side may require a new one on the other.

It cannot be allowed to be a just definition of a miracle, that it is a violation of the laws of nature. It is the act of God, not of man. For what man may know, it may be wrought in perfect consistency with those very laws which he admits. Nothing, certainly, can be properly miraculous in the sight of God. Yet what is strange and unaccountable may seem miraculous to man.

A miracle may justly be defined, a wonder, or an apparent deviation from the common course of nature. This definition may be thought to include eclipses and other common appearances, before they could be resolved into their proper causes. Nor can it be denied. Let natural causes be found for those which are called miracles. The only question can be, whether they were facts. But no natural cause can account for the restoration of a

dead

dead perfon to life. Was fuch a perfon ever reftored? Not in the experience of mankind for
many ages paft. But the New Teftament relates
that Jefus Chrift was raifed from the dead.

This account is given by Matthew and John,
two of his apoftles; by Mark and Luke, of whom,
if they were not eye-witnesses, Mark had his information from Peter, and Luke from Paul, and
Paul profeffed to have been converted by Jefus
from the blindeft attachment to jewifh fuperftition.
Were thefe men honeft? It is not denied. Did
they not know? It cannot but be admitted that
they did. Where, then, is the force of the objection? Not a fact in hiftory is more ftrongly
authenticated. If, then, human teftimony can
prove the reality of any incident, it can prove the
reality of a miracle, and in fuch circumftances it
would be more extraordinary, or, as Hume expreffes
himfelf, more miraculous, that human teftimony
fhould be falfe than that the miracle fhould not be
true. Improbable, is the proper word; it being
abfurd to reprefent teftimony as being miraculous.
—This point is well eftablifhed in the firft paper of
the third Number of the Chriftian Mifcellany.

The evidence for popifh and heathen miracles has
been often proved to be weak and groundlefs, and
in no book fo well as in Douglas's Criterion. If
the refurrection of Jefus Chrift be eftablifhed, many
of the other miracles will follow of courfe. There
will be no occafion for any farther difpute. There
will be no contention for thofe which are not de-
cidedly miracles. If whatever Jefus did and faid,
was by the authority and with the commiffion of
God, chriftianity is true. No one could perform
fuch wonders, unlefs God was with him; and it
cannot be fuppofed that the Deity would permit
miracles to be wrought, or, more properly fpeak-

ing,

ing, work them himfelf in the caufe of error and fuperftition, or for the fake of a character which was not good, and of a religion which was not true, excellent and divine. I. H.

Art. II. *An Illuftration of Pfalm* 110.

In the Chaldee paraphrafe the firft verfe is tranf-lated, the Lord, or Jehovah, faid in his word, or Jehovah faid faying, fit thou at my right hand. This, however, it appears was not the reading in the time of Jefus Chrift. Mat. xxii. 44.

Perhaps, however, the pfalm was originally ap-plicable to Solomon. David calls him his lord or mafter, becaufe he was his fuperior, or a far more glorious king. The proper tranflation of the firft verfe is, Jehovah faid unto my lord, mafter, or fuperior. Where *Lord* is in capitals, there gene-rally is Jehovah in the original. The other word, tranflated lord, can fignify nothing more than mafter or fuperior. If Afaph, or any other jewifh fubject, had written this pfalm, he might with the utmoft propriety call Solomon his lord, mafter, fuperior, or fovereign. If David wrote the pfalm to be fung by Afaph or any other fubject, the ex-preffion would be equally proper in the mouth of the finger.

" Sit thou at my right hand until I make thine enemies thy footftool."

The right hand feat was the feat of honour, and after a victory it was ufual, as appears from Jofhua x. 24. to trample on the necks of the vanquifhed. Thus was it the opinion of David that the kingdom or the reign of Solomon would be, what it indeed was, glorious and triumphant. He was to build a temple to Jehovah, which David was not allowed

to

to do becaufe he had fhed blood. Hence it is faid that Jehovah would fend the rod of his ftrength out of Sion, and that Solomon would be allowed to rule in the midft of his enemies.

In the greek bible the third verfe is rendered thus : " With thee is the government in the day of thy power, in the brightnefs, or with the fplendour, of thy faints ; from the womb I begat thee before the dawn."

If this be faid by David for himfelf, it needs no explanation ; if in the name of Jehovah, it fignifies that Jehovah had appointed Solomon to reign in Jerufalem. But according to readings of the greateft authority, the third verfe fhould be tranflated thus : " Thy people fhall be willing or obedient in the day of thy power, in the mountains of holinefs, or in mount Zion ; from the womb of the morning or early in the morning, dew fhall be upon thee, or the dew fhall be thine ; I have begotten thee." Solomon was allowed to build the temple, whence he might be ftiled, a prieft for ever, or for the age or difpenfation. He was ever, at leaft in his own time, confidered as a prieftly character, uniting, like Melchizedec and the ancient princes of Peru and of other countries, the offices of king and prieft. Accordingly, we find him dedicating the temple to Jehovah, and offering up prayers as the head of his people. 1 Kings viii.

The three laft verfes fignify the fplendid nature of Solomon's victories, and the extent of his dominion and authority. The laft verfe is particularly obfcure.

It may, however, be afked, how came Jefus to apply any part of this pfalm to himfelf? how came Peter to join with him in fuch an application? and whence does the author of the epiftle to the Hebrews ftile Jefus the true Melchizedec?

Q 3

The

The only suppofition which muft be made is that Jefus and his apoftles, with the confent of the jews, confidered not this pfalm as a prophecy, but only quoted it in an allufive manner. Our faviour feems to have referred to it, Mat. xxii. in order to teach the Pharifees that the kingdom or reign of the meffiah was not temporal but fpiritual, and that the meffiah was not a mere regular defcendant from David, defigned to fit on his throne, to rule the jews, or to vanquifh their enemies, but fo fuperior to David as not improperly to be called his lord, mafter, or fuperior. If Solomon was his lord, mafter, or fuperior, Jefus was more efpecially fo, being appointed to found a fpiritual kingdom which would prevail over all the kingdoms of the world, to eftablifh a religion which, when it fwayed all hearts, would render men happy for ever. With great propriety, therefore, was Jefus ftiled a prieft for ever after the order of Melchizedec. The chriftian religion was only figuratively called a kingdom, but Jefus was a prieft in a more literal fenfe, a holy righteous character, attentive to all the duties of devotion. He founded a religion which hath a tendency to grow and increafe till all men become fubject to its power, and are conducted in the way to everlafting happinefs.

The pfalm, as far as it is clearly underftood, is, indeed, fo happily applicable to the meffiah that many have readily been led to confider it as an actual prophecy. With what intention, or on what occafion, it was compofed, it is not eafy to difcover. Thofe, however, who are verfed in poetry, are naturally led to find paffages which feem to them applicable to their own private occurrences and fentiments, even fometimes more applicable to fuch occurrences and fentiments as the poet was not acquainted with than to thofe which he had in

his

his view when he was writing. Whether this obfervation apply to the pfalm in queftion, is left to the determination of the candid, the impartial and the judicious.

ART. III. *On the Infinity of the divine works.*

The fpangled heav'ns, a fhining frame,
Their Great Original proclaim.
In reafon's ear they all rejoice,
And utter forth a glorieus voice;
For ever finging, as they fhine,
" The hand that made us is divine."

ADDISON.

Maria was repeating thefe lines as we were walking on the grafs-plat one evening in the month of September. The reapers had juft finifhed their labours, and the farmers were rejoicing that they had collected and laid up the fruits of the autumn. It was a fine ftar-light night, and the moon illuminated the place where we ftood. I have been reading, faid fhe, Fontenelle's Plurality of worlds, and cannot help feeling a pleafing aftonifhment on confidering thefe planets as abounding with inhabitants, and thofe ftars as fo many funs, communicating light and heat to many orbs full of life and happinefs.

It would fill me with horror to believe them empty of living beings, or containing creatures incapable of difcovering the Deity by his works, and of improving their natures by virtue and devotion. Of this, faid I, there is no probability. Let us rejoice that the weight of evidence lies on the fide of chearfulnefs. If we be in the wrong, we muft be contented till we know more. Then, I truft, though we cannot now difcern the ends of creation,

Q 4

they

they will appear the wifeſt and beſt within the com-paſs of poſſibility or almighty power. But what, continued I, if the univerſe be without bounds, if this hoſt of ſtars extend through all ſpace, multiply-ing to a degree which human imagination cannot conceive. It may, ſaid ſhe. be a magnificent, but to me it is an incomprehenſible, idea. You learned men delight to ſtrike out paradoxes. Remember the philoſopher who fell into the water as he was viewing the heavens. I will, Maria; but you muſt not de-cide before you have heard. I will not, ſhe re-plied. Proceed, and I will liſten with attention. At leaſt then, ſaid I, you muſt acknowledge that we can ſet no bounds to ſpace. Place yourſelf where you pleaſe in its dominions, the proſpect is all around immeaſurable. If, therefore, we conſider the bound-leſs extent of ſpace, its connection with the almighty power of God, is there any thing in the nature of either which forbids the boundleſs extent of the univerſe? I cannot, ſaid ſhe, ſet bounds to ſpace, or to the power of the divinity. Does, then, the perfect wiſdom of the Deity oppoſe the idea that there is an innumerable hoſt of ſuns and worlds? I ſee not that it does. Or his goodneſs? No. Hence, then, concluded I, if God had a power to create at all, he had a power to create farther than we can con-ceive, and if his wiſdom and goodneſs have been diffuſed or communicated in any degree, they may be in a greater than can poſſibly be imagined. Can you conceive, Maria, of creation as being confined within certain limits, and beyond them an immenſity void of all being? Can you imagine God every where preſent, and no marks of his preſence, power, wiſ-dom, or goodneſs in the boundleſs extent of ſpace? Compared with this mighty void, Maria, a finite univerſe is only a point. Well, really, exclaimed ſhe, this idea is too ſhocking to be entertained, and

yet

yet the contrary carries inconfiftency and incomprehenfibility on the very face of it. To quiet your fcruples, faid I, confider what were the divine intentions in the work of creation. Benevolence feems to have been the only motive, and happinefs the only end, of the great Creator. Now, would perfect benevolence be content to impart finite and partial happinefs? Hence, faid I, it is probable that there are endlefs orders of beings rifing one above another in the fcale of exiftence.

Here we were filent a few minutes; when, at length, Maria defired to know how far the conclufions, drawn from fpeculation, were warranted by facts. Good eyes and common telefcopes, faid I, have long difcerned 3000 ftars. But do you fee that white circle over our heads in the heavens? It is called the milky way, and has been ufually fuppofed, and is now found, to confift of an endlefs multitude of ftars at fo great a diftance that they appear one luminous track, and the beft telefcopes can fcarcely diftinguifh them. Fields of ftars, containing 50 or 100, have prefented themfelves at once, and it has been computed that 50,000, fpread over a track or belt 15 degrees broad and 20 deep, have paffed over the plane of the telefcope in an hour. Hence more than a million would pafs in 24 hours, or whilft a belt of 360 degrees revolved, or rather appeared to revolve, round the earth. If the milky way extend to the poles with the fame proportion of ftars, the product from pole to pole will be 180,000,000.

Have we not, then, fomething more than a prefumption that the ftars, like their author, have their centre every where, but their circumference no where?

Such a calculation, faid fhe, feems aftonifhing, not to fay, bold and extravagant. At leaft, however, I replied, it muft be acknowledged that the

power

power of God is wonderfully difplayed in the creation of funs and worlds fo inconceivably numerous, that thoufands of thofe which are moft diftant from us might, without our knowledge, be expunged from the univerfe.

Yet in the nature of infinitude, Maria, there are unfathomable difficulties, inconfiftencies and paradoxes, which, perhaps, will always be inexplicable to the human mind. Infinity, like eternity, is a depth which we cannot fathom, a height to which we cannot foar. I fhould, therefore, be difpofed only to fay that there are many, very many, more funs and worlds, and creatures than I can conceive.

Here the converfation clofed, and we returned to the houfe.

ART. IV. *An Addrefs to thofe Chriftians who attend not the lord's Supper.*

Jefus Chrift commands or requefts his difciples to eat bread and to drink wine in remembrance of him.

If this be a command, what can excufe difobedience? If it be a requeft, is it not reafonable and ufeful to comply? Vifible things imprefs thofe ideas, to which they are annexed, moft ftrongly upon the mind. While we eat the bread, we naturally and eafily reflect on him who calls himfelf *the bread of life*, on that religion which feeds and fupports our fouls. While we drink the wine, we meditate on the death of the faviour of the world, and we rejoice in the fpiritual confolation which he offers to the mourner, in the rewards which he holds out to the meek, to the humble, to the pure in heart, and to thofe who hunger and thirft after righteoufnefs.

The lord's Supper is not a meal, but it derives many advantages from its refemblance to one. It

blends

blends the benevolent difpofitions with an act of religion. It raifes a fpirit of chearfulnefs, which fhould never be banifhed from the houfe of God. It is the meeting of friends, to remind them of a friend who has left the world. It is the meeting of difciples, to commemorate the death of a teacher fent from God. It is the meeting of chriftians, to excite them to obey the excellent precepts of the gofpel, and to imitate the perfect character of Jefus Chrift.

The Corinthians (I. xi. 29.) are blamed by Paul for converting the lord's Supper into an intemperate feaft. They did not difcern the lord's body, they did not diftinguifh the lord's Supper from a feftival in honour of their idols. This was unworthy behaviour, and calculated to draw down upon the Corinthians the damnation (or judgment or difpleafure) of almighty God. Certainly thofe receive the lord's Supper worthily, who attend with a fincere and ferious intention to improve. Examine then yourfelves, whether you have this fincere, ferious intention. You may fafely attend;—ye will certainly improve.

TO THE EDITOR OF THE CHRISTIAN MISCELLANY.

SIR,

If the following pages, as exhibiting a view of the progrefs of the Unitarian fentiments and worfhip, and tending to enforce a conduct confonant to inward convictions, be deemed worthy a place in your publication, it will gratify

A FRIEND TO YOUR DESIGN.

Art. V. *A View of the Progrefs of Unitarian Sentiments and Worfhip.*

The progrefs of truth muft neceffarily be very flow, when it has to overcome the prevailing modes

of

of thinking, to which a length of time has given a sanction, which habit has fixed in the mind, and which national authority has continued to support. Few at first will entertain even a suspicion of the divine foundation of opinions which have been for ages held sacred, and which always blend themselves, by custom, with every devout affection and religious duty. When a suspicion of their rectitude is admitted, it is only cautiously intimated to others; or if divulged with freedom, it gives a shock to the minds of the generality, who have not exercised their own judgment on established doctrines. The opposition of prejudice, authority and interest prevents its being even examined; of course, impedes its progress. The sentiment, which is repugnant to the received creed, must be brought forward again and again, before it can meet with a candid attention, or a general consideration. This has been remarkably the case with respect to the rise and progress of unitarian sentiments and worship. It was about an hundred years from the time when the doctrine of the trinity was denied (near the commencement of the Reformation) and unitarian sentiments were avowed, before a Society formed on these principles was collected, under the humble and pious Mr. Biddle *. This Society subsisted but a few years, and doth not appear to have survived its founders, though the public spirited and zealous Mr. Thomas Firmin was a member and patron of it. This excellent man exerted himself, by publishing and dispersing many tracts on the divine unity, to promote and disseminate just sentiments of it.

  Indeed, notwithstanding his ardent concern to diffuse his own opinions, he acted on a plan which, contrary to his wishes, was calculated to annihilate the
uni-

* See Toulmin's Life of Biddle, p. 78, &c. And Mr. Lindsey's Historical View of the state of the Unitarian Doctrine and Worship, p 301.

unitarians, as a diſtinct party. He cauſed a paper to be publiſhed, to explain the trinitarian forms of the church of England conſiſtently with unitarian principles *. At the ſame time, he was ſo affected with the deep hold which a tritheiſtic conception of the trinity had of the minds of ſome learned men and of the majority of vulgar chriſtians, that he propoſed, and was earneſtly deſirous of ſupporting, aſſemblies for divine worſhip, on the ſimple idea of the unity of God, not as ſeparations from the national church, but as *fraternities* in it; who " would undertake a more eſpecial care of that article for the ſake of which, it is certain, both the Teſtaments were written." For he feared, " without ſuch aſſemblies, " the continual uſe of terms which, in their ordinary " ſignification, are confeſſed by all to imply three " Gods, would paganize in ſome time the whole " chriſtian church, which is heathen already in the " majority of its members, by occaſion of theſe " terms."

It is ſurpriſing that Mr. Firmin, with theſe ideas, could think of holding ſuch aſſemblies without an entire ſeparation from the church, or could ſuppoſe that they would have the deſired effect. For the conduct of their members, when, at the ſame time, they continued to aſſociate in the eſtabliſhed trinitarian worſhip, would evidently be inconſiſtent, repugnant to their belief, and at variance with itſelf. Under ſuch circumſtances no habit of ſteady, uniform attachment to their diſcriminating principle could be formed; the teſtimony they gave to the doctrine of the divine unity, not being regular and uniform, would be far from being complete and perfect; and while they could reconcile it to themſelves,

at

* An Account of Mr. Firmin's Religion, p. 18, 19. and Mr. Lindſey's juſt reflections on it in his Hiſtorical View, p. 299, 300.

at times and even frequently, to join in trinitarian worſhip, it would appear to them, at moſt, as only a matter of expediency and utility to hold ſuch unitarian aſſemblies. Expediency and utility are but feeble motives to weigh againſt the conſiderations of intereſt, the fear of popular odium, and a dread of ſingularity, if a ſenſe of duty does not act with them, and impel, as it were, to a particular courſe of conduct. Their conforming to trinitarian worſhip could not appear to them ſinful. It was an obvious concluſion, that what could be ſometimes and frequently done without ſin, might be always done with innocence; and if no guilt, endangering their acceptance with God, were incurred, why, they would argue, ſhould they expoſe themſelves to great inconveniences, if not ſufferings, for the ſake of ſpeculations and verbal differences.

So the human mind, in ſimilar ſituations, reaſons. It is natural to ſuppoſe that the unitarians of the laſt century reaſoned thus, till they were loſt in the common maſs. A conſiderable interval of time elapſed, before the queſtions, concerning the divine unity, produced a ſecond ſeparation from the prevailing modes of worſhip. The ſubject was kept out of ſight, or was only the ſpeculation of a few inquiſitive minds, ſcattered here and there, without being able, or being diſpoſed, to act together, in forming a congregation on the unitarian principles.

We read of no ſociety of ſuch chriſtians, till the years 1704, and 1705, when the heavy ſufferings of Mr. Emlyn, an eminent, reſpected and beloved diſſenting miniſter, colleague with Mr. Boyle, in the ſervice of a congregation at Dublin in Ireland, exhibited him to public view, as the conſcientious aſſerter and perſecuted advocate of unitarian ſentiments. Theſe ſufferings, which were occaſioned by his publiſhing a piece, entitled, " an Humble Inquiry into the Scrip-

" ture

" ture Account of Jefus Chrift," awakened the attention of fome to the queftion, and raifed in their bofoms an attachment to the virtuous, pious fufferer, like what had been felt and exemplified by the friends of Mr. Biddle. Mr. Emlyn, having been releafed from his imprifonment, went to London; where a few, who were convinced by his writings and admired his virtues, gathered a fmall congregation, to whom he preached, once every Sunday, till it was diffolved by the principal perfons; though this liberty of preaching, which he enjoyed, gave great offence to fome, and was made an article of complaint to the queen, from the lower houfe of convocation *.

The next congregation, of which we hear, arofe under the miniftry of the great Mr. Peirce, of Exeter, whofe paraphrafes on fome of the Epiftles have fpread his name beyond the feas, and will perpetuate it for ages to come.

At the beginning of life, Mr. Peirce had been fettled at Cambridge; where he commenced an acquaintance with the celebrated Mr. William Whifton, and with whom he occafionally correfponded, after his removal from that place, Mr. Whifton has, in the Memoirs of his own life, preferved a letter of Mr. Peirce to himfelf, on the report of his embracing unitarian fentiments; in which he expoftulated with him, in a very friendly ftrain, on the confequences of his opinion; and remonftrated earneftly on the invalidity, as he conceived, of the grounds on which thofe opinions refted. He particularly intimated his fufpicion that Mr. Whifton did not firft derive his notions from the holy fcriptures †. For Mr. Peirce had been educated in the commonly received fentiments

* See Emlyn's works, vol. 1. Memoirs of his Life, p. 45, 48.

† Memoirs of Mr. Whifton. 1753. 2d vol. p. 121—124.

ments concerning the doctrine of the trinity, and, according to his own confeffion, was fond of it to a great degree of uncharitablenefs *.

It is a ftriking inftance and proof of Mr. Peirce's tenacioufnefs on this head, that though Mr. Whifton, in reply to this letter, waved all argument and referred him to the papers which he was about to publifh; yet, after the publication of them, under the title of Primitive Chriftianity Revived, he did not give them a perufal, till accidentally meeting with Mr. Whifton at a bookfeller's in London, his ferious attention to them was awakened by the ftrong and folemn remonftrance on his neglect with which this upright and blunt man urged him. I afked him, fays Mr. Whifton, whether he was reading my volumes. He confeffed he was not, and began to make fome excufes why he was not bound to read them. Upon this I fpoke with great vehemence to him; " that a perfon of his learning, and acquaint-
" ance with me, while I had publifhed things of fuch
" great confequence, would never be able to anfwer
" his refufal to God and his own confcience." †
This mowed him. Mr. Peirce procured Mr. Whifton's books, and read them carefully, and likewife Dr. Clarke's Scripture Doctrine of the Trinity. The weight of argument, contained in thofe pieces, difpoffeffed him of his former ideas, and produced in his mind a conviction of their repugnancy to the holy fcriptures.

With this change of fentiments, in the year 1713, Mr. Peirce removed to Exeter; where, as he was careful to exprefs fcripture doctrines in fcripture words, and his ftrain of preaching was plain and practical, his minifterial fervices were very acceptable. For feveral years he went on in the difcharge of
them

* Britifh Biography, 8vo. vol. 10. p. 110, 111.
† Whifton's Memoirs, p. 125.

them with great peace and comfort; 'till, in the year 1716, when he was abfent from his congregation, an orthodox minifter, who officiated for him, took that opportunity to found an alarm of damnable herefies which were gaining ground amongft the diffenters at Exeter. The zeal of this man evidently out-ran his wifdom, and embarked him in a caufe which he was ill-prepared to fupport; for he afterwards confeffed that he had not ftudied the controverfy.

But the weakeft minds can do mifchief. The people, by this alarm, were thrown into a ferment. The prudent and peaceable conduct of Mr. Peirce was ineffectual to quench the rifing flame. As the clamour fubfided, new machinations were purfued to renew it. The fufpicions of the people and of the minifters, in the city and neighbourhood, fixed particularly on Mr. Peirce and his two colleagues, Mr. Hallet the elder, and Mr. Withers. Tefts were propofed to them, to clear themfelves from the imputation of herefy. The affair was, once and again, referred to the affembly of the united minifters of Devon and Cornwall. After various meafures, in which no defigns of peace were purfued, nor candour or even equity obferved, the proprietors of the chapel; where Mr. Peirce and Mr. Hallet ufed to officiate, took up the keys and fhut the door againft them. In the following week, the proprietors of the other chapels were folicited to take the like ftep. A meeting being held for the purpofe, it was determined that they fhould have no houfe at all for public worfhip. Thefe proceedings were peculiarly iniquitous, as thefe two worthy men were ejected, without confulting the people whom they ferved, and for whom the proprietors of the places of worfhip were only truftees.

R   This

This attempt to silence them proved, however, impotent and vain. They had friends by whom they were esteemed and loved, who valued their ministry and respected their integrity ; and who, while they were cast off by others, still adhered to them. Having, though with difficulty, procured a place for the temporary exercise of their ministry, they opened it on the 15th of March, 1718-19, being the first lord's day after their ejectment ; when Mr. Peirce preached a sermon, which he afterwards published, under the title of " The Evil and Cure of Divi- " sions ;" which, under such irritating circumstances, breathed an excellent spirit of candour and peace, as well as conveyed just and manly sentiments on christian liberty.

The attachment of Mr. Peirce's friends was steady and active ; as they were strong enough, both in numbers and wealth, to erect a new chapel ; which was opened on the 27th of December, 1719. Mr. Peirce again addressed his people on a subject suitable to their peculiar circumstances. The topic, which, on this occasion he handled and applied, was, " The Sufferings of the Apostles a Furtherance of " the Gospel," from Phil. i. xii.

The observations, with which he brought home his subject to that occasion, are, besides being weighty and just in themselves, pertinent to our purpose ; which is to trace the progress of unitarian societies, and to shew on what principles they may and have been formed.

'I take,' says he, 'what has happened to us to have fallen out very much to the furtherance of true, proper gospel worship. If I am able to understand any thing of my bible, the true scheme of christian worship, there delivered, is that of worshipping the one only living and true God, through Jesus Christ, the one only mediator, by the assistance of the one spirit.

fpirit. If we may take our faviour's word, "the "true worfhippers," in the times of the gofpel, "were to worfhip the Father in fpirit and in truth," John iv. 23. Our "coming" according to the apoftle, is to be "to God," but "by Chrift," Heb. vii. 25. And, in general, the method of chriftian worfhip is fummarily delivered by the apoftle, Ephef. ii. 18. "For through him, (Chrift), we "both (jews and gentiles) have accefs by one fpirit "unto the Father."

' This notion and fcheme of chriftian worfhip is fo obvious in the New Teftament, that it has generally prevailed; nor was it ever heard of, I believe, till lately, and here in our learned part of the world, that we are to pray to the Father, fon and holy fpirit, through the fon the mediator; or that the fon was to be confidered as a mediator between himfelf and finners; or that we are to blefs the Father, fon and fpirit for fending his (or rather, if they would fpeak properly, *their*) fon, and pray that he would give us his fpirit. That this is not fuch worfhip as the gofpel directs is, I think, evident from hence, that the gofpel never reprefents Chrift as the fon of any other than the Father. No man can there difcover any fuch abfurdity as that the fon is the fon of himfelf, or that the fpirit is the fpirit of himfelf.

' They, that find fault with us, are not able to deny that our worfhip is agreeable to the chriftian doctrine; but 'tis ftrange they fhould avow a worfhip fo utterly deftitute of all foundation therein. And if I miftake not, the things that have happened unto us, have fallen out rather to the furtherance of the gofpel in this refpect. You are fenfible that after this manner I have all along chofen to order my worfhip among you. This was done peaceably and quietly for a long time, without any one's pretend-

ing

ing to be offended at it. But when the spirit of contention began to work, what was innocent before came to be much censured and condemned; and the great aim and design was utterly to put us down, that such a constant adherence to the scripture worship might be effectually stopt. For this end were we denied any place of worship, and they, who drove us into an obscure and inconvenient corner, took that advantage of insulting both us and our worship.

'But, through the good providence of God, who has raised up a noble and generous spirit in a few persons, the contempt, our neighbours treated us with before, is now turned to envy. We are now got out of our dark corner, and are not like a "candle put under a bed or bushel," (that I may allude to our lord's words,) but like a "candle set upon a candlestick," or "a city set upon a hill." And the men, who thought to disgrace us, have rather made us conspicuous, as they have, though in a very bad way, been the occasion of our being the first congregation who openly declare for the true worship of the gospel; and, through the good hand of our God, have we now built an house to his honour, which our worst enemies cannot contemn, and wherein none need be ashamed to appear and join with us. And what has been done to disgrace our worship, has, at length, fallen out to the honour of it' *.

The society, which thus arose from the unjust measures which indiscreet and bitter zeal pursued against Mr. Peirce, has, amidst every revolution to which voluntary societies are subject, subsisted with reputation, as a monument of the scriptural principles on which it was at first formed; and it now continues to afford its explicit and marked testimony

to

* Peirce's Fifteen Sermons, p. 352, 353, 354.

to the unity of God, and its proteſt againſt every ſpecies of trinitarian worſhip.

[*To be continued in the next Number.*]

ART. VI. *A View of Perſecutions, containing an account of the riſe of the Reformation.*

No. III.

In the preceding numbers, ſome ſpecimens have been given of the fortitude and patience which diſtinguiſhed the early profeſſors of chriſtianity. The number of thoſe who thus honoured their profeſſion, is amazing. It was originally my intention to have cited more examples of primitive firmneſs; but I ſhall content myſelf with referring thoſe who wiſh for farther information to Dr. Prieſtley's Hiſtory of the Chriſtian Church. Nor do I mean to dwell upon thoſe conflicts occaſioned by the trinitarian controverſy, in which both the arians and the orthodox ſo ſhamefully diſgraced themſelves, and outraged the mild ſpirit of chriſtianity. I ſhall proceed to notice ſome martyrs of later date; preparatory to which, it will be neceſſary to give a ſhort ſketch of the hiſtory of the reformation.

It was from cauſes ſeemingly fortuitous, and from a ſource very inconſiderable, that all the mighty effects of the reformation followed. Leo X. when raiſed to the papal throne in the year 1513, found the revenues of the church exhauſted by the vaſt projects of his two ambitious predeceſſors. His own temper rendered him incapable of ſevere economy, whilſt his attachment to pleaſure and to pomp involved him daily in new expences; in order to provide a fund for which, he tried every device that the fertile invention of prieſts had fallen upon, to drain the credulous multitude. Among others, he had re-

courſe

courfe to a fale of *indulgences*. According to the doctrine of the Romifh church, all the good works of the faints, over and above thofe which were neceffary to their own juftification, are, together with the infinite merits of Jefus Chrift, depofited in one inexhauftible treafury. The keys of this were committed to St. Peter, and to his fucceffors, the popes, who may open it at pleafure, and, by transferring a portion of this fuperabundant merit to any particular perfon for a fum of money, may convey to him, either the pardon of his own fins, or a releafe to any one in whom he is interefted, from the pains of purgatory *. Such indulgences were firft invented in the eleventh century, by Urban II. as a recompence for thofe who went in perfon upon the meritorious enterprife of conquering the holy land. They were afterwards granted to thofe who hired a foldier for that purpofe; and, in procefs of time, were beftowed on fuch as gave money for accomplifhing any pious work enjoined by the pope.

Julius II. had beftowed indulgences on all who contributed towards building the church of St. Peter at Rome; and, as Leo was carrying on that magnificent and expenfive fabrick, his grant was founded on the fame pretence. The perfons, who had the privilege of retailing thefe indulgences, executed the commiffion with great zeal and fuccefs, but with little decency; and though, by magnifying exceffively

---

* In conjunction with this reprefentation of Dr. Robertfon's, it is but fair to fubjoin the account which is given by that liberal catholic, Mr. Berrington. ' The *guilt of fin* or *pain eternal* due to it, is *never* remitted by what catholics call *indulgences*; but only fuch *temporal punifhments* as remain due after the guilt is remitted: thefe *indulgences* being nothing elfe than a *mitigation* or *relaxation*, upon juft caufes, of *canonical penances* enjoined by the paftors of the church on penitent finners, according to their feveral degrees of demerit. Reflections Addreffed to the Rev. J. Hawkins, p. 115.

sively the benefit of their indulgences, and by disposing of them at a very low price, they carried on for some time an extensive and lucrative traffic among the credulous multitude, the extravagance of their assertions, as well as the irregularities of their conduct, came, at last, to give general offence. Even the most unthinking were shocked at the scandalous behaviour of men who often squandered, in drunkenness, gaming and low debauchery, those sums which were piously bestowed in hopes of obtaining eternal happiness; and all began to wish that some check were given to this commerce, no less detrimental to society, than destructive to religion. ———

Such was the favourable juncture, and so disposed were the minds of his countrymen to listen to his discourses, when Martin Luther, a native of Saxony and an Augustinian friar, began to call in question the efficacy of indulgences, and to declaim against the vicious lives and false doctrines of the persons employed in promulgating them. Having found a copy of the bible, which lay neglected in the library of his monastery, he devoted himself to the study of it with the utmost eagerness and assiduity, and began to consider it as the great standard of theological truth. It was the licentious use of indulgences and the vices of the monks who published them, that first roused the attention, and called forth the invectives, of our reformer. He was at first far from intending that reformation which he afterwards effected; and would have trembled with horror at the thoughts of what, at last, he gloried in accomplishing. The knowledge of truth was not poured into his mind, all at once, by any special revelation. He acquired it by industry and meditation; and his progress, of consequence, was gradual. By degrees he discovered the inutility of pilgrimages and penances, the vanity of relying on the intercession of saints, the

idolatry

idolatry of worfhiping them, the abufes of auricular confeſſion, and other erroneous opinions and practices, which had obtained an eſtabliſhment in the chriſtian church. The detection of what he conceived to be ſo many errors, led him of courſe to conſider the character of the clergy who taught them; and their exorbitant wealth, the ſevere injunction of celibacy, together with the intolerable rigour of monaſtic vows, appeared to him the great ſources of their corruption. From thence it was but one ſtep to call in queſtion the divine original of the papal power, which authorized and ſupported ſuch a ſyſtem of errors. As the unavoidable reſult of the whole, he denied the infallibility of the pope, and appealed to the word of God as the only ſtandard of theological truth.

To this gradual progreſs, Luther greatly owed his ſucceſs. The prejudices of his hearers were not ſhocked, they were conducted inſenſibly from one doctrine to another, and their faith and conviction were able to keep pace with his diſcoveries. (Robertſon's Hiſtory of Charles V. vol. ii. p. 114---121, and 144---146.)

To the ſame cauſe were owing the inattention and even indifference with which pope Leo viewed Luther's firſt proceedings. Profeſſing and entertaining the greateſt reſpect for the pope, our reformer was ſuffered to proceed ſtep by ſtep in undermining the conſtitution of the church, until the remedy came too late to produce any effect beneficial to the church of Rome.

At laſt, however, on the 15th of June 1520, a bull was iſſued. Forty-one propoſitions, extracted out of Luther's works, are therein condemned as heretical, ſcandalous, and offenſive to pious ears; all perſons are forbidden to read his writings on pain of excommunication; ſuch, as have them in their cuſtody,

cuſtody, are commanded to commit them to the flames, he himſelf, if he did not, within ſixty days, publicly recant his errors and burn his books, is pronounced an obſtinate heretic, is excommunicated, and delivered unto Satan for the deſtruction of the fleſh, and all ſecular princes are required, under pain of incurring the ſame cenſure, to ſeize his perſon, that he might be puniſhed as his crimes deſerved.

This ſentence, which he had for ſometime expected, did not diſconcert or intimidate Luther. He declaimed, with greater violence than ever, againſt the tyranny and uſurpations of the pope, and exhorted all chriſtian princes to ſhake off ſuch an ignominious yoke. Nor did he confine his expreſſions of contempt for the papal power to words alone. Leo having, in execution of the bull, appointed Luther's books to be burnt at Rome, he, by way of retaliation, aſſembled all the profeſſors and ſtudents in the univerſity of Whittemberg, and with great pomp, in preſence of a vaſt multitude of ſpectators, caſt the volumes of the canon law, together with the bull of the excommunication, into the flames ; and his example was imitated in ſeveral cities of Germany. By this he declared to the world that he was no longer a ſubject of the Roman pontif; and that, of conſequence, the ſentence of excommunication againſt him, which was daily expected from Rome, was entirel yſuperfluous and inſignificant. (Moſheim vol. 3. p. 321.

It is not my intention to preſent a compleat view of the progreſs of the reformation. To mark every important ſtep which was taken, to repreſent the various ſtruggles of contending parties, in which ſtruggles religion was, on each ſide, too frequently loſt ſight of, would interfere too much with the general purpoſe of delineating the ſufferings of conſcientious men. In the ſpace of ten years, the favourers

vourers of the new doctrines had gained much ground. Moft of the princes, who had embraced Luther's opinions, had not only eftablifhed in their territories, that form of worfhip which he approved, but—not to the honor of their liberality—had entirely fup- preffed the rites of the romifh church. Many of the free cities had imitated their conduct. Almoft one half of the Germanic body had revolted from the papal fee; and its dominion, even in that part which had not hitherto fhaken off the yoke, was confider- ably weakened by the example of the neighbouring ftates, or by the fecret progrefs of thofe doctrines which had undermined it among them. (Robertfon, p. 44.)

The diffentients were now become fo numerous and refpectable that they concluded a league of mu- tual defence againft all aggreffors, by which they formed the proteftant ftates of the empire into a regular body, refolving to apply to the kings of France and England, imploring them to patronize and affift the new confederacy. The confequence of this was a long and dreadful war, which was not fi- nally terminated till the year 1555. On the 25th. of September in that year, it was agreed, by the con- tending parties, that the lutheran princes fhould be permitted to profefs the doctrine and exercife the worfhip authorized by their own confeffion of faith,* that the proteftants, on their own part, fhould give no difquiet to the princes and ftates who adhered to the tenets and rights of the church of Rome, and that, for the future, no attempts fhould be made towards terminating religious differences but by the gentle and pacific methods of perfuafion and confe- rence.†

Happy would it have been, if they could have learnt this wifdom without the effufion of fo much blood!

* The Confeffion of Augfburg.
† Robertfon, v. 4. p. 200, and Mofheim, p. 378.

blood! Happy would it have been, had each party been satisfied with suffering truth to have made its way by its own evidence! What animosities, what tumults, what conspiracies, what dangers to princes, what havock in nations, what wars, what massacres, have been occasioned by the interference of the civil power in matters of religion! Religion naturally produces peace on earth and good-will among men. The professors and the ministers of religion are naturally mild and forbearing. It is the magistrate, interfering and establishing religion, that renders them proud, tyrannical, intolerant, seditious, cruel. It is the prince that converts the priest into the curse, instead of the blessing, of society. When will the rulers of the earth learn, then, to confine themselves to their proper province? At that time, religion, instead of alternately decorating, and shaking the the throne, will render it firm and happy; instead of being the engine of ambition, will be our guide in life and our consolation in death.

ART. VII. *An Essay on Catechizing.*
(concluded from the last Number.)

But here will come in, I am well aware, the old objection of difficulty and tediousness. " To call to " memory the irksome hours in which we went " through this dull round of questions and answers, " and to hear a poor child repeat, without the pos- " sibility of his understanding them, a series of " words by rote, must be inexpressibly painful and " disgustful." Here I am ready with all my heart to join issue. I am not going to recommend the string of trifling or worse than trifling, metaphysical and theological distinctions, whether sanctioned by a convocation of episcopal, or an assembly of presbyte- rian, divines, which compose the greater part of the

autho-

authorized catechifms of our two eftablifhed churches. The catechifing I would recommend is of a very different kind.*

Suppofe, for inftance, a parent, as foon as his child could fpeak, and began to be amufed with trifling converfations, inftead of repeating to it the trafh of rhymes and ftories current among nurfes, fhould felect fome of the fimpler hiftories of the Old Teftament, and relate them in language intelligible to a child, the exchange would not, certainly, be reckoned for the worfe. The inculcating of brotherly love by a ftory formed upon the plan of Cain and Abel, or of the treatment of Jofeph by his brethren, would probably be as likely to engage the attention, and would certainly be productive of greater advantages than the repetition of nonfenfe, or, what is worfe, the introduction of confufion and terror into the mind by tales of ghofts and hobgoblins. This I would call the firft ftep in a courfe of catechetical inftruction. As the child advances, let fome other perfon, an elder brother or fifter, for inftance, be made to read a ftory, at firft in fimpler language than that of the fcriptures;† afterwards, perhaps, in the words of the bible; and let it then be made to relate, in its own way, the ftory which it has heard

to

* There are two general ways of teaching children the truths of religion. Some make ufe of catechifms, which children are made to get by heart. This is an exercife of the memory, but not of the underftanding; and, therefore, nothing is more common than to find children who can repeat a whole catechifm without knowing any thing more than how to repeat it. The hardeft catechifms are certainly the worft; but the moft plain are nothing more than an exercife of the memory.—The other method is by hearing them read fome little hiftories of fcripture, and by afking them queftions to fet them a thinking and judging for themfelves. This is an exercife of the underftanding.

Robinfon's Village Difcourfes. p. 373.

† Many of thefe may be found in the *Magazine des Enfans*, or, more fimply related ftill, in an Abftract of the Hiftory of the Bible, for the Ufe of the Sunday Schools; printed for Johnfon. price 6d.

to any of the family who may have been accidentally, or defignedly, abfent. As yet, perhaps, the mention of names would be better omitted, or only communicated, and that as a favour, when afked for. By this means the child's curiofity would be increafed, and he would, infenfibly, become mafter of a great number of fcripture names and hiftories, merely in the way of amufement.*

Our young pupil may now be fuppofed to have learned to read a little, and may be allowed, now and then, if he fhould requeft it, but not frequently at firft, to perufe a ftory for himfelf, which his inftructor fhould be careful to choofe from fuch as it is eafieft to read and underftand.†

Children, by this time, begin to take great notice of the things they fee around them, and grow exceedingly inquifitive about their origin and ufe; more efpecially, they are ftruck with the beauties of the field and garden, the viciffitude of the feafons, and, above all, with the glorious luminaries which they obferve in the heavens. Now a judicious parent

may

* In this early ftage of religious inftruction the affiftance of pictures and prints of the chief fcripture hiftories, places, &c. is by no means to be defpifed. I have read fomewhere of a family, the younger branches of which became acquainted with almoft every incident in the Old Teftament before they could read, by liftening to explanations of the tiles which adorned the chimney piece. Fafhion has deprived our children of the benefit of this contrivance, but there are feveral fets of prints of this kind, particularly one lately publifhed by Marfhall.

† There is a very ufeful book for this purpofe, entitled, An Introduction to the Reading of the Bible, by a Lady; printed for Johnfon, price 1s. But I am entirely of opinion with Dr. Prieftley, (Inftit. Introd. p. 23.) that it is a falfe tafte, and a pretended reverence for the fcripture which has banifhed them fo much out of the hands of children; and I cannot think that they would afterwards read them with lefs pleafure in future life for having been the companions of their early youth. I would, therefore, have the bible itfelf, its hiftory, fentiments, and language, familiarized to their minds, when the ftrongeft impreffions are left by the objects which are prefented to them.

may eafily anfwer the early queftions of his offspring
in fuch a manner as to lead them to form a tolerably
correct, though by no means an adequate, idea of a
fupreme all-governing mind.*—How venerable would
be the fight of an affectionate father who, attentive
to catch thofe happy moments which the curiofity of
his child might afford him, fhould take an opportunity
of addreffing him in fome fuch manner as this.

" The little time you have been in the world, my
dear child, you have fpent wholly with me; you look
upon me as your only benefactor, and the caufe of
all the happinefs and pleafure you enjoy. But, my
child, though you think yourfelf fo happy becaufe
you are with me and have hold of my hand, you
are now in the hands, and under the tender care, of a
much greater father and friend than I am, whofe
love to you is far greater than mine, and from whom
you daily receive fuch bleffings as no mortal can
give. That God whom you have feen me daily
worfhip, whom I daily call upon to blefs both you
and me, whofe wonderous acts are recorded in thofe
curious hiftories which you conftantly read, who
created the heavens and the earth, who faved Noah
in the ark, who was the God of Abraham and Ifaac
and Jacob, who protected the amiable Jofeph, the
meek Mofes, and the holy Daniel, who fent his fon
to inftruct mankind,—that God who has done all
thefe great things, is your living father and friend,
your good creator and nourifher, from whom, and not

from

---

* See Mrs. Trimmer's Eafy Introduction to the knowledge
of Nature; a very pretty, though not altogether an unexceptionable, book. For young readers of a higher clafs M. Trem-
bley's *Inftructions d'un Pere*, is by much the beft calculated of
any book which I have feen for leading " through nature up to
" nature's God." It is indeed, upon the whole, fo excellent
that I am furprifed it has not, long before this, been introduced
to the knowledge of the Englifh reader. If the Chriftian Mifcellany fhould be thought a proper place for this, I would engage to furnifh a monthly article out of this pleafing work.

from me, you received your being. You see, my child, this widely ftretched-out firmament, where fun and moon and ftars appear in their turns. If you were to be carried up to any of thefe, you would ftill fee many more as much beyond you as the ftars you fee are diftant from the earth. And yet, my child, fo great is God, that all thefe bodies, added together, are but as a grain of fand in his fight. And yet you are as much the care of this great God as if he had no child but you, or there were no creature for him to love and protect but you alone. He numbers the hairs of your head, he watches over you fleeping and waking, and has preferved you from a variety of dangers which neither you nor I know any thing of. Therefore, my child, fear and worfhip and love God. Your eyes, indeed, cannot fee him ; but all the things you fee are fo many marks of his power and pre-fence : and he is nearer to you than any thing you can fee. Take him for your lord, your father and your friend. Look up unto him as the caufe of all the good you have received through my hands, and reverence me only as the bearer and minifter of God's good things to you. And he that bleffed your father before you was born, will blefs you alfo when I am dead."*

Such a view as this of God and his providence, inftilled into his mind at a proper time, cannot but be attended with the beft influence upon his whole behaviour. More efpecially, it will lead him to en-quire more eagerly into the hiftory of the divine difpenfations, and will enable him to comprehend them more fully, and in a way more honourable to the divine perfections than is as yet become common, or than, I fear, the good man thought of who composed

---

* See Law's Serious Call to a Devout and Holy Life, p 322; a judicious abridgment of which book would be very ufeful.

pofed it, and who certainly forgot his theological fyftem when he gave us this beautiful reprefentation of an univerfal providence extending to each individual, under the direction of the whole train of moral perfections comprehended in the one idea of unbounded goodnefs. In this moft ufeful branch of knowledge the books already recommended will, for the prefent, be fufficient; particularly, the fecond and third parts of the Abftract of the Hiftory of the Bible. In a more advanced ftage, the parent will derive much affiftance from Dr. Prieftley's Scripture Catechifm of Queftions without Anfwers, and from Dr. Watts's Short View of the whole Scripture Hiftory. The preparation of an anfwer to a queftion out of the former, every evening, would furnifh no unpleafant exercife, which would be ufefully followed by a careful perufal, under proper directions,* of the latter. And, in the mean time, the young perfon will be well prepared to learn by degrees the doctrinal and preceptive parts of the fcriptures. Of thefe many fummaries have been drawn up and publifhed, fome of them more, fome lefs, exceptionable. The catechifms of Henry, Watts, Bourne, Taylor, (of Warrington and Dublin,) Read, Prieftley, Porteus, Catlow, Townfend, &c. will be had recourfe to by different perfons, according to their various connections

---

* I have mentioned Dr. Watts's as a proper book for the ufe of young people; though it muft be confeffed that, in common with the other theological works of that excellent writer, it contains many exceptionable things, which it is probable he lived to wifh to fee corrected. If the ingenious author could be prevailed upon to fill up the fcheme of hiftorical lectures which have lately been delivered to his young hearers by Mr. Wood of Leeds, he would certainly obtain the thanks of a numerous train of readers.

There is a pretty Hiftorical Catechifm, in which the author feems to have followed bifhop Law pretty clofely, by the Rev. Daniel Watfon, M.A. Rector of Middleton Tyas, Yorkfhire.

tions and views. I fhall only obferve that thofe appear to me the beft which are moft free from points in difpute among chriftians, and from every thing which favours of a party fpirit, which prefent us, in a fmall compafs, with every thing that revelation contains which can influence the hearts and lives of men, all that is of practical ufe, and, confequently, all that is properly fundamental in religion. And particular care fhould be taken that they be not repeated merely by rote, which may be prevented by occafionally afking the children fome plain queftions, not in the catechifm, but formed upon thofe which are; which will keep them upon their guard, and thoughtful of what they are about.*

I have all along treated this important bufinefs as a branch of family duty, becaufe I look upon it as the proper bufinefs of the parent, which he ought by no means to neglect, on account of its benefit to his children, which parental affection ought to induce him to confer upon them; as it is a debt he owes to fociety to provide for the introduction of ufeful members into it; as it is the beft provifion he can make for the peace and comfort of future life; and becaufe, as I faid before, it is calculated to give himfelf, as well as his children, a more perfect knowledge of important facts and truths.

And if, after parents had conducted the bufinefs thus far, minifters were to complete the religious education by a fhort courfe of lectures on the evidences and doctrines of natural and revealed religion, and on the hiftory of the corruption and reformation of the chriftian church, young perfons would be much better prepared for attending with advantage

---

* See, as a fpecimen, the Queftions formed upon the Scripture-fentences in the Appendix to Mr. Holland's Ed. of Henry. N.B. This Appendix would well bear enlargement.

advantage on the stated preaching of the word than under the present absurd management, which is not more improper than if any one were to expect to make a man an astronomer by reading to him, now and then, a detached proposition of Newton's Principia, without giving him a previous knowledge of the elements of the mathematics.

It is much to be feared, however, in the present state of things, that, notwithstanding the public and private admonitions of their ministers, in neither of which they should suffer themselves to be wanting, parents will be found very backward to undertake this excellent work, so much for their interest as they must acknowledge it to be. Ministers must, then, endeavour, according to their opportunity, to supply the defect; and happy will he find himself who shall possess the spirit to avail himself of his opportunities to the extent to which they have been carried by the indefatigable Priestley.* But such activity is not the lot of every man, nor is every society disposed so chearfully to second the exertions of their minister. But every minister may, at least, hear his young people repeat, a few times every year, some short and plain summary of doctrinal and practical religion, which he may afterwards endeavour to render still more intelligible by a familiar explanation. For an exercise of this kind, I know of nothing so proper as the late Mr. Holland's abridgment of Matthew Henry's Plain Catechism for children. It possesses all the requisites I formerly mentioned; being intirely free from all points in dispute, and insisting chiefly upon the practical applications of religious truth, in a manner sufficiently short, yet clear, and comprehensive. This catechism has been used with good

---

* For a very full account of Dr. Priestley's plan, see the *preface* to his pastoral sermon preached at Hackney, and entitled, *A particular Attention to the Instruction of the Young recommended*, &c. 1s.

good effect, not only by the excellent Editor, but by several other ministers.

This catechism has been also found very useful in the instruction of Sunday scholars, whose less favourable situation scarcely admits of their going through a regular course of religious education, like that described above, either at home, because their parents are generally as ignorant as themselves, and too frequently profligate and thoughtless also ; or at school, where so much time is taken up with giving them the necessary previous instruction. A single plain catechism is as much as they can be taught with advantage during their continuance at school. A minister, however, may, with good effect, insist more at large upon the several articles of their catechism, and express himself in a more familiar manner in his lectures to such catechumens, than is necessary to the better-instructed children of his stated hearers. Such a course of lectures, upon the catechism abovementioned, I happen to possess; and, as the plan is in some measure new, and the children for whose use they were drawn up belong to an institution which still engages a considerable share of the public attention, I have thought they might be no unacceptable present to your Christian Miscellany. They may possibly be found of use to the directors of some other Sunday schools. They may also be useful, with a few variations, to many heads of families, especially among the lower classes, who may find them an agreeable Sunday evening's exercise, to read to their children, after the repetition of the catechism in question.

Leaving it to your discretion to publish them or not, and, if published, at what intervals you think fit, I am, Sir, with the best wishes for the success of your undertaking, Your's,

POEDOPHILUS.

ART. VIII. *The Preface to a catalogue of the books in a Congregational Library belonging to a Society of Protestant Diffenters at Bolton in Lancashire.*

Religion, it is fcarcely neceffary to obferve, is a fubject of the greateft importance. The chriftian religion, in particular, is the common concern of all who profefs themfelves the difciples of Jefus.

But nothing truly valuable is likely to be obtained without labour and attention.

The knowledge of duty is ufeful in the practice. An acquaintance with the beft principles of action may correct many errors in the conduct, and lead perfons to be uniformly and fteadily good.

Example, alfo, is of admirable and ftriking ufe, in conducing to moral and religious improvement. It is more forcible than precept, and better remembered than fentiment.

They, who make the fcriptures the rule of their lives, are in duty bound to ufe all the means in their power to gain the jufteft ideas concerning the real meaning of the various paffages in that excellent volume, which, by way of diftinction, is called THE BIBLE, the book of books. If the feveral parts be well underftood, the tenour of the whole will eafily and thoroughly be comprehended. The more carefully the holy volume is ftudied, the more pleafing, interefting and ufeful will it become. It contains a religious hiftory; it is a volume of providence; it is a book fitted to make mankind wife unto falvation, and to render every human creature virtuous and happy and bleffed for evermore.

The Bible, and the Bible alone, fhould be the religion of chriftians.

When, therefore, every needful help is obtained for the right underftanding of the fcriptures, they

fhould

should be suffered to speak for themselves, and to furnish their own comment.

It would be an endless business to examine all the religious controversies which have been carried on in the Christian world; yet a respectful, an impartial attention should be paid to every important question. They, who study to keep their minds open to conviction, bid very fair to attain the truth; at least they will learn to agree to differ, and will, probably, become well disposed for the diligent cultivation and constant exercise of christian meekness, gentleness, and candour. With pleasure will they reflect on the important truth, in which all Christians agree, that there is one wise, powerful, good God, who, by Jesus Christ, hath brought life and immortality to light.

Every one, whatever be his belief, should be able to give a reason for the faith which is in him.

Some, indeed, are engaged in worldly occupations, which may, possibly, prevent their perfect acquaintance with every religious subject. Yet, if there be any persons who enjoy not some leisure hours which may profitably be devoted to the attainment of religious knowledge, one may truly say that they are too much engrossed by the cares and business and concerns of the present transitory state.

It may, however, be expedient, especially for the young, to read with some kind of regularity and method. What is called natural religion, or that knowledge of God, of our duty, and of a future state, which may be obtained without consulting the bible, seems to demand that it should be studied first. Then revealed or instituted religion, which, if it be not the foundation, is the support of what is natural, will forcibly require attention. The reasons of dissent from the church of Rome, and from the church of England, will then claim a diligent

regard.

regard. Ecclefiaftical hiftory may throw great light upon the opinions of chriftians, and, perhaps, may enable the candid, the impartial, and the judicious, to decide for themfelves on the refpective merits of every important queftion.

But different perfons may ftrike out their own plans, according to the different objects which they may have in view.

An attention to thofe practical writings which are addreffed to the heart, and are fitted to improve the difpofition, may juftly be expected from all. Knowledge and virtue, wifdom and holinefs, are never parted from one another, but to their mutual difadvantage. Yet, better is it to pay a fole attention to the active duties of life, than only to fpeculate upon religious principles, or to make them the mere objects of thoughtful contemplation. The defign of fuch principles is to aid the weaknefs and imperfection of human nature; to teach the proper government of appetite, paffion and affection; to fupport the mind in time of affliction, in the feafon of temptation; and continually to lead mankind to a greater degree of improvement in purity, benevolence and holinefs.

Since, then, it muft be acknowledged that theory is an admirable fupport or foundation of virtuous practice, chriftians might greatly abridge the procefs of religious enquiry, if they took proper opportunities freely to communicate their knowledge and fentiments upon the moft important fubjects. Wherefore fhould religion be fo generally banifhed from familiar and ferious converfation? It may, indeed, be unfeafonably and improperly introduced; but it is not, therefore, unfeafonable and improper, becaufe it is unfafhionable and rare. If religious ideas be fo very important, converfation, it fhould
be

be remembered, gives knowledge a pleafing drefs, and fixes it deeply in the mind.

If lectures, alfo, be given on natural and revealed religion, on the bible, on the reafons of diffent, on ecclefiaftical hiftory, on the corruptions of chriftianity, and on the opinions of early chriftian writers ; references may be made in a regular and orderly manner to fuch books as are calculated to convey clear and methodical ideas on the fubjects in queftion. Such clear and methodical ideas have a natural tendency to infpire a genuine, folid and lafting efteem for religion. If this efteem be planted in a fincerely good mind, it may grow up into perfect habit, and produce the bleffed fruits of unfullied purity, of fteady integrity, of active, generous charity, and of unaffected piety. Thefe are the virtues and graces, which the gofpel demands from thofe who are defirous to become the faithful difciples of Jefus. Thefe are the virtues and graces which are expected in thofe who wifh to join the company of the bleffed, and to fhare in the happinefs of the heavenly world.

ART. IX. *On Humanity to Animals.*

In an age like the prefent, when every thing which regards the happinefs of man is fo much ftudied, and fo well underftood, it is a matter of furprife to fome that a fimilar attention fhould not be extended to the lower claffes of animals, which have an indubitable claim to our humanity. Many of them experience harfh treatment during their lives, and others, at their deaths, are expofed to a greater degree of fuffering than is neceffary.

Till lately, it has been the cuftom to flay and broil eels, and other kinds of fifh, alive. It has

now

now been shewn that these animals may be easily killed by cutting them deep across the back part of the head, along a groove very near the neck. It is much to be wished that this should be attended to, and it is applicable to all fish, particularly to those which are killed with difficulty. Might not also a similar mode be adopted in killing shell-fish, previously to boiling them? The custom of crimping fish appears a wanton piece of barbarity.

The easiest way of killing *any animal* for food is by cutting through its brain, just between the head and the adjoining bone of the neck. If the animal requires bleeding, it may be bled after it has been dispatched. It is not necessary to enforce the duty incumbent on us to save pain to these animals in all cases.

ART.

ART. X. *A View of Mrs. Wollstonecraft's Rights of Women.*

Full many a gem of pureft ray ferene
The dark unfathom'd caves of ocean bear;
Full many a flower is born to blufh unfeen,
And wafte its fweetnefs on the defert air.

GRAY.

They, who have perufed Mrs. Wollftonecraft's firft volume on the Rights of Women, will not think the preceding lines improper to be placed at the head of a paper defigned to detail the principles of fuch a performance.

What can be wanting to enable the females, in like circumftances and with like advantages, to make an equal progrefs with the males of the human kind in whatever it is thought valuable to obtain? Women may not, indeed, have an equal ftrength of bodily conftitution; yet it may bear a queftion, whether thofe among them are juftifiable, who have altogether neglected fuch decent and active exercifes as are fitted to procure it, and to harden them againft the fhocks and inclemencies of the weather. Why fhould not girls, as well as boys, tofs the ball, or engage in other innocent and enlivening games. The practice of archery, it cannot be doubted, may have a favourable influence in bracing the conftitution. Walking and riding are certainly of advantage, as they have a tendency to promote the fame end. If hunting and fhooting were clearly virtuous amufements, wherefore might they not be recommended to women as well as to men, as of admirable ufe in ftrengthening the bodily frame? Perhaps, a ftrong outward conftitution may afford the beft foundation or capacity for ftrength of mind, but it is not found that the length, breadth, or vigour of the body is any abfolute or certain index of the mental powers.

Let

Let the mind be what it will, it certainly arifes from what, as it cannot be feen, cannot be known. Be it only the power which fprings from the particular conformation and arrangement of the brain, this conformation is not to be difcerned, this arrangement is not to be perceived. If the appeal be made to fact and experience, how feldom does a good education fail? And, where it does, the failure is not fo much to be afcribed to the nature of the fex as to the nature of the individual. Be it granted that there is a peculiar character and fome natural diftinction, it is one thing to preferve this character, and another thing to indulge it; it is one thing to obferve the diftinction, and it is another thing to carry it to excefs. It is juftly deemed a difgrace to a woman not to be able to regulate certain domeftic concerns. Thofe mothers are fcarcely better than the greateft criminals, who do not take a proper care of their children, who do not, as far as they can, feed and clothe them, and make the beft provifion for their health. There may be diftinct and proper employments which ought never to neglected. But ornamental accomplifhments fhould always be made to yield to ufeful attainments. Surely finery, trifling and foolery fhould give way to the cultivation of the rational powers. Women as well as men, who have the means to procure an education, may and ought to be taught the great principles of geography and chronology. The art of writing and the practice of arithmetic no one will deny to be moft eminently ferviceable to them. Juft and general notions of the hiftory of the world are as much within their reach as in that of men; and it may with truth be faid that whatever particular knowledge it becomes the male fex to acquire in any certain fituation, in a like fituation women ought to turn their attention to the like purfuits. The works and word of God lie

open

open to the infpection of both, and both ought to render themfelves fuperior to frivolous and irrational behaviour.

Gentlenefs, it may be thought, fhould be the peculiar talent of woman. But of what value is gentlenefs, if it be not a moral quality founded on affectionate, kind and benevolent difpofitions and feelings! Whatever elfe bears the name, is infincere, affumed and affected. If, then, women poffefs more true gentlenefs than men, men do not poffefs enough; and if men poffefs enough, women have too much the appearance without the reality.

The great traveller, Ledyard, bears honourable teftimony to the fuperior benevolence of the female fex. In the moft inhofpitable and favage countries, the women treated him with kindnefs. Nothing rude or harfh fell from their lips. Chearfully and readily, they fatisfied his hunger and quenched his thirft. Probably, the benevolent Howard had made like obfervations, which led his good heart to find great delight in the company of virtuous women, and to declare that no human fociety was perfect or happy without them.

It is difficult as well as odious to draw comparifons; and it is neither politic nor juft to pafs cenfures on general bodies, either of men or of women. Probably, each fex has its diftinguifhing excellencies. Befides, the fuperiority which it has been fo often fuppofed man has over woman, may not be fo readily allowed by the females. If the lions had been ftatuaries, they would not have reprefented the man fubduing the lion.

Mofes, it is thought, has given an account of the creation of Eve which to fome may feem to imply that fhe was inferior to Adam. Perhaps, however, this account may be rather poetical than hiftorical. What cannot be underftood, cannot be explained, and

and may be safely and properly neglected. Paul, it may be said, recommends to wives submission; and where there should be submission, it may be imagined, there must be inferiority and weakness. Yet, let it not be forgotten what a stress the apostle lays on love and affection, and that, where these are, they will stand in the place of submission, and render it totally unnecessary. But it is also certain, that wisdom will, in the end, rule; for knowledge is power. In barbarous, uncivilized ages, might has been right; but the progress of information will spread the principle of benevolence, and mutual benevolence will supersede all authority and every command.

If all the children of men be creatures capable of reason, (and who will dare to deny it) it should be considered as the duty of all to possess and to cultivate reason, and to act consequentially through the whole course of their lives. If, then, the capacity be not doubted, a good education might remedy all the evils which have arisen from considering women as inferior beings, might raise them to their proper rank in society, and render them, not the pretended angels or idols, but the friends and companions of men. The proper objects and method of female education may, perhaps, deserve a more particular attention.

It cannot signify by whom this paper is written; but, perhaps, it may remove the prejudices of some readers, to be informed that it is not the production of a female.

I. H,

POETRY,

POETRY.

ART. XI. *Spring.*

Diffusing benefits around,
   Bespeaking God's parental care,
Fresh show'rs have fertiliz'd the ground,
   And gentle winds have warm'd the air.

Leaves fill the trees, grass clothes the plain,
   And verdant ranks of corn appear,
To raise the hopes of beast and man
   Of constant plenty through the year.

The gardens, dressed in all their pride,
   Perfume the air, attract the sight;
Their use and beauty are allied,
   For man's support, for man's delight.

Will God, from whom these blessings spring,
   Vouchsafe to hear the songs we raise?
To God alone our thanks we bring,
   The object of our love and praise.

Our grateful hearts sincerely feel
   The pleasures we at present have;
Yet we expect with greater zeal
   The future joys beyond the grave.

Jesus hath sown the precious seed;
   May no neglect destroy the crop!
If we extirpate every weed,
   The harvest will exceed our hope.

THE

THE REVIEW.

Art. 1. *Conversations on Christian Idolatry* in the year 1791. Published by Theophilus Lindsey, M.A. 8vo. pp. 169. 3s. Johnson.

In the Introduction to this work, Mr. Lindsey remarks ' that from the rapid progress of free inquiry, and improvement in the knowledge of the scriptures, for some years past, still daily increasing ; and from the very great plainness and perspicuity with which the doctrine of the divine unity is delivered throughout the bible ; it cannot fail but that the gross deviations from this doctrine among all bodies of christians, but particularly discernible in the liturgy of the church of England, a form of devotion in other respects most admirable, must soon be descried by multitudes of that communion, and excite no small ferment and disturbance amongst them, without some preparation and instruction given them relating to it.

' To allay, or rather to prevent, such religious heats and convulsions, of all others the most to be avoided, I believe (continues Mr. Lindsey) it would be of use to give to the public what presented itself on the subject to a select society of serious persons of good sense conversing upon it ; viz.— the strong evidence that was produced from scripture of the absolute unity of God, and that the blessed Jesus received his existence and all his powers from him ;

——that in the account of God himself, and of Jesus Christ, it is idolatry to pay divine honours to a creature, and, of course, to worship this humble but now exalted saviour ;

——that, however, this idolatry of christians in worshiping Christ, which has been of so long duration

tion and fo widely extended, is of a very different nature from the heathen idolatry, fo feverely condemned in the facred writings, and will not affect the future happinefs of thofe who are fincere in it, and who, having had no opportunities of knowing better, live up to the light they have; although it be a thing much to be lamented, and a continual difgrace to the gofpel, and hindrance to its reception in the world;

—and, after various arguments, ineffectually propofed, to take off every fcruple of joining with others in prayer, where it was in part offered to wrong objects in the efteem of the worfhiper, fomething turned up at the laft concerning what might beft be done by thofe who could not remain in the communion and worfhip of the church of England, for fear of the reproach and condemnation of their own minds in worfhipping Jefus and the holy fpirit; whom they did not believe to be gods, or to be worfhiped.'

Thefe extracts afford a fufficient view of the *plan* of this work. The remainder of the article muft be deferred till next month.

Art. 2. *Reafons for Unitarianifm; or, The Primitive Chriftian Doctrine.* Addreffed to the ferious confideration of the Inhabitants of the Diocefe of St. David's. With a Preface, containing Animadverfions on the Bifhop of St. David's Charge; and an Appendix, in which the different Arian Tenets are ftated and examined. By a Welfh Freeholder, 8vo. p. 200. 2s. 6d. Johnfon, &c. 1792.

This work confifts of five parts. The *firft* part contains the ftate of ' the heathen world at the time of Chrift's appearance:' the *fecond* exhibits ' proofs from

from reason and from scripture, that the doctrines of the divine Unity of the Necessity and Efficacy of good works, and of the Resurrection, form the principal articles of the christian faith:' the *third* treats ' of the origin and rise of certain Corruptions which prevailed in the christian church:' the *fourth* explains ' the importance and beneficial effects of christianity on Unitarian principles;' and the *fifth* gives ' a short account of Unitarianism, and its present state.'

With this publication it cannot, from the *object* of it, be expected that all will be pleased. Nevertheless, it contains many things which deserve attention. The language of it is plain, but sufficiently forcible; and, though some of the writer's explanations of scripture may be erroneous, it will prove useful in extending the knowledge of genuine, uncorrupted christianity.

CORRESPONDENCE.

The communications of ' Candidus' and ' F. R.' will be inserted in the next Number.

' An Inquiry whether or not Christianity has, in its consequences, been beneficial to mankind,' will likewise appear next month.

It is requested that all communications for this Work be sent (post paid) directed to the Editor of the Christian Miscellany, at Mr. Stalker's, No. 4, Stationers-court, Ludgate-street, London.

It is wished that those correspondents, whose essays are designed for the current Number, would transmit them as early in the month as possible.

N. B. Publications, which are calculated to promote religious knowledge, or the practice of virtue, are advertised on the cover of the Christian Miscellany at considerably less than the usual prices.

ERRATUM.—In the last Number, page 129, line 10, for *possession* read *profession.*

THE

Chriſtian Miſcellany,

For JUNE, 1792.

====

ART. I. *An Account of the Four Evangeliſts.*

WHENEVER we read a book by which we are much intereſted, we always wiſh to know ſomething of the author. Nothing, therefore, can be more natural than for a chriſtian to feel ſome curioſity reſpecting the writers of the New Teſtament, and, eſpecially, concerning the four excellent perſons to whom we are indebted for the hiſtories of our maſter's public miniſtry. But other principles than vanity induced them to take up their pens; on which account, it is not wonderful that they ſay ſo little of themſelves in the courſe of their narratives. And yet it is to theſe, principally, that we muſt have recourſe for information upon this head, ſince we can meet with but very little authentic intelligence from later writers. Thoſe incidental expreſſions and brief anecdotes, which do tend to throw any light upon their hiſtories, have been very carefully and judiciouſly collected by the great and excellent Dr. Lardner; of whoſe uſeful labours I ſhall avail myſelf as much as poſſible, in giving what information can be obtained relating to the four evangeliſts. It will be natural to begin with Matthew.

Matthew, called alſo Levi, was a publican, or toll-gatherer under the Romans. His office ſeems more particularly to have conſiſted in gathering the cuſtoms of commodities that came by the ſea of Ga-

T.　　　　　　　　　lilee,

lilee, and the tribute which paffengers were to pay, who went by water. He was, undoubtedly, a native of Galilee, as the reft of our lord's apoftles were; but of what city in that country, or which tribe of the people of Ifrael, is not known.

As he fat at the receipt of cuftom, by the fea-fide, in or near the city of Capernaum, Jefus faid unto him, 'follow me. And he arofe and followed him.' There is no neceffity, however, to fuppofe, that he was in fuch hafte to accompany Jefus, as to neglect to make up his accounts with thofe by whom he had been employed and entrufted.

Afterwards, he made an entertainment at his houfe, where Jefus and many of his difciples were prefent. And there fat at table with them feveral publicans, or toll-gatherers, and others of no very reputable character in the eye of the pharifees. Matthew, it is likely, was defirous that they fhould converfe with Jefus, hoping that they might be taken with his dif- courfe. And Jefus, with the view of doing good, and to fhew that he did not difdain any man, made no exceptions to this defign of his new difciple. All the evangelifts have recorded this inftance of our lord's amiable familiarity and condefcenfion, which is one of the diftinctions of his fhining character.

Jefus now called Matthew to be with him, as a witnefs of his word and works, and he put him into the number of his apoftles. Henceforward he con- tinued with him; and, after his afcenfion, he was at Jerufalem, and partook of the gift of the holy fpirit with the other apoftles. Together with them, he bore teftimony to the refurrection of Jefus; and, as may be fuppofed, preached for fome while at Jeru- falem, and in the feveral parts of Judea, confirming his doctrine with miracles, which God enabled him to perform in the name of Jefus.

This

This is all which can be said with certainty relating to the history of the evangelist Matthew. It is a common opinion, that he died a martyr in Ethiopia; but this is a fact by no means sufficiently authenticated. As to his gospel, many learned men are of opinion that it was drawn up in the hebrew language; the apostle having undertaken the work in compliance with the request of the jewish believers. This however is doubted by some. Nor is it certain in what year it was published. Dr. Lardner, after considering a variety of circumstances, concludes that it was done about the year 64, that is, not till about 30 years after our lord's ascension. He also supposes that Mark's account of Christ's public ministry was written about the same time.

Mark was the son of Mary, a pious woman at Jerusalem, and an early believer, at whose house the disciples used to meet, and that in troublesome and difficult times, as well as at other seasons. It is uncertain at what period he became a disciple of Jesus. We find him spoken of in the the xiith chapter of the Acts, where we read that Barnabas and Paul, upon leaving Jerusalem, (which was about the year 44) took with them John, whose surname was Mark. He went with them to Antioch, and, some short time afterwards, accompanied them as their minister into other countries. They went to Cyprus, and preached the word in that country; but when they returned to the continent, and came on shore at Perga in Pamphilia, he parted from them and returned to Jerusalem. Some time after this, when Paul and Barnanabas were again at Jerusalem, and were about to visit their converts in different cities, Barnabas proposed taking Mark with them again, but Paul objected to it, thinking that he had behaved improperly in leaving them at Perga. This difference of opinion produced a separation of the two apostles;

T 2

and

and Barnabas took a different circuit from Paul, and availed himself of the services of his nephew Mark. Dr. Lardner justly considers this as an instance of the amiable temper of Mark ; and from the epistles it appears that Paul was afterwards perfectly reconciled to him, having probably discerned plain proofs of his good dispositions. He mentions him in several of his letters from Rome, and, in one to Timothy, says, " take Mark, and bring him with thee, for he is profitable to me for the ministry."—This is the most which we can learn of the history of Mark. It is the opinion of some christians that he died a martyr ; but this is altogether uncertain.—We shall now proceed to say something concerning Luke.

The first time that we find any mention of Luke in the books of the New Testament, is in his own history of the acts of the apostles. (Acts xvi. 10, 11.) From thence it appears, that he was with Paul at Troas, and accompanied him in his voyage to Macedonia. It may also be gathered from what is said in the xxth chapter of the Acts, that he was with the apostle when he was a second time in Greece, and was setting out for Jerusalem, with the collections which had been made for the poor disciples in Judea. From the sequel of the history it appears, that when the apostle was sent a prisoner from Cesarea to Rome, Luke was in the same ship with him, and continued with him at Rome during the whole time of his two years imprisonment in that place. This is evident, not only from his own history of the Acts, but from the epistles which were written by Paul during his confinement.

It is the opinion of many learned men that " Luke, the beloved physician," mentioned in Col. iv. 14, is the evangelist. Many antient writers speak of him as a physician ; and it seems, upon the whole, to be probable
that

that he was by birth a jew. The notion that he was a painter is without foundation; no notice having been taken of it by antient writers. The firſt chriſtian authors ſpeak of Luke as a diſciple of the apoſtles. It has been thought that he was one of the ſeventy whom Chriſt commiſſioned to preach the goſpel in his life time, that he was the Lucius mentioned by Paul in the epiſtle to the Romans, and that he was one of the two diſciples who met Jeſus in the way to Emmaus.

We do not exactly know when Luke formed the deſign of writing his two books. During Paul's impriſonment in Judea, which laſted more than two years, and was a time of inaction for the apoſtle, Luke had an opportunity of completing his collections, and filling up his plan. For in that time, unqueſtionably, Luke converſed with many early jewiſh believers and eye-witneſſes of the lord, and ſome of the apoſtles, who were ſtill at Jeruſalem. Nor can we heſitate to allow the truth of what is ſaid by ſome of the antients, that Luke, who, for the moſt part, was a companion of Paul, had likewiſe more than a ſlight acquaintance with the reſt of the apoſtles. Whilſt he was with Paul at Rome, it is likely he had ſome leiſure for compoſing and writing. When Paul left Rome, Luke, probably, accompanied him no longer, but went into Greece, where about the year 63 or 64, he finiſhed and publiſhed, one after the other, his two books, which he inſcribed to Theophilus, an honourable friend and a good chriſtian in that country. Here Luke died, and, perhaps, ſomewhat in years; nor need it be reckoned an improbable ſuppoſition that he was older than the apoſtle.

Having thus ſaid a little of three of the evangeliſts, it remains that we ſhould give ſome account of the apoſtle John.

John

John was the son of Zebedee, a fisherman, upon the sea of Galilee, probably of the town of Bethsaida. Though his father was a fisherman, it does not follow that he was poor and necessitous; for it appears that he was not only master of a boat, but had hired servants. It has been supposed that Salome, his mother, was related to our lord. If it were so, it might have been the ground of her petition that James and John should enjoy the two first places in Christ's kingdom, and of the particular intimacy between John and Jesus, and also of our lord's committing to him the care of his mother, so long as she should survive him.

It is said of Peter and John that they were ignorant and unlearned men; which, indeed, is nothing else, but that they were neither magistrates nor doctors, but men of private stations, who had not been educated in the school of the rabbies. It was at the commencement of our lord's public ministry, as he was walking by the sea of Galilee, that he called James and John to attend upon him statedly. Mark informs us that he surnamed them sons of thunder; by which name he prophetically represented the resolution and courage with which they would openly and boldly declare the truths of the gospel. From the time they were called by Christ, they were regularly with him. They heard his discourses, and saw his miracles. They were two of the twelve whom Christ sent forth upon a commission to preach in the land of Israel; which was of great use to them. Thereby they learned to trust in God, and were prepared for the greater difficulties of the apostleship afterwards. At one time, they were so filled with indignation at the treatment which Jesus met with, that they said 'Lord, wilt thou that we command fire to come down from heaven and consume them, as Elias did?' But he turned and rebuked

buked them; saying, "Ye know not what manner of spirit ye are of."

The two brothers, James and John, and Peter, were the only disciples that were admitted to be present with our lord at the raising of the daughter of Jairus. The same three disciples were taken up by Jesus into the mount, when he was transformed in a glorious manner, and Moses and Elias appeared talking with him. The same three were admitted to be present at Christ's devotions in the garden, when he retired from the rest. But they all failed to watch with their lord as he had desired. It was to these disciples he especially addressed himself, when he delivered the predictions concerning the great desolation coming upon the jewish people. John and Peter were the two disciples whom Jesus sent to prepare for eating his last passover. Our lord sitting at supper with his disciples, said, " One of you willbetray me." Peter beckoned to John, who leaned towards the bosom of Jesus, that he should ask who it was of whom he spake: which he did; and Jesus gave him a sign, by which he might know whom he intended. This is an instance of the freedom which John might take, as the beloved disciple and friend of his master. Whether John followed him to the hall of Caiphas, is uncertain; but he attended the crucifixion, and seems to have been the only one of the twelve who did so. ' Now there stood by the crofs of Jesus, his mother. When, therefore, Jesus saw his mother, and the disciple standing by whom he loved, he faith unto his mother, Woman, behold thy son. Then faith he to the disciple, behold thy mother. And from that hour, that disciple took her unto his own home.' John saw his lord expire on the cross; and, which was a more delightful sight, he was one of the first to witness his resurrection From all whic we perceive that he was present at most of the things related by him in his gospel, and that he was an eye and ear-witness of our master's labours, journeyings, discourses, miracles, his low abasement even to an ignominious death, and his being alive again, and then ascending to heaven. Having been favoured, together with the rest of the apostles, with an effusion of the holy spirit of truth, Peter and John healed the lame man at the temple, and, upon that occasion, preached to the people who assembled about them; for which they were brought before the jewish council, and, after some debates, were dismissed with orders not to preach any more in the name of Jesus. Some time after this, John, with the rest of the apostles, was again imprisoned, but was released by an angel, and persevered in preaching Jesus as the Christ.

From ecclesiastical history, we learn that this apostle was banished by the Roman emperor to the isle of Patmos, that in his latter days he resided in Asia, particularly at Ephesus, and that he died in a good old age. His last account of Jesus was published, at least, four years later than those of the other evangelists.

The reader is now, I believe, in possession of all the well-authenticated information which can be procured relating to those worthy men, to whose labours we are principally indebted for our knowlege of the greatest personage that ever appeared upon the theatre of life. I shall only add, that the little intelligence which we can procure about the four historians of the ministry of Christ, is a circumstance highly in their favour. Had vanity prompted them to write, had they entertained a foolish desire of transmitting to posterity their own names and characters, they would frequently have taken occasion to mention themselves, and there would have been no difficulty in learning their histories.

ART. II.

ART. II. *Remarks on a paper entitled, " Obfer-*
vations on Luke's account of what paffed between
our lord and thofe who were crucified with him."

TO THE EDITOR OF THE CHRISTIAN MISCELLANY.

SIR,

In your Mifcellany for March, are fome " obfervations on Luke's account of what paffed between our
lord and thofe who were crucified with him." The
reafons, therein affigned for the variation in the
accounts given by Matthew and Mark and that given
by Luke, appear to me to fap a very grand and important truth, viz. the infallibility of the truth of
the fcripture. Nor do thofe reafons appear fo probable as fome others. If any thing, recorded by
Matthew or Mark, is not true, the fame may be
objected to the writings of Luke or John; for, if it
is true of the New Teftament, as of the Old, that
" holy men fpake as they were moved by the holy
ghoft," I fhould rather affent to the whole as true,
though I cannot reconcile all its parts, than reject a
part of it as untrue, to make it fquare with my opinion. Refpecting the accounts, given by Matthew
and Mark, differing from that given by Luke, I
fhould fuppofe it arifes from the two former having
related one part of the affair, and the latter another
part; and that, foon after the unhappy criminals
were extended upon the crofs, they both reviled Jefus
Chrift, as related by Matthew and Mark; but one
of them, being afterwards convinced of his fins and
enlightened as to the true character of Jefus Chrift as
the meffiah, chearfully embraced the falvation offered, and died a true believer of Jefus, making that
requeft to him recorded by Luke.

Refpecting the fuppofition that unwarrantable
and dangerous conclufions may be drawn from this
passage,

paffage, as leading men to truft to what is called a death-bed repentance, I cannot fee the force of it. That many men of vicious lives have wrefted the fenfe of fome texts to countenance their vices, is a truth. But that is the cafe with many others as well as this. Nor is it any reafon why a glofs fhould be put upon it which the hiftory and its connection do not warrant. I think John Bunyan's plain comment on this paffage is as juft as any I have feen. He fays, " God did this once, that none might defpair; though he did it but once, that none might prefume." I think this a much more rational way of explaining the matter than raifing fuppofitions which the hiftory by no means warrants.

I would farther notice what is faid upon the character of the thieves, as they are called in our tranflation of the bible. I can fee no reafon to fuppofe that they were patriots, " and fuffered death for having taken up arms upon a principle of religion, or that God was the only governor of the Ifraelites, and the Romans were not to be fubmitted to." No fuch thing appears from the account given of them. It does not even appear that they were jews, though it is probable they were; but, for any thing the evangelifts fay upon the fubject, they might be perfons of any other nation or religious profeffion. And refpecting the crime for which they fuffered, it appears, from the man's own confeffion, that it was an atrocious one; his words to his fellow fufferer, who was ftill railing on Jefus, plainly demonftrate it. " Doft thou not fear God, feeing thou art alfo in the fame condemnation? We, indeed, receive the *juft reward* of our deeds; but this man hath done nothing amifs."—We can hardly fuppofe this would been his language, had he taken up arms in defence of his rights as a man, and his religion as a jew.

ART.

ART. III. *Some general Remarks on what is called the Double Sense of Prophecy.*

Precision, clearness and accuracy are the essentials of good writing. In all works and treatises of note, we expect that the meaning of the author be one, clear and determinate. If he express himself in a vague or ambiguous manner, so that what he asserts is applicable to different subjects, we, without hesitation, pronounce him an indifferent writer, who either had not clear conceptions of things, or was not able to express his sentiments in intelligible terms.

Now there seems to be no good reason wherefore we should try profane authors, as they are called, by one rule, and the composers of the holy volume by another. Hence, though we should allow that the sacred penmen were not eminent in literary character, yet we should expect that the historians, prophets, lawgivers and other composers of the bible would express themselves so as easily to be understood by the most illiterate and vulgar.

As their only end must have been to convey knowledge, so, if their meaning be not clear, they have written to no good purpose. Neither the historian, the poet, nor the orator in other languages has two or more meanings. Why, then, should we suppose that the hebrew poets have? They may, indeed, express themselves ambiguously, but not on purpose.

Unity of design is a beauty in a poem or picture, and unity of meaning seems equally necessary in all books intended for the instruction and improvement of mankind.

If we admit the double sense of prophecy, we can never tell when the prophecy is fulfilled. For if it has two senses, it may have more. Where shall we stop? On this ground, the jews will tell us that,

though

though we may imagine that Jesus Christ has fulfilled the prophecies, another and another messiah is yet to appear, who will accomplish them in their exact and literal meaning. According to the doctrine of the double sense of prophecy, fancy has an unlimited range, and may find a type and hidden meaning of Jesus Christ in every verse of the bible.

Eastern imagination required strong expressions, especially when the minds of the hebrew bards were animated with the hopes of better times.

The jews also quoted the Old Testament as we quote the poets, accommodating and applying various passages from it, to their own peculiar situations and circumstances. Hence it might possibly happen that what was written for one occasion, might more properly suit another, for which it was not intended. But the just meaning of passages must be gathered from their original connection, and not from any after applications.

These sentiments, it is presumed, may serve as principles to direct an inquiry into an interpretation of such passages as have laid the foundation for the notion of what has been termed the double sense of prophecy.

I submit them, Mr. Editor, to you and to your readers, prepared either to defend or surrender them, as they shall be attacked or refuted.

I believe I am indebted for them to a tract written by one Johnson, which may be found in Watson's collection.

I wrote down my thoughts some years ago, after I had read the piece.

SIMPLEX.

ART.

ART. IV. *Remarks on the Manner of conducting Public Worship and Instruction.*

TO THE EDITOR OF THE CHRISTIAN MISCELLANY.

SIR,

I have read with great pleasure the plans for promoting religious knowledge, described in Art. V. and VI. of your Miscellany for March; and am one of many readers who must esteem ourselves obliged to " a Friend to Truth," for proposing his inquiries. Those schemes appear *generally* calculated to serve the cause of religion in the world at large; but as the attention of your readers has been invited to this subject, I am induced to offer you a few cursory remarks on the manner of conducting public worship and instruction in societies of professing christians.

Whatever may be the issue of those inquiries respecting the nature of government, and the principles of general policy, which now engage the attention of mankind, I am disposed to ask whether the principle of republicanism, carried into religion, would not be likely to produce the happiest effects. In all civil governments, whether monarchical or aristocratical, certain priviledged individuals seem to think that the people are made for them, and claim their authority as property; which has been the case with ecclesiastical as well as civil officers, and, indeed, has uniformly prevailed in every establishment of religion. But with establishments, where the few dictate to the many on subjects of universal interest, I have no concern, upon a question to the discussion of which christian liberty is indispensible. I turn to the dissenters; a description of men who, to act consistently with their principles, must be disposed to innovate whenever they can do it with advantage, and, being neither *allies* nor *engines* of the state, are free to adopt any mode which may promise to advance

the

the purpofes of moral edification. Yet among diffenters, though we cannot boaft of a rich bifhoprick, or a fat living, we fometimes hear of a good intereft; that is, a falary raifed for the fupport of an individual, who, being precluded, by the prejudice of cuftom, from thofe advantages which an attention to trade and commerce might afford, is fometimes reduced to the neceffity of lamenting over a declining intereft, when a rich fubfcriber, even though a man of bad morals, leaves his ufual place of worfhip. But does not this idea of the abfolute neceffity of raifing fifty or a hundred pounds a year, in order to carry on the fimple worfhip and inftruction of the chriftian church, convey an impreffion to the mind, that the kingdom of Jefus Chrift muft be fupported by the riches of this world?—Yet I have often thought that the kingdom of Chrift might be carried on without riches, without fplendour, without any particular favour from the government; by a few fincere men meeting together, inftructing each other in the knowledge of the fcriptures, and joining in breaking of bread and prayers.

A plain man, willing to adhere in all ecclefiaftical matters to the examples of the firft chriftians, [except when thefe appear to have been local or temporary,] would find that they met on the firft day of the week to break bread; that they did not " neglect affembling themfelves together;" that, when met, they attended to the words of Chrift and his apoftles, " He that is of God heareth us." But would he learn that the firft chriftians fupported one man to ftudy the fcriptures for them, while their attention was engroffed all the week about their worldly bufinefs? Were not, rather, the united abilities of all called into exercife one way or other, privately or publicly, for the edification of the affembly? [See Rom. xii. 3, 4.] And in the prefent day,

day, might not committees be annually chofen, for exercifing the various duties and offices in the church? Would not private members of the firft talents be thereby brought forward to exercife their powers for the fupport of chriftianity, in focieties of the moft learned chriftians? Might not the poor and unlearned, alfo, in the fame manner inftruct each other, and might not this plan be adopted where the focieties confifted of two or three perfons, to two or three hundreds or thoufands? Religion by this means would never be in the cradle, nor upon crutches, as Paine fays of government; public worfhip would not be fufpended by the indifpofition of one man; and, when he died, religion would not die with him. Among a thoufand advantages which might be mentioned, this plan appears eminently calculated to promote the great branches of public religion; viz. inftruction, fellowfhip or giving to them that need, breaking of bread, and prayer, offered up in a folemn, fhort and fervent manner.

I am well aware that many thinking perfons have been averfe to the public miniftrations of thofe who are not divines by profeffion; and I am not ignorant of the caufe of this averfion. Some well-meaning, but injudicious chriftians, have affected to defpife the advantages of learning, if within their reach; or elfe have neglected to improve their religious knowledge by a fober and diligent attention to the connected fenfe of fcripture. Thefe men, probably actuated by an honeft zeal, but unqualified for their employment, have gone out to inftruct the world: preffing the text without examining the fenfe, they have expofed religion to contempt, by delivering the groffeft abfurdities in the folemn tone of infpiration. Thefe are not the inftructors I would encourage; and I hope, if any of your correfpondents choofe to difcufs this fubject, thay they will bear this remark in their remembrance.

remembrance. I hope, also, that nothing I have said will be misconstrued into the smallest disrespect towards dissenting ministers. In a familiar intercourse with some of them, I enjoy the purest pleasures of a virtuous friendship. To the valuable labours of such men I am indebted for very important assistance in pursuing the most interesting of all inquiries; and, indeed, when I think how many of that body of christians have adorned human nature, I am willing to offer them all the veneration that man ought to pay to his brother-man. But I cannot help observing that such men, whatever had been their trade or profession, must, upon the plan I am recommending, have borne a distinguished part in the religious services of any christian society with which they were connected; while, at the same time, the instructions of a Locke, a Barrington, a Hartley, a West, &c. would not only have taught in the closet, and influenced in the world, but also have edified the public assembly; and though such distinguished talents are but sparingly distributed, yet in almost every congregation might be found persons with good natural abilities, able to speak or write their native tongue with propriety, and well acquainted with the scriptures; such persons as your sensible correspondent (p. 105.) thinks sufficiently qualified to become public teachers of religion. And here it should be particularly noticed, how the exertions of younger christians, thus animated by a worthy emulation, and encouraged by the example of their elder brethren, would be cherished to maturity; 'till, (besides their assistance in public) at the head of every family would preside, not merely a reader of the labours of others, but, a man fitted to be a priest and instructor in his own house.

I regret that theological enquiries are not esteemed (as they ought to be) the most important business

and

and the firſt pleaſure of a chriſtian's life; but I would aſk your readers who have ſtudied human nature in the hiſtory of the world, whether a material reform in this particular can be expected, while chriſtian ſocieties from infancy to old age, inſtead of practiſing mutual inſtruction, depend on the teachings of one man, exalted above his brethren, not, perhaps, by any ideas of ſelf-importance, but by a ſilly affectation of ſuperior ſanctity, which cuſtom has impoſed upon him in the form of a reverend title, and a garb of perpetual mourning, moſt unſuitably connected with the joyful ſound of the chriſtian ſalvation? Theſe rattles, I hope, will ſoon be put away, with other childiſh things, and conſigned to the place which Milton has provided for

" cowls, hoods and habits,
" White, black, and grey, with all their trumpery."

Or, to be more ſerious,—a practice, very indifferent in itſelf, may yet be detrimental to the intereſts of truth and virtue, if it encourages the young and the inconſiderate to regard, as the excluſive requiſite of ſome chriſtians, that regularity of manners and decorum of character which is the duty, and ſhould be the ornament, of all. And, indeed, it appears to me not a little inconſiſtent for a diſſenting miniſter, who is a brother among brethren, to aſſimilate ſo much to the appearance of the hired ſervants of the eſtabliſhment; perſons of quite another deſcription. —But, to return to the ſubject—what changed the mechanic of America into a ſoldier, but the neceſſity and the honourable occaſion of employing ability and courage in the ſervice of his country? My chriſtian brethren will improve the alluſion, and make an inference for themſelves. I ſpeak to wiſe men, who are not enſlaved by cuſtom, and with whom a precedent is nothing till they have aſcertained its ſuperior excellence.

U

A diſ-

A diftinguifhed fcholar has lately argued againft the obligation of focial worfhip. I have no doubt but his opponents will be able to fhew that his arguments are inconclufive, and that, amidft all its errors, the chriftian world has not been univerfally miftaken on this fubject. When that writer takes the trouble to recount the eccentricities which have been connected with public worfhip, he feems to have overlooked the very common maxim, "ab abufu ad ufum non valet confequentia." But I peculiarly regret that a chriftian and a liberal fcholar fhould fometimes exclude the forbearing fpirit of his religion, and the politenefs of a gentleman, from his part in this controverfy.---Yet I am pleafed that the attention of the religious world has been called to this fubject; as the enquiry will expofe fome defects in the prefent forms of focial worfhip, and promote an examination of the moft fcriptural means to perfect the chriftian character, and to furnifh the man of God to every good work.

R——n.   F. R.

ART. V. *Chriftianity proved to have been in its confequences beneficial to mankind.*

Soon after I had fettled in my chambers at Lincoln's Inn, I was vifited by a much valued friend, who had been the companion of my ftudies and amufements both at fchool and at the univerfity. During fupper, (which I had ordered from the neighbouring coffee-houfe) we indulged ourfelves in a pleafing converfation concerning thofe paft events of life in which we had been engaged together. We amufed ourfelves in recollecting the different characters of our college acquaintance. The joviality and wit of one, the ftudious difpofition and folemn
gravity

gravity of another, had made such deep impressions on our minds, that our memory enabled us to relate to each other many of those curious anecdotes of which persons of the characters I now mention are generally the source. But when the waiter had removed the cloth, and had retired from the room, our conversation gradually turned into a more serious channel. My friend had taken orders a few months before. It was natural that we should talk of his profession; and from this, we were led to the subject of religion in general. My companion, though a clergyman, was one of those men who thought it impossible for religion to frown on the innocent gaieties and harmless pleasures of life; but still he held religion in the greatest respect and veneration. He expatiated with much warmth and animation on the happy effects that a pure system of religion had on the morals of mankind. I was pleased that religion had become our theme, as I had some difficulties on this head, which I wished to have removed. I, therefore, made the following observations to my friend.

" The object of religion (said I) is not merely to force devotional supplications and thankfgivings from the creature to the Creator, but to secure the happiness of mankind, by recommending the practice of those rules of conduct which will promote among them mutual benevolence, harmony and peace. Now history records that religion, so far from accomplishing this purpose, has been the source of more contentions and animosities than all the fatal ambition of kings. Without turning our eyes to the human victim who expires, a grateful sacrifice, on the altars of pagan superstition,---without disgusting our enlightened reason with viewing the cruel impositions of heathenish priests,---not to dwell on the arts which they practised to make religion a pre-

text

text for bloody wars;---let us confine our enquiry solely to the christian religion. You say that the Deity condescended to introduce this religion into the world. If so, it should be a religion which not only has for its basis good precepts and peaceful maxims, but also, as the Deity sees into endless futurity, it should, in its consequences, be beneficial to mankind; it should, above all things, contribute to universal harmony and good will. But, alas! has it done so? Have not almost eighteen centuries passed over our heads, since it was founded? and yet this is, of all periods of history, the most remarkable for wars undertaken in the name of religion. When we consider the excruciating tortures and the accumulated miseries, which the primitive christians suffered in support of their religion, our blood freezes with horror; yet our feelings would excuse christianity as the cause of these unhappy events, if it had at last given to the world the predicted blessings of general peace and harmony; if it had, when established, ' turned our swords into ploughshares, and our spears into pruning hooks.' But mankind have experienced the reverse of this; they have found that christianity bears the seeds of discord and reciprocal intolerance. Had it not been to support the honour of this mild and benevolent religion, (as its votaries term it) the inoffensive Saracen would have retained possession of his native land, unmolested by the blood-thirsty, superstitious crusades of christians. What horrid persecution does this mild religion promote? Its doctrines are so obscurely expressed, that no two men can view them exactly in the same light. They necessarily involve men in dissention of opinion; and, therefore, not only the christian persecutes the heathen, but the christian persecutes the christian; one sect of christians persecutes another. We shudder when we read of

men

men being the devoted victims of pagan idolatry; yet what are they in number, who have perished in this unfortunate manner, compared with those christians who have been murdered by their fellow-christians, under the pretence of supporting the pure principles of christianity! Thirty thousand protestants were massacred at Paris in the year 1572, by the roman catholics. Historians say that, in those civil wars of France, which were carried on merely on account of religion, more than a million of men perished: many escaped death, only to endure the bitterest sorrows of life; and immense treasures were expended, which to have collected, industry must have been severely taxed, and poverty itself must have felt an additional pressure of affliction.

When this open war between the two sects had terminated, a spirit of persecution still prompted to cruelty and oppression; still was one sect harrassed and rendered miserable by the other. If you will read Voltaire's history of religion during the age of of Louis the XIVth, you will there find that, from animosities of which the christian religion had been the cause, nearly five hundred thousand persons were driven to the sad extremity of abandoning their native country, and many, who were detected in endeavouring to escape, were punished on the rack, or suffered some other heavy misfortune. I allude to the revocation of the edict of Nantes. These, then, were the miseries with which the roman catholics afflicted the protestants.---But, among the roman catholics themselves, you will observe, in Voltaire's history, how numerous are the disputes which christianity cherished, and how numerous the mischiefs which the most trifling disputes occasioned. Christianity has not caused in Britain evils quite so dreadful. However, in perusing our history we find,

from

from the perfecution of the Lollards down to the perfecution of Dr. Prieftley, numerous intervening calamities which chriftians of one fect inflicted on chriftians of another. Even to this day, we fee a numerous body of citizens deprived of fome of their deareft rights, becaufe they differ in opinion from the ftronger party concerning the obfcure, the dubious doctrines of chriftianity. Now, my friend, if fuch are the effects which fpring immediately from chriftianity,---if, as is plain from the experience of ages, the chriftian religion is the never-failing fource of reciprocal ill-nature, jealoufies, wars, maffacres, and various other calamities,---I cannot difcover its utility ; for I apprehend that the ufe of religion is to make mankind happy. Neither can I fuppofe chriftianity of divine original ; for it would fully the benevolence, that moft beautiful attribute, of the Deity to fuppofe that the all-comprehenfive Being to whom there is no diftinction between things paft, prefent and future, would introduce a religion which he knew would bring additional mifery on the fons of men."

My friend, on hearing my concluding fentence, fhook his head, and gave a fmile that was expreffive of difapprobation. After a few moments' reflection, he replied to me, as nearly as I can recollect, in the following terms.

(To be concluded in the next Number.)

ART. VI. *A View of the Progrefs of Unitarian Sentiments and Worfhip.*

(Continued from p. 189.)

The progrefs of knowledge and truth, and of the reformation of the corruptions under which chriftianity hath been difguifed, is flow ; efpecially, when
both

both the fashion and the emoluments of this world are on the side of those corruptions. Otherwise, it would be a matter of great wonder, that from the year 1719 to the year 1774, when the society in Essex-street was formed, no body of men had broken off from the established church, or from the dissenters in large and populous places, and united together for religious worship on unitarian principles: for those principles have, in this period, been continually gaining ground and spreading, though, indeed, under considerable opposition and obloquy.

But, though out of the number of separations which, in the mean time, have taken place amongst protestant dissenters, scarcely any or none had their origin in a disapprobation of trinitarian worship, and in a conscientious concern to maintain, pure and uncorrupted, the worship of one God the Father; yet many of their societies, by the peaceable and prudent conduct of their ministers, have been, in a manner silently and insensibly, brought over to strict unitarian worship. And this period of time has not been without public declarations in support of such worship.

In the year 1735, the learned and excellent Mr. Joseph Hallet, jun. first, colleague with, after the death of his father, and then successor to, Mr. Peirce, published a small piece on this question, entitled, " An Address to Conforming Arians, both among the Clergy and the Laity;" which was afterwards reprinted in a collection of tracts, entitled, " A Cordial for low Spirits." What effects this Address produced, we cannot say; but that it was not wholly unsuccessful is evident from a letter which Mr. Whiston received from an unknown hand : the writer of which owns himself to have been seriously and strongly impressed by it. The scruples, which it raised in his mind, induced him to propose this question to

Mr.

Mr. Whiston; viz. " As hypocrify is, undoubtedly, a fin odious to God and man, I, with *many others*, fhould take it as a fingular favour, if, in fome of your important writings, you would difcufs this important queftion; viz. with what church or fect the Arians, in the prefent corrupted ftate of things, ought to communicate, till it pleafes God more compleatly to reform the chriftian world? whether with that eftablifhed, or whether they ought to feparate, and go over to the diffenters, as many arian minifters are fuppofed to be amongft them."

Mr. Whiston was much difturbed with the contents and purport of his unknown correfpondent's letter; his former difficulties on the fame head were awakened; he was led into a review of the principles on which he had defended his conduct, when accufed of joining in idolatrous worfhip, and of *bowing in the houfe of Rimmon*; he was diffatisfied with the defence which he had fet up, and, in 1747, entirely withdrew from the worfhip of the church of England; and, by his publickly joining with the diffenters, did, in this cafe, honour to the confiftency and integrity of his own character, and exhibited an explicit teftimony in favour of unitarian worfhip.* It is remarkable that this change and determination was, at leaft indirectly, brought about by the influence of Mr. Hallet's tract at the diftance of eleven years from its firft publication. When the feed has lain in the earth, for a length of time, invifible, and, in human apprehenfion, is perifhed, it will fpring up and produce fruit. The efforts of the friends of truth and piety will have their effect, though their operation is unobferved and flow.

Mr.

* See Mr. Lindfey's View of the State of Unitarian Doctrine and Worfhip; p. 406, &c.; or, Memoirs of Whifton's Life, 2d Edit. p. 370.

Mr. Hallet's piece was followed, in the year 1738, with another serious, close and weighty tract, particularly pointed at that part of trinitarian worship which consists of prayers and praises offered to the holy spirit; and levelled, more especially, at the unscriptural doxologies in use amongst the dissenters. It was written by a virtuous sufferer and an able writer in the cause of the divine unity, Mr. Martin Tomkins, who was ejected from a dissenting congregation at Stoke-Newington in 1718. His tract was entitled, " A Calm Enquiry, whether we have any warrant from scripture for addressing ourselves, in a way of prayer or praise, directly to the Holy Spirit; humbly offered to the consideration of all Christians, particularly of Protestant Dissenters."

This pamphlet, which has had its designed effect with many minds, and contributed much to abolish, amongst dissenters, the use of the trinitarian doxology, concludes with this solemn monition. " Upon the whole, while we follow the direction of our blessed lord and saviour, *asking of our Father, who is in heaven, that he would give his holy spirit to us*; while we imitate the inspired apostles, those first and most glorious christians, *bowing our knees to the Father of our lord Jesus Christ, that he would grant unto us that we may, according to the riches of his glory, be strengthened with might by his spirit in the inner man; blessing the God and Father of our lord Jesus Christ, who hath blessed us with all spiritual blessings in heavenly things, in, or through, Christ*; while we join with the *many angels round about the throne, and the living creatures, and the elders, saying, worthy is the lamb that was slain, to receive power, and riches, and wisdom, and strength, and honour and glory and blessing; and with the whole creation, saying, blessing and honour, and glory, and power be unto him that sitteth upon the throne, and unto the lamb for ever and ever*;

ever;——we know that we are fafe, we are fure that this is acceptable worſhip. If any, not content with this, will be ſo officious as to offer up direct addreſſes to the holy ghoſt, and give him equal honour with the Father, they may do well to conſider what they will anſwer, when the *Lord our God, who is a jealous God,* ſhall ſay unto them, *Who hath required this at your hands ?*"

The reaſonings of Mr. Tomkins' tract were directed only to this ſingle point, the addreſſing of prayers and praiſes to the holy ſpirit. From the references in the preceding paragraph to the doxologies in the Revelations, the reader will, juſtly, conclude that he ſaw no objection lying againſt offering aſcriptions of praiſe to Chriſt, but thought the practice juſtified by the example of the angels round the throne, and of every creature in heaven, on the earth and under the earth. That, in general, judicious and cloſe writer did not advert to the peculiar circumſtances under which theſe aſcriptions of praiſe were made, viz. in a ſcenical repreſentation, nor reflect, " that what was tranſacted in a viſion, where Chriſt was ſuppoſed to be preſent, can be no precedent for chriſtians, his followers, to addreſs prayer or praiſe to him, or to ſuppoſe him every where preſent to hear them; eſpecially when there is no authority whatever for it, from any precept of his own, or of his apoſtles from him; or from their practice."*

Mr. Tomkins, in another work, appears an advocate for the worſhip of Chriſt as mediator, and for offering up of prayer to him.† This called forth the remarks of a ſenſible, anonymous writer, in the controverſy occaſioned by Dr. Middleton's Free Enquiry. His piece was entitled, " An Impartial Enquiry, What is the Teſt by which we may judge of

* Commentaries and Eſſays, vol. i. p. 452, &c.
† Sober Appeal to a Turk or Indian, 2d Ed. p. 254, &c.

of the miracles done by our faviour and his apoftles and know that they were really done? Or what is the difference between them, and thofe that are pretended to have been done fince thofe times; fo as to make the one credible, and the other incredible? In a Letter to the author of Two Queftions previous to Dr. Middleton's Free Enquiry. To which are added, Serious Advice to the Proteftant Advocates for the Miraculous Powers in the Primitive Church; and a Letter to the author of a Sober Appeal to a Turk or an Indian, concerning the plain fenfe of fcripture, relating to the trinity, upon the fubjeft of prayer. Printed for Noon, 1750."

The Letter to the author of the "Sober Appeal" may be confidered as a folid and explicit declaration in favour of the worfhip of one God, the Father; and, though it does not appear to have been followed with any eclat, yet, as coming in aid of the former attempts in that caufe, and carrying on Mr. Tomkins's defign to a fuller extent, it deferves particular notice.

The author obferves, that "the Appeal had been more properly made to a Jew or a Turk, than to an Indian, becaufe neither Jew nor Turk will be reconciled to chriftianity, whilft chriftians maintain, in exprefs contradiction to the revelation under the Old Teftament, and to the light of reafon, that more perfons than one are the only true God. But this gives no offence to the heathen, becaufe he profeffes to believe in more Gods than one."

This remark the writer then applies to the queftion concerning worfhip, and pertinently afks the author of the Appeal, " But do not you, Sir, very well know, that chriftians offering up prayer to more perfons than one, or to any other perfons befides the only true God the Father, of whom are all things, gives no lefs offence to the Jew and to the Turk?

Turk? This you ought to have taken notice of. But, inftead of doing this, you argue for the offering up prayer to Chrift, as if it gave no offence to the Jew or the Turk."

This unknown writer then proceeds thus. " It is, indeed, impoffible, in the nature of the thing, to be true, that God is more perfons than one, or that more perfons than one are the one fupreme God. But it is not impoffible, that God might have commanded that prayer fhould be offered up to one or more perfons befides himfelf; notwithftanding that, in the revelation under the Old Teftament, he has exprefsly forbidden the offering up of prayer to any other perfon or being befides himfelf; and that the light of reafon directs, that all prayer be offered up to the one fupreme felf-exiftent God.

" But though there be, as I fay, no *impoffibility*, that God might, if he had pleafed, have commanded the offering up of prayer to his fon and to his holy fpirit, and even to the angels; yet, I confefs, it feems to me to be incredible that God fhould do this, as well for his own glory, as for this reafon; that, as he would have all men, both jew and gentile, to believe in his fon Jefus Chrift, fo certainly the moft fure way to effect this is, that Chrift fhould teach no doctrine that is contrary either to the light of reafon, or to the revelation under the Old Teftament.

" Neverthelefs, as God may, if he thinks fit, give his glory to another, (his effence, indeed, he cannot, if I may fo fpeak, give to another,) fo, if he has done this, we may moft certainly conclude, that he has, in the moft plain and exprefs words, commanded, in the New Teftament, that prayer be offered up to one or more perfons befides himfelf."

The writer then obferves, that " nothing can reflect greater difhonour upon chriftianity, and upon
the

the divine authority of it, than to fuppofe that Mofes delivered the moft plain and exprefs commands to the jews, how they ought to pray; and that Chrift has not given as plain and exprefs commands to chriftians, how *they* ought to pray."

This principle, carrying its own evidence with it, the writer of the letter expreffes his furprize, that neither the author of the appeal, nor any other writer on the fubject of prayer, has firft enquired what is the form and manner of prayer commanded in the New Teftament; and then, what was that form and manner of prayer, which was practifed by the apoftles, and firft chriftians.

" One other thing" he adds, (addreffing himfelf to the author of the Appeal,) " I am equally fur- prifed at, is, " that you and they feem purpofely to avoid ufing the word *prayer*, and make ufe of the word *worfhip* inftead of it; which is a word of ambi- guous fignification, and does not, ftrictly fpeaking, neceffarily imply direct invocation or prayer. The only queftion, therefore, now before us, is this; whether there be any plain and exprefs precept or example, in the New Teftament, for offering up prayer to the fon."

In reference to certain paffages which the author of the Appeal quoted, and on which he laid a great ftrefs, as being a repeal, with refpect to chriftians, of the obligation of the firft commandment; the writer of the Letter afks; " What is there in all this, that has any relation to the offering up prayer to the fon? Is God's requiring men to honour the fon, as they honour the Father; that is, that all men fhould believe in and obey the fon, as they do the Father—is God's commanding all the angels to worfhip him, as they are prefent with him, and be- hold his glory—is God's commanding that every knee fhould bow at the name of Jefus, and every

tongue

tongue confeſs that he is lord, to the glory of God the Father ; by which no more is intended than this, that all men ſhould acknowledge him to be their lord, their only ſaviour and redeemer ; is all this any proof, that we ought to offer up prayer to the ſon ? is this the plain account which the New Teſtament gives us, of offering up prayer to our bleſſed ſaviour as one diſtinct from the ſupreme God and Father of all ? is this a repeal of that abſolute prohibition, as delivered at Mount Sinai, of any other object of worſhip, beſides the only true God ? this the plain and expreſs declaration of Chriſt and his apoſtles, that prayer be offered up by chriſtians to our bleſſed ſaviour ? Pardon me to ſay, that it aſtoniſhes me to hear you ſay this."

The author of the Appeal had alledged the ex-hortation given to Saul by Ananias, as an argument and precedent for offering up prayer to Chriſt. On this the Letter-writer remarks, " Now, ſuppoſing it to be true, ' that the phraſe calling upon the name of the lord, be meant of worſhiping him,' though it is, I think, plain from the context, wherever that phraſe is uſed, that no more is meant by it, than the profeſſing to believe in Chriſt ; yet nothing can be more forced than to ſay, ' that when Ananias ſaid to Saul, " Ariſe and be baptiſed, and waſh away thy ſins, calling upon the name of the Lord," he in-tended to direct him to offer up prayer to Chriſt. What connexion has the praying to Chriſt with Saul's being baptiſed, and waſhing away his ſins ? But his profeſſing his belief in Chriſt, which is all that Ananias means, by " calling on the name of the lord," has an immediate connexion with his being baptiſed and waſhing away his ſins, without which profeſſion, his being baptiſed could avail him nothing, or be of any efficacy to waſh away his ſins. The proof or argument from ſcripture muſt run

very

very low indeed, when fuch texts as thefe are preffed into the fervice."

The author of this piece, having noticed the directions on the duty of prayer given by Chrift, to inftruct his difciples how to pray while he was with them, obferves, " it is plain from hence, that our faviour commanded all who believe in him, to offer up all prayer to the one God and Father of all, as the Jews were commanded to do."

He then proceeds to remark that Chrift, in his laft difcourfe with his difciples, a little before his fufferings, refumes the fubject of prayer, and gives them the plaineft and moft exprefs directions how they were to pray, when he left them and returned to the Father.

" Thus, John xiv. 13, 14. " Whatfoever ye fhall afk in my name, that will I do ; that the Father may be glorified in the fon. If ye fhall afk any thing in my name, I will do it." This is the firft mention that our lord makes, of prayer being offered up to God in his name. And it is remarkable, that though he tells them that he will do thofe things for them which they fhall afk of the Father, yet he does not bid them to afk thofe things of him, but of the Father in his name. Surely, if in any cafe he had intended to direct to offer up prayer to him, it would have been in thofe cafes where he would be the perfon to *do* thofe things for them which they afked.

" Is not this inference neceffarily to be drawn from hence, that our faviour intended to inftruct his difciples that prayer was the *peculiar* honour due to the Father, the fame as under the Old Teftament, and as the light of reafon directs ?

" Again, chap. xv. 16. Our lord repeats the fame command to them, to pray to the Father in his name. In the next chapter, he not only gives
them

them the fame directions to pray to the Father in his name, but, left they fhould miftake, and think they were to pray to him for any thing, when he left them and returned to the Father, he exprefsly *forbids* them to do it. "In that day, fays he, ye fhall afk me nothing." And, left they fhould have any doubt that the Father would not give them what they prayed to him for, unlefs they likewife prayed to the fon, he gives them the greateft affurance to the contrary. "Verily, verily, I fay unto you, whatfoever ye fhall afk the Father in my name, he will give it you." And then, as a ftanding and perpetual direction to them and to all who fhould hereafter believe on him, he adds;—"Hitherto have ye afked nothing in my name. Afk, and ye fhall receive, that your joy may be full. At that day, ye fhall afk in my name."

or "Had our faviour intended to direct his difciples, to pray directly to himfelf, he would, moft certainly have told them;—hitherto, whilft I was with you, ye have offered up all your prayers to the Father, but, when I leave you, and return to the Father, then ye fhall offer up prayers to me alfo. And is it poffible to believe that, if they were to pray to him, he would not plainly have told them fo in this his laft difcourfe with them, wherein he refumes the fubject of prayer?"

We cannot better conclude our large extracts from this letter than by giving the paragraph which follows the preceding. The fpirit, in which it is written, is truly candid, pious and edifying. "If you think me miftaken in this, or that I have put a wrong fenfe on thefe directions of our faviour, let me, Sir, earneftly defire of you to fet me right; for I am very ferious in it, and would not be miftaken. I would not *knowingly* refufe my lord and only faviour that honour which is due to him; nor

X   *dare*

dare I give that honour and glory to the son, which, I verily think, and am fully perfuaded, ought to be given to the Father *only*."

The tract, on which we have dwelt fo long, is, it is conceived, fcarcely known. The plainnefs and force of the argument, exhibited in the extracts which we have given, joined to this confideration, will, it is hoped, excufe to the reader the length of our review of it.

(To be concluded in the next Number.)

ART. VII. *Biographical Anecdotes of* J. B. BASE-DOW, *extracted from the Appendix to the Seventh Volume of the Monthly Review.*

When any one has diftinguifhed himfelf by the difplay of great talents, or by his ardent zeal to promote the public good, we naturally entertain a defire to know fome leading particulars of his private life : the qualities which he may have received from nature ; the education which may have prepared and ripened thefe qualities, or have proved a check to their early and vigorous exertions ; and alfo fuch adventitious circumftances as may have directed their operations into any particular channel.

J. B. Bafedow is defervedly placed among this clafs of refpectable characters. To his diffatisfaction with the common mode of educating youth, and to his unwearied endeavours to introduce a better, Germany is indebted for the very confiderable changes that are now making in moft of their feminaries. To his diffatisfaction with the religious tenets in which he was educated, and which confti-tute the *orthodoxy* of the German meridian, his countrymen are in a great meafure obliged for that free fpirit of inquiry which is now pervading the

Lutheran

Lutheran church; where also the human mind, feeling its vigour, and claiming its rights, is powerfully struggling against the shackles of established creeds.

This ingenious person was born at Hamburgh, in the year 1723. His father was of the lower class of illiterate burgers, and of an hasty and morose disposition. Instead of cherishing the early sparks of genius, and directing the distinguished talents of his son in a proper manner, he endeavoured, by every species of severity, to suppress and extinguish them: but his endeavours had no other influence than to alienate the affections of his son at a very early period. The melancholy temper of his mother farther contributed to render his parental residence so comfortless, that his chagrin had frequently tempted him to destroy himself. On leaving his father's house, he became servant to a land-surveyor at Holstein. The mild and engaging disposition of his master rendered his situation under this roof extremely happy, and inspired him with that philanthropy to which he had been a stranger at home. After he had passed a year at Holstein, which, in his most advanced age, he pronounced to have been the happiest in his life, his father recalled him, and placed him in the public school at Hamburgh. Here he suffered all those hardships and marks of tyranny, to which indigent youth is so frequently exposed both from masters and scholars, while he remained in the *lower* classes; but, as he advanced; his industry and superiority of genius gave him the ascendancy over his school-mates. He made himself necessary to the ignorant and indolent, by assisting them in their exercises; by making verses, and by other methods, he was able to subsist at the age of sixteen, independently of his parents. When he was advanced to the higher class, he attended the lectures of professors Richey and Reimarus, with whose

friendship

friendſhip he was honoured; and from whoſe in-
ſtructions he derived great improvement, particularly from thoſe of Reimarus: but, as he afterwards
complained and confeſſed, he did not apply to the
ſciences, in any regular ſeries, nor in a manner ſufficiently ſyſtematic; and, by his becoming the favourite companion of the richer ſcholars, he began to
lead an indolent and an irregular courſe of life. He
remained ſome time undetermined concerning the
choice of an occupation. When a youth, he had no
diſpoſition for ſtudy. It was only the ambition of his
father to *make his ſon a clergyman*, that impelled him
to the profeſſion; and when the reſolution was finally
taken, the want of proper means of ſupport detained
him ſome time longer from entering on an acade-
mic courſe. This difficulty being at length ſur-
mounted, in ſome degree, he went to Leipſic in
1744, to proſecute his ſtudies, particularly in *theology*. Here he continued for two years, and attended the Lectures of profeſſor Cruſius, who had
diſtinguiſhed himſelf at this period, by rejecting the
viſionary ſyſtems that had been ſo much in vogue,
and by uniting *philoſophy* with *religion*. The inſtruc-
tions which he received from the ſchool of Cruſius
had an important and permanent influence on his
mind:—but his vigorous genius was wearied by the
ſlow proceſs of public lectures; he applied himſelf,
therefore, with unremitted diligence, to ſtudy his
maſter's ſyſtem, by reading the moſt diſtinguiſhed
authors that had written in oppoſition to it, or in
ſupport of it. The writings of Wolf, to which he
alſo applied, rendered his mind unſettled reſpecting
many doctrines that he had imbibed for chriſtianity;
and a ſceptical diſpoſition being once excited, he
began to entertain ſome anxious doubts reſpecting
the truth of the chriſtian revelation itſelf:—till, at
length, by reading the beſt authors on this intereſt-

ing

ing controversy, he became a firm believer of the truth of Christ's mission, though he denied most of those doctrines which many christians think an essential part of their faith.—During his abode at Leipsic, his finances were so scanty, that it was only three times in a week that he could afford himself a comfortable meal.

In the year 1749, he was appointed private tutor to the son of a gentleman in Holstein. This situation gave him an opportunity of bringing to the test of experience, the plan of an improved method of education, which he had, for some time, held in contemplation. The attempt succeeded to his wishes. His young pupil was only seven years of age, at the time when he was appointed his preceptor, and could merely read the German language. We are informed that, in the space of *three* years, he was able not only to read Latin authors, but to translate from the German into that language, and, also to speak and write it with a degree of fluency. The young gentleman had moreover made considerable progress in the principles of religion and morals, in history, geography, and arithmetic. This success procured to his preceptor much renown, and encouraged him to prosecute his plan with redoubled assiduity.

Mr. Basedow was chosen professor of moral philosophy and *belles lettres* at the university of Sorde, in the year 1753, where he enjoyed farther opportunities of pursuing his favourite object. While in this station, he published several works, which were well received, particularly a treatise on practical philosophy, for all classes, in which the particulars of his plan are fully explained; and also a grammar of the German language. He applied himself, with great assiduity, during his residence in this place, to the study of theology; from an eager and conscientious

tious

cious, desire of forming just and consistent ideas of religion, and to avoid the absurdities which attend the established system on the one hand, and the doctrines of infidelity on the other. From Sorö he was nominated to a professorship at Altona. He now employed his leisure hours in communicating to the world the result of his theological inquiries. It was in vain that his friends advised him to tread in the path of discretion. In vain did they preach to him the necessity of following their example, in believing one set of doctrines and professing another. His mental optics were so peculiarly constructed, that he could not see the honesty of this conduct; and he was, notwithstanding his general acumen, so dull of apprehension, that he was not able to conceive how any one could be a faithful minister of Jesus, while he preached doctrines opposite to the genuine spirit of christianity. He had the imprudence, therefore, to become the strenuous advocate for what he deemed to be TRUTH, in opposition to SYSTEM and CREEDS established by LAW.

His biographer informs us that the writings of M. Basedow excited the most violent opposition on every side; particularly among the clergy, and more especially among his townsmen, the clergy of Hamburgh; among whom, the Rev. Messrs. Goffe, Winkler, and Zimmerman distinguished themselves: they not only preached but published against him, seconding their arguments with all the force of invective. They represented his doctrines as inimical to religion and morals. They calumniated him as a visionary and dangerous sceptic, a mad projector of reforms, a detestable heretic, and an apostate from christianity, unworthy of station or stipend, and deserving exemplary punishment. The

' The populace of Hamburgh were excited to tumults; and it becoming the universal opinion among
them, that to stone the apostate to death, would be
a meritorious act, he was obliged to absent himself
from the city. At length, the magistrates, partly
from the importunity of the clergy, and partly to
appease the clamours of the people, prohibited the
publishing and reading of his works; warned citizens not to put any of his institutes into the hands of
their children; and forbade schoolmasters from using
them in their schools, under the pain of banishment:
while, on the other hand, they encouraged every
publication against him.'

The biographer farther informs us that M. Basedow stood firm against the violence of opposition,
continued to justify his sentiments from misrepresen-
tations, and supported them with additional arguments, by every method which those parts of Germany, more distant from the seat of contest, left open
to him. He also remarks, that clamours and
invectives did not prove of any essential service to
the cause which they were intended to support; and
that, twenty-five years after these violent commotions,
M. Basedow could contemplate with pleasure the
progress of his peculiar sentiments concerning religion, through every part of Germany.

ART. VIII. *A View of Persecutions, continued from*
P. 195.

Though we have, as yet, spoken of Germany
only, the spirit of opposition to the doctrines and
usurpations of the romish church, was not confined
to that country. An attack no less fierce, and occasioned by the same causes, was made upon them
about the same time in Switzerland. The fran-
ciscans,

cifcans, being entrufted with the promulgation of indulgences in that part of Europe, executed their commiffion with the fame indifcretion and rapacioufnefs which had rendered the dominicans fo odious in Germany. They proceeded, neverthelefs, with uninterrupted fuccefs till they arrived at Zurich. There Zuinglius, a man of uncommon fagacity and not inferior to Luther himfelf in zeal and intrepidity, ventured to oppofe them; and, being animated with a republican boldnefs, and free from thofe reftraints which fubjection to the will of a prince impofed on the German reformer, he advanced with more daring and rapid fteps, to overturn the whole fabric of the eftablifhed religion. (Robertfon v. 2. p. 137---8)—It is, however, to be lamented that Zuinglius did not, upon particular occafions, difcountenance the ufe of violent meafures againft fuch as adhered to the faith of their anceftors.* Mofheim p. 320.

Whilft Luther and Zuinglius were thus exerting themfelves in Germany and in Switzerland, the light of the reformation fpread itfelf far and wide. Before the middle of the 16th century, fome of the moft confiderable provinces of Europe had already broken their chains, and openly withdrawn themfelves from the difcipline of Rome and the jurifdiction of its pontiff. The reformed religion was propagated in Sweden, foon after Luther's rupture with Rome, by one of his difciples, whofe name was Olaus Petri, who was the firft herald of religious liberty in that kingdom, andwho tranflated the bible into the Swedifh language.

Reformation was alfo encouraged in Denmark, and that fo early as the year 1521; and it was not feven years from that time, when king Frederick

X 4 procured

---

* See alfo Brant's Hiftory v. 1. p. 57. Fol.

procured the publication of an edict, which declared every subject of Denmark free either to adhere to the tenets of the church of Rome, or to embrace the doctrine of Luther. (Mosheim p. 343—7.)

The kingdom of France was not inaccessible to the light of the reformation. Margaret, queen of Navarre, sister to Francis 1, was extremely favourable to the new doctrine. There where, so early as the year 1523, in several provinces in that country, multitudes of persons who had conceived the utmost aversion both against the doctrine and dominion of Rome, and among these, many persons of rank and dignity, and even some of the episcopal order. As their numbers increased from day to day, the authority of the monarch and the cruelty of his officers intervened, to support the doctrine of Rome by the edge of the sword, and the terrors of the gibbet.

From the constant intercourse which subsists between Germany and the Netherlands, it was impossible but that the new opinions must have been early propagated from the former to the latter; and accordingly, in the month of May 1521, the emperor Charles had published an edict, in which all the penalties of high treason were denounced against those who should be found guilty of holding any of Luther's tenets, or of republishing or vending any books written by him or his followers. In the execution of this edict, which Charles from time to time renewed, all the fury of persecution was exercised; and it is affirmed by several contemporary historians, that, during the reign of Charles, fifty thousand of the inhabitants of the Low-Countries were put to death on account of their religious principles. These principles, however, far from being extirpated, were more and more diffused in the midst of those severities which were employed to suppress them. (Watson's Philip II.)

So

So irresistible was the spirit of innovation, in the age of which we are speaking, and so great is the force of truth, that the opinions of the reformers had found their way even into Spain, and were embraced openly by great numbers of both sexes, among whom were both priests and nuns. (Ib. 137.) It is said that those very divines, whom Charles took with him into Germany to combat the reformers, imbibed their doctrines instead of refuting them, and, upon their return, propogated them in Spain. But the inquisition reigned triumphant in that country; and, by racks, gibbets, stakes and other such formidable instruments of persuasion, soon terrified the people into a profession of the romish faith, and suppressed their desire of novelties. (Mosheim 388.)

The seeds of the reformation were very early sown in Scotland, by several noblemen of that nation, who had resided in Germany during the religious disputes that divided the empire. But the power of the Roman pontiff, supported and seconded by inhuman laws and barbarous executions, choaked, for many years, those tender seeds, and prevented their taking root. At length, however, the papal cause was ruined, chiefly by the exertions of John Knox; and, from the latter part of the 16th century to the present time, the form of doctrine, worship, and discipline that had been established at Geneva by the ministry of Calvin, has been maintained in Scotland, and every attempt to introduce into that kingdom the rites and government of the church of England has proved impotent and unsuccessful. Ib. p. 380.

Having given this general view of the rise and progress of the reformation in some foreign countries, it will be proper to reserve an account of the sufferings of the martyrs to integrity, to a future number. The affairs of England will claim separate notice.

For

For the present, I shall dismiss the subject by observing, that one cannot but see and lament the footsteps of human frailty and passion in the conduct both of the romanists and of the protestants. The former, not contented with opposing the doctrines and arguments of Luther and his adherents, attack their persons, their liberties and their lives; whilst the latter fly to arms in defence of their religion, and establish the truth by the terrors of the sword. Such behaviour was, surely, very unbecoming christians. It is a plain proof, that God was not altogether with either party. Had they been perfectly acquainted with the principles and doctrines of the gospel, and and had they fully imbibed its spirit, they would have acted a more liberal and more amiable part; they would have more exactly followed the example of Jesus and his apostles. We should learn from hence to be cautious how we adopt implicitly, and without inquiry, either the doctrines of the church of Rome, or the doctrines of the reformers; nor should we be more ready to ascribe infallibility to the latter than to the former.

THE REVIEW.

Art. 1. *Conversations on Christian Idolatry, &c.*
Published by Theophilus Lindsey.

(Concluded from p. 215.

Having in the last Number, enabled the readers of the Christian Miscellany to form some idea of the design and plan of this work, it may be proper to afford them a specimen of the information and pleasure which they may derive from it. The following extract relates to the learned and excellent Dr. Clarke,

' the

' the celebrated Rector of St. James's, Weftminfter.'

' This eminent perfon was under very extraordinary convictions of the neceffity of reforming the liturgy of the church; and, for fome years before his death, had employed himfelf, at his leifure hours, in making amendments in it throughout. The principal and moft ftriking alterations, made and propofed by him, were in the devotional parts, with refpect to the object of worfhip.

' And here he took the liberty of blotting out all thofe paffages in which the fon or the holy ghoft, (or holy *fpirit*) is called God, or divine worfhip afcribed to either of them; retaining only thofe prayers and invocations which were addreffed to the one true God, and Father of all.

' This was done by him when his judgment and faculties were in their full vigour, having been finifhed juft before he was unexpectedly taken off by a fever, in his 54th year, anno 1729.

' This invaluable labour of his father's, his worthy fon, Mr. Clarke, prefented to the Britifh Mufeum, about 20 years ago; that it might be depofited, and preferved, among the moft precious things of the nation (*f*). And there it is now to be feen by you, Volufian, or by any other perfon.

' I cannot, however, finifh what I had to fay on this invaluable depofit, without adding, that there is in the library here an extract of a letter from archbifhop Herring to Dr. Jortin, after the bifhop had gotten a fight of this work of Dr. Clarke's. And his character of it, to fo eftimable a perfon, and fine a fcholar, as Dr. Jortin, well marks the high opinion both of them had of thefe emendations

(*f*) ' Dr. Clarke's own title is, " Amendments, humbly propofed to the Confideration of thofe in authority, of the Book of Common-Prayer, &c,"

tions of Dr. Clarke, and the concern it gave the archbishop, that the temper of the nation would not permit them to be adopted; although it might have been wished, that he had taken some way to express these sentiments before the public, as well as to his friend in private, to whom he thus writes:

Croydon, Aug. 7, 1753.

(t) " I have seen Dr. Clarke's common prayer-book. I have read it; have approved the temper, and wisdom of it. But into what times are we fallen, after so much light, and so much appearance of moderation, that we can only *wish* for the success of truth. The world will not bear it."

It is added, that ' there is no small ground of presumption to believe, that he would therein have had the countenance of his late majesty George II.; but, most assuredly, of his consort, queen Caroline; who was intirely in Dr. Clarke's sentiments, with respect to the athanasian trinity and worship. One circumstance is reported on good authority, that by both their majesties he was so highly esteemed, that, had he lived, he would have been raised to the bench of bishops; and perhaps the see of Canterbury might have been offered to him.'

It

(t) ' See New Review, vol. 1. p. 241, by Henry Maty, A.M. learned, ingenious, and of most singular integrity. He was a confessor of the truth of the divine unity; suffering the loss of many things for it. The admission of the amendments of the liturgy, proposed by Dr. Clarke, would have kept him in his station in the church.

To these testimonies of approbation of Dr. Clarke's reformed liturgy, may be added that of another prelate, more lately gone off this mortal stage, the learned, gentle and humane Dr. Law, bishop of Carlisle; than whom no one ever had a mind more open to truth, or was more communicative of it. Very signal proofs might be produced, how joyful an event it would have been to him, if he could have seen Dr. Clarke's reformation of the liturgy adopted throughout the nation.'

It now only remains to say of this work, that the whole is written with a very commendable spirit of temper and moderation. The opinions of *some* of the readers of the Christian Miscellany may, perhaps, be widely different from those of our author; but it must surely be acknowledged that the subject is, in itself, highly important, and that the manner in which it is treated renders the work before us worthy of the perusal and attention of *all*. The easy, familiar stile of the performance will, likewise, make it more interesting than theological productions in general.

Art. 2. *Two Practical Sermons on Private Prayer and and Public Worship.* To which is added, A short Address on the proper Manner of employing the Lord's Day. By. J. Charlesworth, M.A. late Fellow of Trinity College, Cambridge. 8vo. pp. 41. 6d. Johnson and Robinsons. 1791.

Art. 3. *A Sermon against Lying.* By a Member of the Society for promoting Christian Knowledge. 12mo. pp. 27. 3d. Johnson, &c.

Plain, practical and rational. Persons in the lower situations of life, for whose use these discourses are principally intended, may consult them with much real advantage.

Art. 4. *Plain Sermons, for Plain People.* By Hannah Sowden. 12mo. pp. 192. 2s. Johnson. 1792.

The design and tendency of this useful little volume cannot more fully be made known to the reader than by extracting the writer's *preface.*

' The

‘ The author of the following difcourfes, in the form of fermons, was induced to offer them to the public from the confideration that they might be conducive to the advancement of religion, among a clafs of people who greatly need inftruction.

‘ Much has been done, no doubt, of late, both by individuals and by bodies of men in this country, for the information of youth among the lower orders; and it is to be hoped that the happy confequences will be felt by the rifing generation. It is neverthelefs, certain, that reading the fcriptures, and attendance on public worfhip, though excellent means of inftruction, are not fufficient, and too frequently fail of the end propofed. Much pains muft be taken to make uncultivated minds underftand even things that to us appear the moft evident. The relation in which they ftand to God and to fociety, cannot be made too plain to their conception, or the duties of it be too ftrongly recommended to their practice.

‘ With this view of things, the following fheets were compofed. The fubjects treated are, chiefly, moral, the language plain, and the difcourfes fhort. They are intended to recommend the pure and undefiled religion of the heart, and to influence the reader to difcharge the duties of his ftation.

‘ The greateft part of the many excellent fermons, that have been publifhed in our language, fuppofe prior information, without which they cannot be fully underftood. The philofophical, the metaphyfical, or the doctrinal preacher, muft not hope to be ufeful to the vulgar; nor muft even the rational moral divine, unlefs he will take pains to inftruct his flock in private, or will condefcend to fuit his public ftile to their capacities.

‘ The influence of religious opinions, and their importance to the well-being of fociety, have lately

been

been difcuffed at large by a man * eminent in public and private virtue; who cannot but be fuppofed to underftand perfectly the true interefts of mankind. He has proved, how much the poor ftand in need of religious principles, as their fituation expofes them to many temptations.

' It is, therefore, to the poorer and lower ranks of mankind that thefe fheets are offered: but, as many among them poffefs neither the opportunity nor the means of obtaining them without the affiftance of their fuperiors in underftanding and in fortune, it can only be through the channel of the latter that the former can receive the benefit intended them. But what mafters would refufe to procure inftruction for their domeftics? Had they no fuperior motive, felf-intereft would be fufficient to inform them how much they muft be gainers by the virtuous principles of their fervants, their tradefmen, and their tenants. But the author does not mean to fufpect the judgment of the public, or to call their generofity in queftion. Convinced of their liberality, and trufting to their candour, fhe is perfuaded that they will readily lend their generous affiftance to promote the defign under confideration; by which a part, at leaft, of the benefit intended may accrue to individuals and to fociety.'

To this account of the publication before us, it is proper to add, that the fermons (which are very fhort) are twenty-one in number; and that the work is executed in fuch a manner as to render it probable that it will meet with general approbation, and be of confiderable fervice in promoting the laudable defign which the writer feems to have had in view. The author's theological fentiments are, thofe which are commonly called *orthodox*; but, though it be to

be

* Monfieur Necker.

be wished that, in a work of this kind, such sentiments had been entirely concealed, it must, at the same time, be confessed that they appear but seldom, and that, when they *do* present themselves, it is in the becoming dress of candour and moderation.

Art. 5. *The Fashionable Preacher*; or, Modern Pulpit Eloquence displayed, 8vo. pp. 32. 6d. Symonds, &c. 1792.

This little essay contains many just observations on a subject which will be allowed, by persons of reflection, to be highly important. The pulpit eloquence of this country, the author considers, and, perhaps, with truth, as in a very deplorable state, and as capable of great improvement. This defect is ascribed, principally, to the *affectation of learning and refinement* which prevails among our preachers, and to the custom of *reading* our sermons, which he exposes with much felicity of expression and clearness of illustration. It might be well if our clergy of all denominations would attend to the sensible advice which is here offered them.

CORRESPONDENCE.

' R. P's Vindication of Rational Religion' will appear in the next Number.

The communication of ' Candidus' is, necessarily, postponed till next month.

It is requested that all communications for this Work be sent (post paid) directed to the Editor of the Christian Miscellany, at Mr. Stalker's, No. 4, Stationers-court, Ludgate-street, London.

It is wished that those correspondents, whose essays are designed for the current Number, would transmit them as early in the month as possible.

THE

Chriſtian Miſcellany,

For JULY, 1792.

ART. I. *A Vindication of Rational Religion.*

AGAINST perſons who hold liberal or rational ſentiments of religion, the charge, that the ſcriptures enſure no permanent good, nor bring to light any important diſcoveries, hath not unfrequently been alledged; and, while it hath been imagined that the doctrines of the trinity, the atonement, and many other ſuch myſtical articles, conſtitute the eſſence, nay, the very exiſtence of chriſtianity, an equally abſurd opinion has prevailed, that the goſpel offers no promiſes, opens no proſpects, and reſerves no rewards, for perſons who practiſe the virtues it inculcates, and who lead lives conformable to the ſpirit of its injunctions. Let us, then, enquire whether divine revelation doth not confer ineſtimable bleſſings, unfold immenſe views, and inſpire with the moſt ardent hopes of immortality thoſe of its profeſſors who reject thoſe ſentiments which to them appear deſtructive of its purity, and ſubverſive of its influence.

In our preſent reſearches, we ſhall enquire what revelation teaches with reſpect to the Deity, our fellow creatures, and ourſelves.

Chriſtianity was, perhaps, neceſſary to confirm rather than demonſtrate the exiſtence of a firſt, intelligent, deſigning cauſe; but what the ideas of the heathens were concerning its nature and excellence,

Y

lence, let their views of religion determine. We shall find that, with a few exceptions, all of them entertained the most degrading notions respecting their Deities; that they conceived of them as not only liable to, but chargeable with, the greatest crimes; that their existence was circumscribed by narrow bounds, their knowledge limited to a few objects, their power confined to a small extent, and their goodness diffused through narrow channels. We find them captivated by a magnificent temple, a rich oblation, and a costly sacrifice. We view them influenced by the detestable passions of anger and revenge. In short, the farther we enquire into their character, the more striking will appear the depravity of their nature. But the scriptures exhibit the most glorious display of the Divine perfections; and the traits of his character, as pourtrayed in them, are consonant with, though, perhaps, not discoverable from, natural appearances. What views too sublime can be entertained of that Being whom christianity represents as the one, only wise, living and true God; as that grand centre in which resistless power and inexhaustible wisdom are united with boundless, unchangeable goodness; as that perennial fountain whose streams roll in such rapid torrents, and carry with them blessings so vast and distinguished; as that life which hath existed from all eternity, and that existence which shall continue when time shall be no more; as that comprehensive mind to whose view all past events and future occurrences are equally present? But the scriptures not only insist on the existence of the Deity, but describe him as the only proper object of our veneration and confidence. And, if he be that assemblage of natural and moral beauty which we have before ascribed to him, if he be that light in which is no darkness, that purity which is stained by no blemish, blemifh, and that goodnefs which knows no change, —can our hearts defire a fubject more entitled to worfhip, an afylum more certain, a harbour more fecure from all the ftorms which blacken around us? If the chriftian religion enjoin us to repofe an unlimited confidence in our Maker, it is becaufe he is that rock of all ages whofe foundations are immoveable and everlafting; if it encourage us to look up to him for the fupply of our neceffities, it is becaufe his liberality is as diffufive as the wants of his creatures; if it reflect a beam of hope on the minds of finful beings, and enable them to implore and obtain forgivenefs of their fins on repentance, it is becaufe, as a father, fo he pitieth his children, becaufe he knoweth our frame, and remembereth that we are duft.

But it is time to view the fcriptures in another light, and fee whether they are not equally excellent in the conduct they enjoin towards our fellow-creatures. A little attention to them will evince their decided preference to other fyftems, both in the fuperiority of the principles they lay down, and the motives whence they originate.—To be fatisfied how low was the ftandard of the morality of the heathens, we have only to confult the writings of fome of their greateft men. The defcription a Roman poet has given us of the depraved manners of his times and the prevailing licentioufnefs of the age in which he lived, is truly deplorable. He has painted, in the moft glowing colours, the crimes unaffifted nature was capable of committing. But what will be our aftonifhment to find the very perfon who lafhes, with an unfparing hand, the vices of his countrymen, become the object of our fevereft cenfure? The writings of Ifocrates *(a)* are, perhaps, the moft perfect fpecimen of morality which has been prefented to us

Y 2

from

(a) See, particularly, his Oration to Demonicus.

from the fchools of Greece; and yet, how contracted their views of human conduct, how confined their notions of real ufefulnefs! Deftitute of that warm philanthropy which ought to be kept alive in every human breaft, infenfible to thofe generous emotions of fympathy of which every heart ought to be fufceptible, they teach us to perfecute our enemies, and to exercife our revenge on thofe weakneffes of our fellow-beings which have a juft claim to our compaffion and forgivenefs.

But, to acquire enlarged ideas of moral worth, we muft have recourfe to the fcriptures. They alone exhibit a model by which the character may be formed to the moft exalted virtue, by which it may be moft eminently fubfervient to the interefts of the world. They alone command us to confider all mankind as our brethren, as the children of God, our common Parent. They teach us never to extinguifh that fpark in our bofoms which will kindle up the nobleft affections of the human mind, feelings which will ever prompt us to relieve the wants of the indigent, which will folicit our protection for injured virtue, which will incline us to forgive, from our hearts, the failings of our offending brethren.

We fhall now examine the motives revelation fupplies us with for the proper difcharge of our duty. It is generally allowed that the *fprings* of human actions are the only criterion by which a judgement of their excellence can be formed; fo that it is poffible that an act of generofity, produced from interefted views, may be juftly reprehended, although efficient of the happinefs of the perfon on whom it is exercifed. If this be the rule by which the virtue of the heathens is to be eftimated, we fhall perceive it to be highly defective. I can dwell with admiration on the character of that perfon who could fa-
GRIFICE

crifice the feelings of a parent to the good of his country; but such examples are seldom to be met with. The *amor patriæ* of the Romans will, with a few exceptions, be found to originate from a selfish principle; and the honour of a triumph or a statue to have summoned that magnanimity which would have been ill supplied from the consideration of preserving their country.—But the grand motive to virtue, laid down in the gospel, is the love of God. This is the true source of all actions which are directed to the public good. If we have a sincere love of God, it is impossible not to love our neighbour as ourselves. For the Deity designed all his creatures for happiness. He created them for no other end. This principle of affection, then, will induce us to co-operate with him in his great design. It will lead us to consider no labour too great to be sustained, no dangers too threatening to be encountered, no life too dear to be sacrificed, when engaged in this glorious enterprize.

Having briefly considered the scriptures as discovering to us what we know concerning God and our fellow creatures, we proceed, lastly, to point out the great blessings they communicate to us as individuals. Here, objects of pursuit the most interesting arrest our attention; rewards the most distinguished, and punishments the most dreadful, all conspire to render our lives conformable to the will of our Maker. The religion of Christ teaches that no man liveth to himself. Here is a doctrine worthy its divine Author, suitable to that universal happiness it was intended to diffuse. By this, man, the rational and immortal creature of God, is taught to view the ennobling privileges of his nature: led, by this, to despise the thought of a life devoted to selfish gratifications, his attention is directed to some great object; he considers himself as born for the

Y 3

world,

world, and as under the moft binding obligations to enlighten and improve it.—Again, the gofpel teaches us that we are beings defigned for a future world. This truth, that our exiftence fhall recommence in a future world, is the confummation of the great plan of divine providence. Deftitute of it, our lives, fo far from being defirable, would prove a fource of the moft diftreffing anxiety. After having formed a few ideas of the divine perfections, difcovered a few of thofe laws by which the immenfe fyftem of nature is regulated, and received the moft exquifite delight from thefe grand refearches, the thought that diffolution will exterminate this noble career, intercept from our view thofe infinite fources of fcience, and bury our intellectual powers in eternal oblivion, were fufficient to difmay a heart deprived of its pureft fenfations. But chriftianity fpeaks a different language. It informs us that, while nature is fubject to perpetual change, and expofed to decay, man, rendered a few years infenfible by death, fhall be reproduced by the energy of that Being who firft fpake him into exiftence ; that incorruption fhall enter into the compofition of his celeftial frame ; that he fhall move in a more exalted fphere ; that thofe bubbles of fcience, which elude his grafp and vanifh into air, fhall be condenfed into a boundlefs ocean, fupplying pure and neverfailing ftreams of the moft exalted pleafure ; that, in the luftre of his glory, he fhall fhine as the ftars of heaven.

Such are the advantages imparted by the gofpel. It draws, in the ftrongeft lines, the unrivalled excellencies of our great Creator. From the defcription of his nature, it encourages us to addrefs our prayers to him, and to repofe the moft unlimited confidence in his goodnefs and mercy. It commands us to exercife our benevolent regards to the
whole

whole race of human beings; and refts them on their proper bafis, the love of our Maker. It prefents to our fouls an anchor, fure and ftedfaft, in the refurrection from the dead to endlefs exiftence; and enforces our obedience to the divine laws, by the moft pofitive affurances of eternal happinefs.—If, then, after this reprefentation of the fcriptures, we be charged with debafing their excellence, and fapping their very foundations, the only punifhment we would defire for fuch perfons is, more enlarged conceptions and charitable difpofitions. While we prefent our petitions to one God, even the Father, let them worfhip as many Deities as their imaginations may fuggeft. While we ufe that reafon, which conftitutes our fuperiority over other beings, in matters of religion, and fet it up as the only ftandard by which we can judge of its doctrine and evidence, let them entirely difclaim its authority, and believe in opinions the moft abfurd, by pleading that they are incomprehenfible. While we reft our hopes of retribution on our perfonal exertions and a fincere though imperfect obedience, let them indulge the vain conceit that the fimple belief in the atonement, inftantaneoufly created at the pleafure of the will, fhall be fufficient to wafh away the fins of a perfon whofe life has been ftained by the blackeft crimes, whofe conduct has been a continued violation of the laws of God and man. While we believe it to be inconfiftent, and contradictory to the infinite goodnefs of God, *infinitely* to punifh a being for crimes he could not fail to perpetrate, let them conceive of it as felecting a few for endlefs enjoyment, and configning the reft to endlefs mifery. In fhort, while we entertain opinions which naturally expand the foul, let them embrace thofe which tend to contract it. While we ground our falvation on the *practice*, let them derive theirs from the *belief* of

the

the doctrines of revelation.—While, therefore, we entertain fentiments fo congenial to the fpirit of the gofpel, let us exercife that charity without which all religion will prove but an empty fhadow. Let us embrace our opinions under the fulleft perfuafion that we are liable to error, and cherifh the warmeft affection for thofe whofe mode of thinking is diffonant from our own. Where the heart is fincere, let us commend the actions it performs. Let us look forwards to that ftate where all religious differences will be abforbed in univerfal harmony, peace and joy.

R. P.

Art. II. *Remarks on Pofitive and Negative Religions, extracted from the Seventh Volume of the Monthly Review.*

In illuftration of a remark of Mr. Burke's, that ' in England, even during the troubled interregnum, it was not thought fit to eftablifh a *negative* religion; but the Parliament fettled the *prefbyterian*, as the church *difcipline*; the directory, as the rule of public *worfhip*; and the *Weftminfter catechifm*, as the inftitute of *faith*;'—the Monthly Reviewers obferve,

True it is, no national church, of which we have read, has contented itfelf with eftablifhing what Mr. Burke here calls a *negative* religion; and we doubt whether the caufe of revelation has not hence received more injury, than from all other caufes put together.

The jews had a *negative* religion handed down to them from heaven, which faid, " thou fhalt not kill, thou fhalt not fteal, &c." but it feems this was not enough for them, and fo they heaped on it the *pofitive* traditions of their elders, till, as we read,

(Matt.

(Matt. xv. 6.) they " made the commandment of God of none effect."

Chriftians alfo had a *negative* religion given them from the fame fource, faying, " call no man your father on the earth :" but this did not content national churches; and fo they created for themfelves, father Dominics, father Francis's right rev. and moft rev. fathers in God, father confeffors, holy fathers of the inquifition, and fuch an innumerable hoft of other *pofitive* fathers, that their Father, which is in heaven, (who, whether we refer to his own prohibitory mandate, " thou fhalt have none other gods or fathers but me," or whether we refer to the great neglect into which he and his precepts had fallen among national churches in comparifon of other fathers and their precepts, might not improperly be called their *negative* father,) was nearly loft and forgotten in the crowd.

Catholics, again, by the *negative* religion which they received from God, were forbidden to make to themfelves any graven image; but, being wifer than their maker, they difcovered that fomething *pofitive* was abfolutely neceffary, to affift and invigorate their devotions, as they pretended; and fo they introduced image-worfhip.

Laftly, both papift and proteftant, both evangelift and reformed churches, were taught by the *negative* religion which was made for them, that " the Lord their God was one Lord, and that they fhould have no other gods but him :" but they made a *pofitive* religion for themfelves. The clear light of heaven, which fhone fo refulgent in the fimple negative propofition, was found to be too dim, obfcure, and *undefined*; and fo they invented their homooufias, their confubftantialities, their hypoftatic unions, their three perfons in one nature, and two natures in one perfon, and all their other patent

lamps

lamps to light those souls on their road to salvation, which had been left in such a benighted and forlorn condition by him who created them. Amid all their care and concern, however, they forgot one thing, without which an ordinary capacity must be in great danger of erring; and if it should err therein, it seems that it must perish everlastingly;—they forgot to point out how men were to distinguish and clearly comprehend the difference between three separate persons all endowed with every attribute of God, and three separate Gods; so as that they might commit no fatal blunder, either by " confounding the persons or dividing the substance."

Much worse, however, than all this,—it has ever been in defence and propagation of their *positive* religions, that men have unsheathed the sword of persecution; that they have harrassed and massacred, and burned and tortured, one another, in every mode which human, or rather diabolical, ingenuity could invent. Gracious Heaven! that such wretches should ever, by their own impudence, or by the sufferance of others, have worn and polluted the most respectable and honourable of all titles, that of a Christian! That men, who made it their business—and to judge from the history of most of these positive gentlemen, one would think they had no other business in the world—who made it their business, we say, to " go about like roaring lions seeking whom they might devour," should pretend to be followers of him who " went about doing good!"—That miscreants, breathing nothing but *hatred* and vengeance, should pass themselves for disciples of a Master, who made it a condition absolutely indispensable in all who would be his disciples, that they must have " *love* one towards another;" and who, by his adding that this should make them manifest to all the world, seems to have considered scarcely any

other

other criterion as effentially neceffary! Were not the fact known to be otherwife, one would almoft be led to imagine, that churches and kirks had impofed the name of *Chriftians* on thefe their myrmidons, in the way of fcorn and derifion : juft as, it is faid, another Kirk, whofe memory, by the uncommon infamy attached to it, is likely to furvive a long time in the weft of England, impofed the name of *lambs* on the brutes who executed the favage barbarities of a commander more brutal than themfelves.

TO THE EDITOR OF THE CHRISTIAN MISCELLANY.

S I R,

If you think the paper herewith worth a place in the Chriftian -Mifcellany, it is at your difpofal. That your work may prove a mean of rouzing the attention of mankind ftill more towards their beft interefts, is the fincere wifh of, Sir,

Your humble Servant,
CANDIDUS.

Art. III. *On the Duty and Neceffity of Religious Enquiry.*

True wifdom confifteth in valuing things according to their degree of importance, in relation to the true happinefs of rational and immortal beings. True religion is the beft *mean* to this the beft of *ends*. However much any other object may deferve man's attention and purfuit, yet, when he values it as productive of that happinefs which is to be found only in true religion, he difcovers a folly that can only be equalled by the difappointment he muft infallibly meet with. To *feel* the worth and importance of religion, implies that it muft firft be known ; and to enjoy

enjoy that happiness it alone can give, implies that this knowledge produce its proper effects in practice. Therefore, to be truly happy is both to *know* and *practise* religion.

Although I believe very few will dispute the principle laid down in these observations, yet many people, eager in the pursuit of happiness, are so apt to run into extremes as to miss the object they aim at. Although the knowledge and practice of religion are inseparably connected, so as to be productive of real happiness; yet, in human characters, these often appear strangely disjoined. Some have studied theology as a science, as a fit subject for the exercise and improvement of the human mind, as a subject that affords much variety of conversation. They have experienced a pleasure in examining the various opinions of mankind upon it, and have, possibly, at last acquired pretty clear and just views of its principles: but it has sometimes appeared that the *practical importance* of these has not equally impressed their hearts; that they have discovered a greater keenness to disseminate among mankind the knowledge of *their own* principles, than the practice of *plain* and *obvious duties*. On the other hand, as the doctrinal points of theology are far from being obvious, as the generality of mankind have not opportunity, or, rather, will not be at the trouble to examine them, as the opinions of those, who have enquired, are various, and as some of this class have not shewn an equal attention to the practical part of religion; it is no matter of surprize, if not only the unthinking and ignorant, but even some of the thinking and intelligent part of mankind, either look upon religious principles as matters of mere indifference, or rest in a blind assent to what they had imbibed in youth, which may be true or false, for them. All that is sufficient for them, say they, is to " fear

God

God and keep his commandments;" and thus very gravely footh themfelves in their ignorance and indolence. The tafk of enquiry affrights them; the prevalent example of mankind deters them; the inconfiftent conduct of fome of thofe, who have enquired, cherifhes their prejudice; and the variety of human opinions makes them conclude that the truth is not to be found, that an attempt to difcover it would be idle and vain. There is, furely, a medium between thefe two oppofite characters; poffibly, nearer to truth and propriety. From the firft, I would by no means be underftood to infinuate that the ftudy of religion in any degree hurts the practice of it; nor, from the laft, be thought fo uncandid as to fay that the lives of many, who are ignorant of the true principles of religion, are irreligious and immoral. On the contrary, I would hope it will appear in the courfe of this paper to be not only the duty of every man to ftudy his religion, but alfo neceffary to produce a truly pious and virtuous life: and I believe there are many, who have never made a regular enquiry, that are pious and virtuous; but I muft add that their piety would be much more enlightened, exalted and rational, and their virtue much more extenfive, fteady and uniform, if they had been well acquainted with the grounds and reafons of a truly religious conduct. As the principles of religion are founded in truth, as thefe are perceptible to human reafon, and ought to be examined by it, and as they afford the beft motives to the beft conduct; fo, when they are ftudied to mend the heart, and regulate the behaviour, then it is that man acts in this manner as becometh a rational creature in the purfuit of happinefs. Things that are the beft in themfelves are often the moft perverted to produce mifchief. No one, however, from this can with propriety argue againft their excellence and importance.

importance. In like manner, however immoral the lives of many profeffing chriftians may be, it would be unfair to conclude that religion is a vain and unneceffary ftudy. Religion, no doubt, contains principles of primary or effential importance, and principles of lefs confequence to man. But none of thefe can be called indifferent, but in comparifon with another of greater importance. Nothing furely is indifferent which God has been pleafed to deliver to man. This very argument might be fufficient to induce mankind to be well acquainted with his revelation.

Every man, who has any regard to religion at all, affents to this truth,—that all ought firmly to believe its doctrines. But men differ in opinion as to what they fhould do or not do, previous to this belief, and not whether they fhould or fhould not believe any thing at all. Many embrace the religion of their fathers, or that of their country, without enquiry or confideration : others will not give their affent to any principle, until they know its grounds and reafons. The former believe, although they cannot give a reafon for their belief; the latter believe, and are acquainted with the reafons of their's. The former call the conduct of the latter, idle and unimportant fpeculation; while the latter, in their turn, call that of the former, weak, fuperftitious and unreafonable. The difference between them is,—the belief of the one arifes from knowledge, that of the other from chance, from influence and ignorance.

The foregoing obfervations were deemed proper to pave the way to the following arguments, tending to fhew the duty and neceffity of enquiring into religion, from the confideration *of its importance*; of man as a *reafonable* creature; of us, in this country,

try, as *chriftians* and *proteftants*; and, laftly, of the *variety* of opinions held on that fubject.

(To be concluded in the next Number.)

ART. IV. *Chriftianity proved to have been, in its confequences, beneficial to mankind.*

(Concluded from page 238.)

" In ftating the dreadful calamities of which chriftianity has been the caufe, your object feemed to be to caft a cenfure on the religion itfelf, and, in the next place, to infer the improbability that it fhould have a divine original, from the confideration that the Deity muft have forefeen thefe ealamities, and, being a benevolent Deity, would never have permitted the caufe of them to exift.

I. If you had intended to caft a real cenfure on chriftianity, you fhould have proved that the calamities happened in confequence of an obedience to its precepts. But I run no danger of a refutation, if I affert that a perfon, but fuperficially acquainted with the fcriptures, would be able to quote, from almoft every page, paffages that fhould pointedly and feverely condemn the immediate authors of every calamity which you have mentioned." (Here my friend produced a number of paffages which formed fo ftriking a contraft to the principles that actuate the fons of ill-nature, of revenge, and of that bi. gotted zeal which wifhes to eftablifh its own opinion through the medium of violence, that I began to doubt the propriety of the argument I had employed. He alfo related fome circumftances of our faviour's life which feemed to prove, in the ftrongeft manner, how much his conduct as well as his precepts condemned perfecution, violence and a want

of

of charity. I am forry that my friend's detail was too long for infertion here. He continued———)
" Having fhewn, then, that the perfons, who were the immediate caufe of thofe miferies which you defcribed, were the enemies and not the friends of the chriftian religion; that, whilft they profeffed to fupport, they in reality violated its moft important precepts;—you muft perceive that, inftead of cafting a cenfure, you have beftowed an encomium on chriftianity. For, had thefe been guided by the precepts of chriftianity, thofe unhappy events would never have been known.

II. As, however, it muft be allowed that they would not have happened, if this religion had not vifited the world, you deny its divine original, becaufe God, forefeeing thefe calamities, would never have introduced the caufe. It is my bufinefs, therefore, to prove that the pofitive good effects of chriftianity exceed the evils which indirectly flow from it.

All thefe evils have been the immediate confequence of the corrupt and pernicious paffions of men. To have prevented, then, the evils which you have related, and thereby (according to your opinion) to have proved the divine original of this religion, it would have been neceffary to have divefted man of thofe paffions to which he is fo liable : a miracle totally unneceffary to the introduction of chriftianity; becaufe chriftianity was introduced for the very purpofe of itfelf annihilating or correcting the paffions. You ought not to wonder, then, if, in effecting this purpofe according to the natural courfe of things, the various conflicts and ftruggles of the human paffions have given rife to calamitous events; nor, confidering the power which the paffions have over the mind, and alfo that, though the times in which chriftianity was introduced were favourable

vourable to its general reception, yet a long night of barbarifm and ignorance foon fucceeded, and the day of reafon has but juft begun to dawn upon the world ;——I fay, confidering thefe two facts, it is no argument againft me that nearly eighteen centuries are paft, and yet chriftianity has not attained its defired purpofe. It is fufficient for me to fhew that we are in a progreffive ftate of improvement in confequence of its precepts. Now the moft ingenious fceptic cannot draw a parallel between modern times and thofe in which our religion was introduced.

1ft. In thofe times, emperors on the throne were gods on earth : their temples were filled with votaries, and the incenfe from their altars wafted its flattering odours to their mental fenfes; or, if divine honours were not paid them while alive, the people decreed them to be gods after their deceafe, fo that no fooner had the hand of death proved them to be mortal, than they were reverenced as immortal. But now the proudeft defpot is content to be the tyrant of his people; he cannot be their god. Chriftianity has taught men to revolt at this daring impiety.

2dly. We are, even in thefe times, too prone to revenge our injuries, but the perfuafive voice of chriftianity has often prompted us to forgive them; and, in obeying this precept, we experience a grateful fatisfaction. Chriftianity blufhed to find, on its introduction into the world, that revenge was reverenced as a virtue.

3dly. There are, comparatively, few of the moderns who can contemplate flavery without an emotion of indignation. The generality of mankind are making the moft ftrenuous efforts for its entire abolition. Chriftianity has dared to whifper in the ears of monarchy and nobility this important truth, that all are equal in the fight of God; and, by this decla-

Z ration,

ration, has undermined the horrid precept of antiquity, which taught that flavery is a neceffary-link in the chain of fubordination.

4thly. Nor can the moft refined civilization of antiquity be compared to that of modern times. A fierce cruelty ftrongly characterized all their actions; but chriftianity has foftened and humanized our manners: and, when we hear of fome daring deed of cruelty and violence, we generally trace it to a wretch on whom the rays of chriftianity have but faintly beamed.

5thly. It fhould be obferved too, that, when we take but an imperfect furvey of the effects of chriftianity, the great mifchiefs to which it has unqueftionably given rife are the firft to force themfelves upon our attention. It is not natural to turn back and gaze upon the filent ftream which foftly glides through the verdant meadow, and, in its progrefs, difpenfes, unobferved, its refrefhing bounties; when before us the rapid torrent, fwelled by previous rains, overflows its wonted banks, and, in its maddened courfe, fweeps down the oppofing bridges, overwhelms the incautious cattle that have ftrayed from the neighbouring paftures, and whirls along the victims of its fury. In the fame manner, the filent bounties of chriftianity are more apt to efcape our notice, than thofe violent mifchiefs of which it is fometimes the innocent caufe, and which, meeting the more boifterous paffions of men, roufe and command their attention in a greater degree.

But, if we obferve the conduct of a good chriftian through the various ftages of his life, we fhall there admire the pleafing, fecret influence of chriftianity. As, however, we have not time to dwell on every particular, let us confine our view to the laft and moft interefting that a chriftian difplays. Let us obferve him on his death-bed. Examine

the

the features of his countenance. Do his ferene looks betray a regret and horror at leaving his worldly poffeffions? Do his laft accents dictate, with the fternnefs of a dying heathen, the bloody mandates of revenge to his furrounding family? Does he, with his laft breath, bequeath to them the care of avenging his wrongs? Ah! no! It is a different picture. His calm brow expreffes the confcioufnefs of a well-fpent life. On it are imprinted the refignation and the hopes of a dying chriftian. It is here that the grand, important doctrine of chriftianity vifibly difplays its confolatory influence. The expiring chriftian expects a future ftate. His laft prayers are for bleffings to his enemies. The contented, gentle fmile, that plays upon his countenance, fpeaks the tender farewell to his weeping friends. He once more directs his eyes to heaven; then clofes them for ever. Each forrowing friend mufes this foliloquy in his breaft,—" Oh! with what peace a chriftian dies!"

It is faid that fome few heathen philofophers had, by the force of reafon, convinced themfelves that there muft be a future ftate. But their conceptions on this point were very abfurd and very confined. They were intelligible only to philofophers; the bulk of mankind derived no confolation from them. When reafon yielded in the ftruggle, imagination took the field; and the poets drew pleafing pictures of futurity. Are we to fuppofe that they were generally believed? They feem too ftrongly tinctured with poetic fiction.—Yet, it is certain that the people believed in the gods, concerning whom thefe fanciful, poetic ftrains were fung.——True. But, on this principle, future ages may think we have believed in the daring and fublime imagery of Milton's Paradife Loft. But, grant for a moment, that the people believed there was a Tartarus, and a

Rhada-

Rhadamanthus rigorous to count the blue fcars which the crimes of a man's life had branded upon his foul;*—this, indeed, might in fome degree infpire terror in the wicked, but ftill it was profitable that chriftianity fhould difpel thefe errors, and introduce a more rational, a more credible fyftem of futurity. This doctrine, now fo well eftablifhed, is a perpetual fource of confolation to the virtuous, a rod fufpended before the wicked to warn them of their danger; and thus fociety at large, as well as the individual, is indebted to chriftianity.

6thly. Reflect, alfo, on what might have been the condition of mankind, if chriftianity had not vifited the world. I have already had occafion to mention the ftate of the world before the general eftablifhment of chriftianity. Mankind feemed little difpofed to improve their principles and difpofitions; they rather receded gradually from true virtue at that time. Can you think, then, that chriftianity (not to fpeak of thofe pofitive advantages which, without it, we fhould never have known), has caufed half the evils which the world might have experienced from barbarous, cruel and revengeful heathens?

I have yet fpoken only of paft and prefent events; but what may we not expect of the future? We find ourfelves in a ftate of gradual improvement; we have already difpelled many of the clouds of fuperftition and error which, foon after the fun of chriftianity had firft begun to gild our horizon, frequently intercepted its genial rays. Yet the calamities and miferies, which you have ftated, happened, chiefly, at a time when thefe inaufpicious clouds ftill troubled the chriftian atmofphere; for popery had, in thofe days, an almoft univerfal influence. Thus, then, are we better practical chriftians

* See Lucian's Dialogues.

tians than our anceftors; and it is not unreafonable to fuppofe that our children may excel us, and that diftant pofterity may almoft clafp perfection."

Here my friend concluded; and fo ftrongly had he rivetted my attention, that I was feldom tempted to break the filence which I had promifed to obferve.

It was now very late at night, and I conducted him to his chamber, and then went to my own bed. However, it was a confiderable time before I could compofe myfelf to fleep. I lay ruminating on what had been faid; and though my friend's difcourfe had made great impreffion upon me, I own I did not feel myfelf thoroughly divefted of my former opinions. I thought I faw objections hovering about my friend's obfervations, which feemed rather forcible at that time; but a little familiar converfation with him the next morning brought me over entirely to his fentiments: and I now believe in the good effects of chriftianity the more firmly, becaufe on that point I was once a fceptic.

ART. V. *A View of the Progrefs of Unitarian Sentiments and Worfhip.*

(Continued from p. 249.)

Since the publication of that piece, two popular works have appeared to give men juft and fcriptural notions concerning the object of worfhip, and to fhew that the trinitarian worfhip is as deftitute of foundation in fcripture as it is repugnant to reafon. One of thefe is afcribed to a clergyman of the church of England, and is entitled "An Appeal to the Common Senfe of all Chriftian People, more particularly, the Members of the Church of England, with regard to an important point of faith and

Z 3

practice,

practice, impofed upon their confciences by Church Authority. By a Member of the Church of England, fincerely attached to her true Intereft." The 2d Edition was printed 1754. The author of the other piece was a perfon in a very humble ftation; but whofe probity, pure manners, love of truth, extenfive reading and philofophical ftudies gave to him, in his lowly condition, an elevation and dignity of character to which numbers in the nobler walks of life have no claim. His fmall tract was called " An Attempt to reftore the Supreme Worfhip of the Father Almighty; written for the ufe of Chriftians, by George Williams, a Livery Servant." This appeared about the year 1763 or 1764.

Both thefe tracts were drawn up in a good fpirit, and written with the beft views; and there is no doubt but they made a confiderable and extenfive impreffion. But, to whatever caufe it may be imputed, whether to long habit, to the timidity of the authors, or to the hope of effecting a change in the public national fervices by other means than by an open feparation from the church which retains the corrupt forms of worfhip, thefe pieces could fcarcely be expected to have any other effect than to correct men's inward fentiments; for the authors recommend it to their readers to continue in the communion of the church where the worfhip of God, the Father, is blended with that of two other perfons, where the prayers and praifes are formed upon principles totally repugnant to thofe, the truth and divine authority of which it is the defign of their pieces to illuftrate and eftablifh. What is this, but to aim to fet right the *faith* of men, but to leave them, nay, advife them, to follow a different faith in their *conduct?* They recommend, it is true, " an honeft and open profeffion" of the truth on this head: but how

can

can that profeffion be *honeft*, which is united with *infincerity* in *religious* acts? Or how is it *open*, if it ftill wears the *mafk of conformity?* Uniformity and confiftency feem effential to an honeft and open profeffion of the truth. What fhould we think of the conduct of chriftians, of their integrity and zeal in keeping themfelves from idols, who, with their lips making confeffion of faith in the One true God, ufually frequented the temples of idols, and worfhipped, as did Socrates, at the heathen altars? " Indeed," to adopt the remark of archdeacon Paley, directly applicable to this point, " where one man " thinks it his duty conftantly to worfhip a being " whom another cannot, with the affent of his " confcience, permit himfelf to worfhip at all, " there feems to be no plea for comprehenfion, or ' or any expedient left, but a quiet feceffion. All " other differences may be compromifed by fi- " lence."*

We are come to a period, when the truth of thefe fentiments hath been felt, and the dictates of truth, in this refpect, have been obeyed. The Rev. Dr. William Robertfon, in the year 1760, led the way in the upright and difinterefted line of conduct purfued by thofe who have, of late years, quitted their preferments in the church, and withdrawn from its devotional fervices. He was urged by preffing difficulties, by affecting pleas, againft fuch a ftep; but a principle of pious integrity overcame them all.

" In debating this matter with myfelf, (fays this worthy man) befides the arguments directly to the purpofe, feveral ftrong collateral confiderations came in upon the pofitive fide of the queftion. The ftraitnefs of my circumftances preffed me clofe; a numerous family, quite unprovided for, pleaded with

Z 4

the

* PALEY's Principles of Moral and Political Philofophy, 4to. p. 363.

the moſt pathetic and moving eloquence; and the infirmities and wants of age, now coming faſt upon me, were urged feelingly. But one ſingle conſideration prevailed over all theſe;—*that the Creator and Governor of the univerſe, whom it is my firſt duty to worſhip and adore, being the God of truth, it muſt be diſagreeable to him, to profeſs, ſubſcribe, or declare, in any matter relating to his worſhip and ſervice, what is not believed ſtrictly and ſimply to be true.*" *

The example of this venerable *father of unitarian nonconformity*, as he has been called, was, it appears, a ſtimulus to the mind of Mr. Theophilus Lindſey, and was followed by his reſignation of the vicarage of Catterick, in Yorkſhire, in the year 1774. Since him, the hiſtory of unitarianiſm has been able to record, and perpetuate with due honour, the names of Dr. John Jebb; of Mr. Tyrrwhit, of Jeſus College, Cambridge; of Mr. Evanſon; of Mr. Maty; of Mr. Harries; of Dr. Diſney,† and of others; who have ſeparated themſelves from the communion of a church in which they could not follow the dictates of conſcience, in paying pure and uncorrupted worſhip to the ſupreme God and Father of all.

Mr. Lindſey has had the peculiar happineſs of ſeeing his reſignation and his Apology drawing on them ſuch notice and attention, as to be the cauſe of his beholding a Society, in every view reſpectable, forming and riſing under him, on the ſcriptural plan of offering up prayers and praiſes to the one only God of the univerſe, the God and Father of our Lord Jeſus Chriſt.

(*The remainder of this article muſt, from want of room, be deferred till next month.*)

ART.

* See Lindſey's Apology, 3d Ed. 225.
† See the hiſtory of theſe worthies in Mr. Lindſey's Hiſtorical View of the State of the Unitarian Doctrine and Worſhip, p. 478—551.

ART. VI. *A View of Perfecutions.*

No. IV.

Of the fufferings of the French Proteftants.

We have feen the kingdoms of Denmark, Sweden, Scotland, and almoft one half of Germany, throw off their allegiance to the pope, and abolifh his jurifdiction within their territories. Nor was the fpirit of innovation confined to thofe countries which openly revolted from the fee of Rome. It penetrated into France, and made a rapid progrefs. In all the provinces of Germany which continued to acknow-ledge the papal fupremacy, as well as in the Low-Countries, the proteftant doctrines were fecretly taught, and had gained fo many profelytes that they were ripe for a revolt. Even in Spain and in Italy, fymptoms of the fame difpofition appeared. The pretenfions of the pope to infallible knowledge and fupreme power were treated, by many perfons of eminent learning and abilities, with fuch fcorn or impugned with fuch vehemence, that the moft vigi-lant attention of the magiftrate, the higheft ftrains of pontifical authority, and* all the rigour of inquifi-torial jurifdiction, were requifite to check and extinguifh it.

In France, the reformation was cherifhed by the king's fifter, Margaret queen of Navarre, " a very generous princefs (fays Mezeray, the french hiftorian,) who, having a great love for learning, had fuffered her reafon to be prevailed upon by thefe broachers of novelties."

" About the end of the year 1534, the facra-mentarians (for fo he names the french proteftants) publifhed fome libels, and pofted up papers, againft the divine myftery of the holy facrament of the altar. King Francis, in the beginning of the year 1534, for reparation of thefe injuries, caufed a general proceffion

* Robertfon's Charles V. vol. iv. p. 356.

proceffion to be made at Paris, whereat he affifted with great devotion, holding a torch in his hand, together with the queen and his children. Afterwards, making diligent fearch for the authors of that fcandal, he committed half a dozen to the flames, who were burnt in feveral places; but, for every one he put to death, there fprang up hundreds of others out of their afhes." (Englifh Tranflation, fol. p. 598.) This fact, one fhould imagine, fhould have convinced the king of the folly and infignificance of his perfecuting meafures. But fo far was it from having fuch an effect upon this monarch, that, in fubfequent periods of his reign, he kindled the flames of perfecution throughout all his dominions. His example was followed in this refpect by his fon, Henry II. who treated the proteftants of France with the moft unrelenting feverity. The fame hiftorian, after informing us that the year 1549 was, for the moft part, fpent in public entertainments, and " in all the vain paft-times which an ingenious and opulent idlenefs could invent," adds; " when the court was weary of thefe fports, the fcene of it was changed, and a fit of piety fucceeded their gallantry. They made a general proceffion to Notre Dame, whereat the king was prefent. This was to teftify, by a public act, the zeal he had to maintain the religion of his anceftors, and to punifh all thofe that would difturb it; which he confirmed by the horrible executions of great numbers of thofe miferable proteftants, who were burnt in the common place of execution. They were hauled up by a pulley and an iron chain, then fuffered to fall down in the midft of a great fire, which was repeated feveral times. He would needs feed his own eyes with this tragical and melancholy fpectacle; and it is faid that the horrible and mournful fhrieks of one of thofe poor wretches left fo lively an impreffion on his imagination, that,

all

all his life long, he had, from time to time, a very frightful and terrifying remembrance of thofe dreadful groans." (p. 628.) Yet (fuch is the power of fuperftition and bigotry) the king was not deterred from continuing to exercife the moft dreadful feverities towards the unhappy proteftants.

Our hiftorian, in his account of the tranfactions of the year 1559, fays, " there was neither city, nor province, nor profeffion, where the novel opinions had not got footing. Men of the gown, men of learning, and the ecclefiaftics themfelves, againft their own intereft, fuffered themfelves to be charmed with them. Punifhments did but make them fcatter and encreafe, and inflame their zeal the more; fo that feveral of the parliament (fome, out of a more tender and merciful nature; others, becaufe they had embraced them,) were of the mind to moderate thofe too fevere profecutions."

The king, knowing this, fent for the prefident, with fome others, and commanded them to execute his edict (againft the proteftants) with the utmoft feverity. So defirous was the king to prevent any mitigating meafures, to which moft members were inclined, that he appeared himfelf before the parliament, commanding them to continue the debate in his prefence. " His prefence, however, did not fo much daunt them, but that three perfons of the affembly proceeded boldly to deliver their fentiments upon the principal points of religion, and concluded by demanding a council, and that, in the mean time, executions might be fufpended. The king, having thus difcovered their opinions, gave orders to feize upon two of them in the place, and afterwards fent to take the prefident and two counfellors, all of whom were carried to the baftille." " Never, (fays Mezeray) did that auguft affembly receive fo great and fo fhameful a rebuke and blemifh. They ap-

pointed

pointed commiffioners for trial of the prifoners." But the death of the king, which happened three weeks after, put fome ftop to thefe vehement profecutions. (p. 653.)

His fon, Francis II. though but a youth of 16, fo far imbibed the fpirit of his predeceffors as to believe " that to execute his father's will was to extirpate all fuch as oppofed the catholic belief. To this end, he created in each parliament a particular chamber or court, which took cognizance of no other matter. They were named *burning courts* (chambres ardentes) becaufe in effect they burned, without mercy, all fuch as were convicted ; and there needed no other proof but the finding of them at fome nocturnal or clandeftine conventicle." Two young men, who were employed as informers, depofed that, in thofe midnight affemblies, they did eat the pafcal lamb and roafted pig, and afterwards put out the lights, and were guilty of criminal practices. The calumny was fpread abroad by the populace, and brought to the ears of the king and queen ; and though thefe witneffes had been convicted of falfhood by the chancellor, that did not hinder it from making fome impreffion on the queen. (p. 660.)

The fame writer bears an honourable teftimony to the manly behaviour of one of thofe members of the parliament who were apprehended by the order of Henry II. " He went to his death with fo much joy and fo great fhew of piety, that his execution was fo far from ftriking any terror, that it begot compaffion in every one, and infpired many with this perfuafion, that the belief which fo good and fo underftanding a man profeffed could not poffibly be bad." (p. 662.)

At length, the proteftants, influenced by fuch a feries of cruel perfecutions as were exercifed againft them, united together to extinguifh thofe flames

which

which were kindled for their deſtruction. Headed by leaders of illuſtrious rank, and of the moſt heroic valour, they combated for their religion with various ſuccefs.

It would have been happy for the French nation, had the conduct of the contending parties been regulated by thoſe ſentiments which the chancellor delivered before an aſſembly of the States, upon the acceſſion of Charles IX. He blamed thoſe violent proceedings which had been adopted on account of religion, aſſured them that a good, exemplary life, and ſound doctrine, were the only means to reclaim the erring, earneſtly exhorted them to lay aſide the opprobrious names of lutherans, huguenots, papiſts, and adviſed every one to extinguiſh all hatred, and to own no paſſion but for the public good. (p. 673.) But ſuch wiſe counſel ſuited not with the temper of the times, or with the ſecret views and intereſted aims of the principal actors in thoſe dreadful commotions. After a bloody war of many years' continuance, the queen-mother, who exerciſed unlimited authority in the government, reſolved to employ other means than open force, to be avenged upon her enemies. She communicated her plan only to five perſons, beſides the king her ſon, who all engaged to maintain the moſt inviolable ſecreſy. Time only brought to light their dark deſign. The proteſtants, they now believed, were not to be overcome by the force of arms; and it was reſolved to have recourſe to fraud and circumvention. In purſuance of this plan, a treaty is ſet on foot with the oppoſite party, the proteſtants are allowed to make a public profeſſion of their religion, the king takes every opportunity of expreſſing his pleaſure upon the reſtoration of tranquillity, the enemies to the proteſtants retire from court in apparent diſguſt, a reſolution is declared of entering into war with the king of

Spain,

Spain, and a marriage is propofed between Charles's fifter and the king of Navarre, a proteftant leader.—— And yet the defign of all thefe appearances of friend-fhip, (fuch is the almoft incredibly diabolical perfidy of courts) the fole defign of all thefe profeffions of regard was no lefs than the total extirpation of every proteftant. " It hath been faid that, at firft, they fpake only of the chiefs and principal men; but that the king, after he was, with much labour, per-fuaded to refolve upon it, added, fwearing in his ufual manner, ' Well then, fince it muft be, I will not have one left alive to reproach me with it.'

Orders, therefore, are given to execute this refo-lution that fame night. A band of military affaffins are chofen. The ringing of the palace bell is to be the fignal for beginning the butchery. But, upon the approach of the moment, the king's mind is in fuch a violent perturbation, that his whole frame is fhaken. It is with much difficulty that they can pofitively obtain his confent. At length, it is granted, and the queen-mother immediately haftens the fig-nal above an hour. The wolves are loofened, and every houfe is filled with blood and flaughter. " This horrible maffacre lafted feven whole days, during which time, were murdered nearly five thou-fand perfons, by divers forts of deaths.' Neither the aged, nor women, nor tender infants, were fpared. Some were ftabbed, others hewn in pieces, others fhot, others thrown headlong from their win-dows, others dragged to the river, and many had their brains beaten out with clubs and mallets. A butcher, going to the Louvre upon one of thofe days, told the king that he had difpatched one hun-dred and fifty the night before; and a gold-wire drawer often boafted that he had killed four hun-dred for his fhare. (p. 719.) It is afferted that, in

all,

all, upwards of fixty thoufand perfons were maffacred upon this occafion. *

On the 3d day of the maffacre, the king returned thanks to God for the precious victory obtained over herefy, and commanded that medals fhould be coined to preferve the memory of a tranfaction which will be an eternal blot in the annals of human affairs (p. 721). The court of Rome, and the council of Spain, were filled with inexpreffible joy upon the tidings of this horrible event. The pope went in proceffion to St. Lewis's church, to render thanks to God for that fo happy fuccefs ; and a panegyrical act thereof was reprefented before king Philip, under the title of " The Triumphs of the Church Militant" (p. 722).

Thefe facts I have, for the moft part, collected from the roman catholic hiftorian, Mezeray ; who ufes expreffions implying the utmoft difapprobation and abhorrence of the perfecuting fpirit which animated the ruling powers in France, and of thofe horridly bloody meafures which it prompted them to purfue. The candour and liberality of this writer will, I truft, have fome effect in foftening thofe averfions and undiftinguifhing prejudices which, perhaps, our education may have imprinted on our minds, againft all who are members of the roman church.

Upon reviewing thofe dreadful tranfactions, it is but juftice to obferve, that religion ought not to be charged with all thofe violations of the public peace and of the rights of human nature which have been committed by perfons, who have called themfelves her fervants. Religion has been abufed to forward the projects of ambitious princes, and to cover the defigns of envious and intriguing ftatefmen. Kings have been zealous to fupprefs herefy, becaufe they have

* Watfon's Philip II. v. ii. p. 28.

have been zealous to maintain their own lawless authority; or they have thought to accomplish some favourite scheme of policy, by appearing zealous to defend the religion of their ancestors and of the multitude[*]. In like manner, the counsellors and ministers of princes have only meant to exalt themselves, or to crush their rivals, by joining a religious faction. They have seen that the people have been uninterested in their personal jealousies and resentments, whilst they have given their souls to them, as the patrons and protectors of the church. They, who are acquainted with the characters of the persons principally concerned in the transactions which have been passing in review before us, will suspect that ambition and state-craft governed the leaders in them, more than a genuine zeal for the catholic, or the reformed, religion. Let real christians learn, then, not to be too eager to take up arms on account of their religion. They are almost sure of becoming the dupes of princes and designing politicians. Very seldom is any good done to the gospel or to truth, by fighting for it. Animosity and a state of war must necessarily cherish principles and feelings unfavourable to a christian spirit; so that religion is forgotten before the contest is finished. Even under persecution, the lawfulness of resistance may, perhaps, be doubted. Resistance, if it be unsuccessful, only licenses a continuation of persecution; and, if it be successful, that success is purchased, probably, with the loss of more lives than would have fallen at the stake,

* Francis I. formed an alliance with the protestant princes of Germany, whilst he was persecuting protestants in his own dominions; and Charles allowed protestant ministers to his German soldiers who were in his service in the Low-Countries, whilst his Low-Country subjects were, at the same time, put to death for embracing the reformed religion. (See Robertson, v. iii, p. 38. and Brand. v. 1. p. 95.)

ftake, and by the facrifice of the principles of meek-
nefs and forbearance in thofe who remain. Though
the French proteftants took up the fword under more
favourable aufpices than moft diffentients in chriftendom ever could; we know how little they benefited themfelves, and what dreadful calamities were
brought upon their country. Had they continued
patiently to *fuffer* for their religion, inftead of *fighting*
for it, they would probably have become the more
numerous and refpectable part of the French nation.

ART. VII. *Remarks on the means of promoting Religion and Virtue, and Rules of a Society for the
Reformation of Manners.*

TO THE EDITOR OF THE CHRISTIAN MISCELLANY.

SIR,

A re-perufal of your valuable Mifcellany, and,
more efpecially, of thofe papers in it figned, " A
Friend to Truth, A Friend to the Poor, Evangelicus,
and P. Y." has fuggefted the following thoughts to
my mind, which if they prove worthy of your notice,
or be found of any ufe in promoting the good defigns
your correfpondents have in view, will afford me
great fatisfaction.

I am not as yet convinced that the plans, fuggefted
by the two former of thefe gentlemen, in anfwer to
the propofer, are practicable to any extenfive degree,
unlefs very ample funds had been previoufly eftablifhed for defraying the expences which muft of
courfe attend them; and to carry them on upon a
very fmall fcale will anfwer no good purpofe. Befides, it appears from the Addrefs, p. 61, that it is intended to inculcate *unitarian* principles only; and, as
P. Y. juftly obferves, this circumftance will " fubject
the defign to great inconveniencies; " for prejudice,

A a   " combined

combined with interest, has occasioned most of the lower classes to believe that, if it succeeds, *christianity will be subverted.*" To which may be added, that the teachers of the faith, now established by *law,* will be greatly alarmed and irritated at such a bold attempt against the great Athanasius, and may vote it to be " both requisite and necessary for the safety " of the souls," of their flocks, to defend the good old cause in the good old way lately exhibited at Birmingham. It is well known that they have a vast army of saints under their command, who are ready to march upon the shortest notice, to renew the attack with the same zeal and in the same manner as they did last year, and to demonstrate again the good effects of the unwearied labours of their ghostly advisers, in making them good christians. It is also no insignificant hint which a very meek, candid writer, and who seems to speak like one in authority, suggests; (See *Appendix to the account of the riots at Birmingham,* p. 23.)—" the bolt, tho' shot, *is not entirely spent*; the Lion will not trample upon the fallen, but if ye *again arouse him*"——Farther this deponent saith not; but, perhaps, it will be no egregious deviation from his meaning, if the chasm was supplied thus : " Your houses shall *all* be burned, your property be seized on, as lawful plunder, by our lamb-like, immaculate friends and fellow —— ; and if, after all, you yet persist, your throats shall be cut for the glory of —— and ——." I would, therefore, advise your correspondents to halt a little, and to reflect upon the dangers which will accompany the execution of their scheme. One of them (p. 101.) has declared that " the character of a great part of the common people is a dreadful mixture of ignorance, superstition and vice." Now if this is a just description of them, while they are said to believe in three Gods, how much worse will they become,

when

when taught to believe in but one? And if, at leaft, ten thoufand holy men, together with an equal number of affiftants and fubftitutes, all deriving their authority from the apoftles, cannot reform their flocks, what can be expected from the labours of a few folitary interlopers, commiffioned by nobody knows who, and preaching a doctrine which will expofe both themfelves and their converts " without doubt to perifh everlaftingly."

My plan, therefore, would be this ; I would let the poor fellows enjoy the athanafian creed, predeftination, and the other glorious peculiarities of orthodoxy, undifturbed, for fear of " aroufing the lion," or rather the devil again : but I would endeavour to put a ftop to thofe evil propenfities which abound fo much among them at prefent, and render them fuch a dreadful fcourge to the virtuous, though heterodox part of the community, whenever the gentlemen of the fable tribe are in the humour to employ them, and to aroufe the lion. In other words, I would try to check the cuftom of drinking, fwearing, fabbath-breaking, thieving, and other fuch like *piccadillos*, which may have been overlooked by their ghoftly fathers, while labouring to preferve the purity of their faith ; and would ftrive to make them fober and honeft : after which, there would be no great difficulty in perfuading them to believe that the chriftian religion has not authorized its votaries to burn their neighbours houfes, or to fteal their property. To effect this, I would try to revive thofe Societies for the Reformation of Manners which were fo general in the laft and the beginning of the prefent century. Some feeble attempts have, indeed, been made for this purpofe, a few years ago ; particularly, in the year 1786, by the inhabitants of Leeds in Yorkfhire, of whofe Rules the following is a copy :

A a 2

RULES

RULES *of the* SOCIETY *for the Reformation of Manners, agreed to by the Inhabitants of Leeds,* 1786.

1. That we meet once a week (for the prefent) at five o'clock on Monday evening, under the penalty of 6d. to confult how we may be moft ferviceable in promoting the execution of the laws againft vice, prophanenefs, &c. &c.

2. That, at thefe meetings, we will forbear all difcourfe foreign to the purpofe of our meeting; and, for order's fake, elect a Chairman, who fhall put all queftions propofed, take notice of the breach of any of the Rules, warn abfenting members of their obligations to attend, and enquire what difficulties any member has met with, in order to find out proper remedies. A fecretary fhall alfo be chofen to enter in a book all our Refolutions and Orders, to read over the minutes at the end of every meeting, and to correfpond with other Societies inftituted for the fame purpofe.

3. That when any queftion is propofed and feconded, it fhall be debated with calmnefs; after which, the majority fhall determine. If the votes are equal, the Chairman fhall have the cafting vote.

4. That we will, on every proper occafion, encourage and affift the various parochial officers in the execution of their duty, particularly in fuppreffing all kind of irregularities, or tipling in the ale-houfes on the Lord's-day, and in fearching for vagrants, cheats, &c. and taking them before the Magiftrates; alfo in giving information ourfelves, where we have perfonal knowledge and proof of the breaking our excellent laws againft fwearing, and other notorious immoralities.

5. That, in all cafes of difficulty, we will previoufly confult the Magiftrates, and others learned in the law, to be certain that our proceedings are ftrictly legal; and that all the money which fhall at any time arife by the penalties on conviction of offenders fhall be diftributed to fome charitable purpofe.

6. That we endeavour, as far as good manners permit, in all companies where thefe proceedings are reflected on, to juftify the neceffity of executing the laws againft open vice, and that we ufe all proper means and folicitations to prevail with perfons of rank and authority to concur with us in the

work

work of reformation; especially the Clergy, Magistrates, Churchwardens and Constables.

7. That we endeavour to encrease our Society with men of prudence and virtue of all religious denominations, but that no person be admitted without the consent of the majority of our body, nor unless he appears heartily and conscientiously disposed to assist in suppressing every species of open notorious wickedness; no persons but members shall be admitted to our debates, except such as are to be witnesses, or assistants in this design.

8. That, as National Reformation must of necessity be preceded by personal and family reformation, we will, therefore, carefully attend to the conduct and morals of ourselves and families, and endeavour to set a good example in our own houses. More especially, that we will use all proper means to prevent our children and servants from prophaning the Lord's day by sports, or other improper recreations. That we will attend regularly with them upon public worship. That we will not hire any servants, unless they come recommended to us by persons of probity and virtue; nor unless they will previously agree to conform to our moral regulations. Neither will we give any servant, who desires us to certify his character, any other than his real one, be it what it may, without fraud or concealment.

9. That we will give our encouragement and assistance to the Sunday Schools instituted in this Town.

If these, or some such-like, Rules were adopted and vigorously pursued by the leading people in every town and village, the schemes of your correspondents would either be found not so necessary, or they would be executed with much greater probability of success.

I. X.

P. S. I beg leave to recommend to the notice of your correspondents above referred to, an excellent pamphlet entitled, "A Narrative of Proceedings tending towards a National Reformation," by a Country Magistrate. London, Robson and Clarke.

ART.

Art. VIII. *Memoirs of the Rev. Micaijah Towgood; taken from "A Sketch of his Life and Writings," by James Manning.* 3s. Johnson.

With the character and writings of Mr. Towgood, most of the readers of the Christian Miscellany are, it is presumed, in some measure, acquainted. The history of so excellent and useful a person, though not enlivened by a succession of striking incidents, may be expected to afford pleasure and improvement to all whose curiosity is chiefly exercised by what is truly valuable, and attended with the happiest influence on conduct.

Mr. Micaijah Towgood (it appears from this publication) was born at Axminster, in Devonshire, on the 17th of Dec. 1700. After a domestic education, he was committed to the care of the Rev. Mr. Chadwick; and, at Lady-day 1717, was placed under the academical instruction of the Rev. Stephen James, and the Rev. Henry Grove, who, in the reign of queen Anne, were joint tutors of an academy at Taunton.

Having gone through the usual preparatory studies, he was invited, in 1722, to become the minister of a congregation of protestant dissenters at Moreton-hampstead, in the county of Devon.

He rose at an early hour throughout the year, and had often spent a busy day before others began to enjoy it. In this practice he continued through life, and thereby secured a portion of leisure for study and composition, which the charge of a large congregation, without such economy of time, will seldom allow.

He was no sooner settled than he applied himself with unremitted attention to the discharge of his duty. He had no conception that the life of a minister was to be an idle and trifling life. He considered the ministry not only as a station of honour but of labour, to be supported not by indolence and

ease,

eafe, but by active fervice. By no means fatisfied with merely performing the cuftomary duties of the fabbath, he devoted a confiderable portion of his time to private inftruction. Once in the week, he had a religious exercife in his own houfe for the benefit of any of his congregation whofe leifure would allow them to attend, and which admitted, in fome meafure, of the freedom of converfation. But his hopes were not fo much in the prefent generation as in the fucceeding. He found it an eafier tafk to prevent vice than to correct it, and to form the young to virtue than to amend the long-contracted habits of the aged. With thefe views, he divided the town into certain diftricts, and cathechifed the children, in each of thefe divifions, in rotation. Many of the catechumens are ftill living, and retain the livelieft gratitude for the happy effects of thofe inftructions.

During his refidence in this place, he married Mifs Hawker, daughter of James Hawker, Efq. of Luppit, in the fame county.

Here Mr. Towgood continued till Chriftmas, 1736, when he received and accepted of an invitation from Crediton; to which place he removed, accompanied with the regret of his friends at Moreton, in the beginning of the year 1737.

As foon as he was fettled with this congregation, he purfued the fame ufeful plans for the moral improvement of his hearers; and, in all his inftructions, one great object, which he had in view, was to lead the people to think for themfelves, and to inculcate the principles of religious liberty.

In the year 1743, during his refidence at Crediton, an event took place which is worthy of recording, on account of the amiable light in which this worthy paftor appeared, and the important fervices he rendered to the inhabitants of the town. In this year

a moft

a most dreadful fire broke out, by which 450 families were deprived of their dwellings. The town consisted chiefly of two streets, and the devastation extended for more than half a mile on one side of the longest of these streets, not leaving a single house standing, and but a small part on the opposite side. The loss sustained was estimated at 40,000l. This awful event was sufficient to excite the compassion of persons however distant and unconnected. It is not, therefore, wonderful that Mr. Towgood, who was an eye-witness of the awful scene, and intimately acquainted with the sufferers, should immediately exert himself to the utmost to lessen the affliction. His house, his purse, was open for their relief. In connection with the Rev. Mr. Stacey, the minister of the established church, he solicited subscriptions, and was particularly successful in procuring a very considerable sum of money. By these benevolent exertions, he secured to himself the esteem of the inhabitants of every description.

In 1749, Mr. Towgood removed to Exeter, as co-pastor with three other gentlemen in the two united congregations of dissenters in that city.

In the year 1759, he met with a severe trial in the loss of Mrs. Towgood. He had lived thirty-five years with his lady, who, like himself, was a model of the conjugal virtues. The separation was painful, and he felt like a man, but not like a man without hope.

About this period, many dissenters in Devonshire thought it expedient to open an Academy in Exeter, for the purpose of educating young persons for the ministry and other learned professions, as well as for civil and commercial life. In this undertaking Mr. Towgood was desired to engage as a tutor; and the province assigned to him was, the delivering, once a week, a critical lecture on the scriptures.

scriptures. In this situation, he encouraged his pupils to think freely and impartially upon every subject of natural and revealed religion which the study of the scriptures brought under their consideration. His lectures were rather the open informations of a friend, than the dictates of a master.

In the beginning of the year 1771, he had the affliction of losing his eldest daughter; and, in 1777, he lost his cousin, Mr. Stephen Towgood, who was co-pastor with him at Exeter.

Notwithstanding Mr. Towgood was now far advanced in life, he took his share in the stated duties of the sabbath, and continued to officiate till, at last, the infirmities of age disabled him from performing the more laborious part of his ministerial functions. Being no longer capable of public duty, he resigned the pastoral office in the year 1782, after more than sixty years of service in the christian church.

From this time, he continued to receive his friends with his wonted kindness. His fortune was sufficient to supply him with every requisite accommodation, and to enable him to assist those brethren in the ministry whose circumstances were straightened and necessitous. His company was coveted by all his acquaintance; and, in the years subsequent to his resignation, he was visited not only by his particular friends, but by many strangers to his person, in whom his writings had excited the greatest respect.

In the decline of life, the weaknesses, even of the greatest men, are frequent and excuseable. But habitual temperance prevented Mr. Towgood from feeling many of the infirmities to which age is subject; and the religion he had inculcated, dispersed the clouds, and diffused a sunshine on the evening of his days. The easiness and sweetness of his temper are not to be described by words; of this nothing but conversation with him could convey a just idea. A

disposition

difpofition fo happy was become habitual, and con-tinued with him to the laft.

> ———— " Though old, he ftill retain'd
> His manly fenfe and energy of foul.
> Virtuous and wife he was, but not fevere;
> His eafy prefence check'd no decent joy."

ARMSTRONG.

There was every thing in his fituation to make old age a ftate of felicity. He could look back on a long feries of public fervice, in which he had been the honoured inftrument of much good. Health, and the continued ufe of his rational faculties, ena-bled him to enjoy the prefent moment; and his fu-ture profpects were joyful and animating.

In the month of January 1791, the ftrength of his religious principles was feverely tried by the death of his only fon, Matthew Towgood, Efq. of London, in the 60th year of his age. He was a gentleman of diftinguifhed public fpirit and ardour of mind, and zealoufly engaged in various undertakings, in which the advantage and honour of the proteftant diffenters were concerned. Mr. Towgood had the fatisfaction of feeing him pafs through the various fcenes of life with great credit and ufefulnefs, and clofe it as be-came the expectant of a better world.

With a delicate conftitution and great application to literature, the fubject of thefe memoirs lived on to an extreme old age; and is one of thofe examples which ferve to fhew that ftudious occupations, if accompanied with uniform temperance and moderate exercife, are not fo detrimental as is generally imagined.

On the 26th of February 1791, he had a paralytic feizure, and, for feveral days, his friends hourly ex-pected his diffolution. Though, to the furprize of the medical gentlemen who attended him, he gra-dually recovered; the oppreffion of his diftemper

was

was so great that it became difficult for him to articulate. His understanding did not appear to be in the least debilitated, but preserved all its energy; the activity of his mind concealed from him much of his real weakness, and his soul continued serene, calm, and resigned to the will of God. From the time of this seizure, he was seldom able to go out of his chamber. He was still, however, glad to receive his friends; and his behaviour in this closing scene of trial was so truly exemplary that none of them could leave his room without admiration and improvement.

In this state of daily-increasing weakness, every one was anxious to contribute something to his comfort; and his paternal care was repaid by the tender assiduities of his affectionate daughter, who had always lived with him, and who now listened to his broken accents, to catch the least intimation of her father's wishes, and watched with anxiety every look, to learn his wants,

> " Explore the thought, explain the asking eye,
> " And keep alive one parent from the sky."

He experienced frequent returns of his disorder, and, after continuing eleven months in a state of great debility, he died on the 1st of February 1792, leaving no good man his enemy, and attended with that sincere and extensive regret which can follow those only who, occupying useful stations, have acquitted themselves with zeal and fidelity.

The publication, by which Mr. Towgood is most known, is the " Dissenting Gentleman's Letters," in answer to Mr. White. This work has had a very extensive circulation. Three editions of it have been printed in America, besides the six editions through which it has passed in this country.

POETRY.

P O E T R Y.

ART. IX. *A Fragment.*

ALL on the side of yonder brow
    An ancient Castle stood,
With turrets, walls and spires enow,
    And half embower'd in wood.

'Twas so when Edgar, kind and good,
    Its new built walls possest;
The friendless trav'ller's hope it stood,
    The weary pilgrim's rest.

Then plenty op'd, with smiling hand,
    The hospitable door;
Then riches, pow'r and wide command
    But serv'd to bless the poor.

Then splendid rooms, then gilded halls,
    Then beauty's brightest ray,
E'en diadems, have grac'd its walls
    On many a holiday.

But now how chang'd!—No monarch here
    His stately head uprears,
Save where the cautious herdsman's fear,
    The crested snake, appears.

The splendid room, the gilded hall,
    E'en beauty's brightest ray,
Relentless time's sad victims fall,
    The debt of nature pay.

The lilly thus must droop its head,
    Nor feel reviving rain;
The rose must lose its blooming red,
    And ne'er be seen again.

And

And furely, in fome future page
 Of time's ftill op'ning book,
The trav'ller of another age
 In vain for Thee fhall look.

Thy ruins, mould'ring ftone by ftone,
 Shall form th' unnotic'd heap,
And thou, like thy poffeffor gone,
 In long oblivion fleep.

The cryftal brook, the filver ftream,
 Shall glide unnotic'd by,
No longer any poet's theme,
 Nor worth the curious eye.

Perhaps the young, perhaps the fair,
 Shall drop the paffing tear;
Thine Edgar's merits fhall declare,
 And fay that " worth liv'd here."

Alas! but, fuch is heav'n's decree!
 Thofe happy days are paft.
Oh that the race of men like thee,
 Edgar, might ever laft!

Of tott'ring age the hoary head
 Should then ne'er drop the tear,
The orphan never want for bread,
 The widow never fear.

All dimm'd with tears, the fparkling eye
 Appears like April's fun;
The beauteous form adorns the fky,
 But all its luftre's gone.

And fhall the tear of pity flow,
 The bofom heave with grief,
Whilft you th' abodes of mifery know,
 And never give relief?

Forbid it, every tender heart;
 Heav'n did thefe feelings give,
To make you act the gen'rous part,
 And bid the wretched live.

THE

THE REVIEW.

ART. 1. *Thoughts on the Neceſſity and Means of a Reform in the Church of England.* By a Friend to Religion and his Country. 8vo. pp. 64. 1s. 6d. Johnſon, Dilly and Knott. 1792.

The object, which this intelligent writer has in view, ſeems to be no other than the welfare of his country, and the meaſures, which he recommends for the attainment of this end, will, it is apprehended, meet with many advocates.

After obſerving ' that crimes abound in this kingdom to an extent unknown in any other civilized country in the world, and that foreigners remark with aſtoniſhment the groſs ignorance of the nature of religion and the diſregard to its inſtitutions, which ſo commonly prevail;' he proceeds to inveſtigate the cauſe of theſe evils. ' That the fault does not lie in the national character, or in the civil inſtitutions for promoting the virtue of the people,' he boldly avers; and, at the ſame time, guarding his opinions from miſrepreſentation, attributes a large portion of thoſe vices and crimes which diſgrace ſociety, to the corruption of the church. Of the truth of this ſtatement he produces evidence.

The articles that fill up the liſt of thoſe vices which, in the opinion of this writer, render the clergy juſtly chargeable with corruption, are, *ignorance; a want, in a great degree, of the ſpirit, and even of the very form and appearance of religion; ſloth and indolence, and a neglect of paſtoral labours; and laſtly, pluralities and non-reſidence.* This portrait, he obſerves that truth compels him to ſay, is a ſtriking likeneſs. ' The features are juſtly repreſented, the colours are not overcharged, and the unſeemly countenance of the picture is owing to the diſguſting viſage of the original.'

In order that his readers may more diſtinctly perceive both the propriety and nature of the Reform required, he next confiders the caufes of this corruption of the clergy. Under this head, he remarks that the evil frequently arifes from *the choice of the perfons deftined for the clerical office*; from *the fyftem of education at the Univerfity*; from *the mode of introducing the clergy into their livings*; from *the ufual method of rifing to the higheft dignities of the church*; from *the unequal diftribution of its revenues*; from *the mode of paying the clergy*; and from *the want, the almoft total want of difcipline among them.*

'That a reform is abfolutely neceffary, who, then, can doubt? But to what quarter fhall we look for this reform? The clergy have long had an opportunity of effecting it, if they had thought proper; but they have not. Indeed, who can reafonably imagine that Satan will caft out Satan; that a corrupt church, more than a corrupt civil government, will ever reform itfelf? To the *people* we muft turn our eyes. To the people of England this important work belongs.'

The remainder of this treatife is employed in ftating two different *plans* of a reform in the church; but for thefe, and various interefting particulars, the reader muft be referred to the pamphlet itfelf. 'The important *object* of the author's labours, and the *manner* in which he purfues it, entitle his performance to a ferious and difpaffionate perufal.

Art. 2. *The Duty of promoting the Welfare of the Rifing Generation*: Reprefented in a Sermon preached at St. Thomas's Jan. 2, 1792, for the Benefit of the Charity School, in Gravel-lane, Southwark. By Rochemont Barbauld. 8vo, pp. 23. 6d. Goldney, Paternofter-Row.

In this difcourfe on the common fubject of charity, from Eccles. i. 4. *(One generation paffeth away, and another generation cometh.)* the reader will meet with fome novelty, and with a very confiderable degree of elegance. It was the writer's intention to offer fome 'obfervations that are calculated, not fo

much

much to imprefs the heart with a fenfe of our being appointed to remain here but for a fhort period, and then to yield the place we occupy to a new fet of guefts, tranfient like ourfelves, as to excite in us the wifh, and to point out to us the means, of ftamping a character of lafting worth on the generation now paffing away, by rendering it beneficial to the generation that is coming in its room, and by thus extending our influence far beyond the term of our exiftence here below.'

With this view, Mr. Barbauld obferves, 1ft. that ' each generation is, by the appointment of our Maker, clofely connected both with the generation immediately preceding, and with that immediately following;' 2dly. ' that fince the children of men, called fucceffively into being, form a lengthening chain, each link of which has a confiderable influence upon the next, it is the duty of each generation to ftudy to promote the happinefs of that which is rifing up in its room;' 3dly. ' that the moft effectual method of being beneficial to the rifing generation, is to give them a religious and virtuous education:' 4thly, ' that we hereby benefit, not one only, but many fucceeding generations;' and, laftly, ' that, as thefe children of mortality are heirs of immortality, and as the time they fpend here below, is to qualify them for future and endlefs exiftence, we become, by giving them a virtuous education, willing inftruments of God's mercy, in conducting them in the path which leadeth to everlafting blifs.'

The chain of reafoning in this fermon is, evidently, both beautiful and juft. The ftyle, likewife, in which it is written, feems well calculated to fecure the approbation of every judicious reader.

CORRESPONDENCE.

It is requefted that all communications for this Work be fent (poft paid) directed to the Editor of the Chriftian Mifcellany, at Mr. Stalker's, No. 4, Stationers-court, Ludgate-ftreet, London.

THE
Chriſtian Miſcellany,

For AUGUST, 1792.

ART. I. *On the Duty and Neceſſity of Religious Enquiry.*

(Concluded from page 279.)

IN the firſt place; If religion be a concern the moſt ſerious and important which can occupy the thoughts and attention of man, then it becometh him to regard it according to its importance. All men acknowledge the utility of the arts and ſciences, of wealth and riches, but none expects, in the uſual courſe of things, the knowledge of the former or the acquiſition of the latter without labour and applica-tion. Is religion, then, the only thing, becauſe of its infinite excellence, that gives its advantages with-out application to know it? Do men expect to be-come rich by any art or employment, while ignorant of its nature? By no means. And ſhall they pre-tend to be rich in good works and ſubſtantial piety, while ignorant of the real ſource from whence theſe alone can flow? Are we ambitious only to acquire the knowledge of preſent objects, becauſe they are fleeting and tranſitory? And are we indifferent about thoſe that are future, becauſe they are ſure and eternal? How prepoſterous is ſuch conduct? How contrary to true judgement? In ſhort, if wiſdom be better than folly, if happineſs is to be

preferred

preferred to misery, if the concerns of eternity be more important than those of time, if religion be the only thing that can ensure us real happiness, and if misery has its abode only where *it* is a stranger ; then, from its dignity and importance, we cannot remain indifferent about what it is in itself, what it bids us believe, what it bids and forbids us to do, and what it promises and threatens,—without discovering the greatest degree of insensibility.

Secondly ; As man is a reasonable creature, to be consistent with himself he should act as such. Even in the matters of common life, mankind seem to be aware of the difficulty of coming at truth. When they hear of any piece of intelligence, they generally wish to learn the origin and grounds of it, before they give it a full assent. So far they act consistently ; and it were to be wished they were as inquisitive in cases of far greater importance. When proper evidence is afforded for any one truth, and that accessible to every man, why should we be more ready in this case, than in the former, to take it off the lips of any man, or trust entirely the authority of any priest or church whatever ? Is it because eternal truths are less worthy of our attention than the trifling occurences of the day ? Is our belief, when we do not ourselves examine the evidence, a rational belief ? Therefore, when we believe merely from custom, chance or authority, we fail in duty as reasonable creatures, we act below our character as such ; and our pretending to believe what we know nothing about is, in the highest degree, contemptible, not to say, worse.

Thirdly ; The obligations on christians to examine the grounds of their religion rise a degree higher. Christians profess a *rational* religion ; a religion which addresses itself to the understandings of men ; a religion

gion founded on reafon and argument. It, therefore, demands to be underftood by *rational enquiry*,
and fpurns to be fupported by blind fuperftition, or
to be huddled up in the dark. To profefs to believe
any thing *excellent* of which we are ignorant, doth
only difcredit that which we mean to honour : and,
in like manner, to make a profeffion of the beft religion in the world, while unacquainted with it, as it
is acting the part of the hypocrite, as it is difhonour-
ing that religion, fo it argues fuch an indifference
and infenfibility of mind as is inconfiftent with what
it is of fuch importance to know, and of fuch excellence in itfelf.

Fourthly ; The argument ftill comes with additional force on proteftants, or, thofe who proteft
againft the errors of the church of Rome. That
church difclaims all enquiry into religion, and holds
that, the pope being infallible, every individual muft
implicitly take his faith from him, as well as fubmit
to the decifions of the church. This, proteftants
declare to be unjuft and unreafonable, and ground
their feceffion from that church upon enquiry ; affert-
ing that the bible alone is the only infallible rule of
faith and manners, and that it is the duty of every
man to take his religion folely from it. Therefore,
do proteftants embrace a fyftem of faith merely becaufe it is the eftablifhed one of their country, and
has the fanction of civil authority ; do they either
wilfully or thoughtlefsly difavow all enquiry ;—they
revert from the grand principle on which they found
their feceffion from the romifh church, and act much
worfe than papifts ; becaufe, while profeffing *oppofite* principles, they act on *theirs* ; and, while declar-
ing that the bible is the only infallible rule of faith,
they blindly adopt the creeds and confeffions of their
country, and thus fhew, by their conduct, that they

believe

believe in the infallibility of these as much as papifts believe in that of the pope, and the decifions of their church. If it be faid that the religion of proteftants is quite free from error, that it has been fufficiently enquired into already by learned and pious men, who affure us that it is fo, and that we fhould, now-a-days, take it upon their authority;—I anfwer, this is exactly the popifh argument; and if the firft reformers had been influenced by it, or other confcientious and able men fince their time, we fhould have been papifts to this day. Nay, was this argument to have dominion, the empire of reafon would foon become extinct among the fons of men.

Fourthly; From the variety of opinions held by men on this fubject, the argument receives additional ftrength. Religion in itfelf is one unchangeable truth. But, when we look around us in the world, we fee it almoft in as many different forms and fhapes, as thefe are different among men. It is, therefore, almoft needlefs to add, that right religion muft be as rare, as error is prevalent. Need there be a ftronger argument to evince the neceffity of every individual enquiring for himfelf? Exclude enquiry into religion, and every man muft embrace that of his country or his parents, whether true or falfe. Upon this principle, had I been born in Turkey, I had certainly been a mahometan; in Spain or Portugal, a papift; in Britain, a proteftant, but only by name. Had my parents been calvinifts, I had been a calvinift too; had they been quakers, I had been a quaker likewife: and fo the idea might be purfued through the various opinions which prevail among mankind.

While the evident tendency of this principle is to cut up all religion by the roots; while it would fupplant all religious knowledge and good fenfe from among

among men; and while it would nourish superstition and error; it, likewise, goes upon the supposition that fallible man is infallible, that a world of darkness needs no light. In short, upon this principle, error could never be exploded, reformation in any one thing could never take place. Hence, the exercise of private judgment in matters of religion becomes absolutely necessary. Although we fall into errors, yet, if our intentions are upright, and our endeavours assiduous in all our enquiries, we have every reason to think these will not be laid to our account. But, if we blindly and negligently embrace error, the case is reversed; because we gave ourselves no trouble to examine how far the opinions, which we embraced, were warranted by the word of God.

Sixthly; I might enlarge on the idea of an improper practice necessarily resulting from erroneous principles; I might call in the authority of scripture to confirm what I have advanced, of that scripture which commended the Bereans of old, because they searched for themselves, to learn whether the things taught them " were so or not," which desires us " to prove " all things, to try the spirits, and to be able to " give a *reason* of the hope that is in us." But, surely, I need say no more on a point so obvious from the nature of man, from reason, from the state of the world, and from revelation.

CANDIDUS,

ART. II. *A View of the Progress of Unitarian Sentiments and Worship.*

(*Concluded from page 288.*)

To some, whose minds are justly and deeply affected with the solemn importance of the subject,

B b 3

and

and with the clearneſs and force of evidence in its favour, it may appear a matter of ſurpriſe as well as concern, that this age of freedom has not furniſhed more, many more inſtances of clergymen making a noble ſacrifice to divine truth, and of laity uniting with them in their conſcientious ſeceſſion from a church whoſe ſervices are, in their opinion, in the moſt eſſential point repugnant to the purity and to the truth of ſcripture.

But, when it is conſidered that all the emoluments and ſanctions of this world are on the ſide of this corrupt worſhip; when it is conſidered, that many candid minds turn away from theological diſcuſſions, through the abhorrence which they feel in the recollection of thoſe evils of which controverſy hath been productive; when it is conſidered, that levity and frivolity characteriſe our times; when it is conſidered, that, in all times, religious knowledge is the purſuit of the few; and when it is alſo conſidered, that it requires great vigour of mind to conquer prejudice and long habit;—when theſe things are weighed, rather than wonder that the conſiſtent confeſſors of the truth have not been more numerous, we ſhall wonder that the times have furniſhed ſo many inſtances of ſelf-denial, integrity and fortitude.

But, even in theſe times of degeneracy and diſſipation, not only ſome miniſters of the goſpel, in a way peculiarly ſuitable to their characters, as ſet for the defence of the pure goſpel, have withdrawn from a church in which unſcriptural forms of worſhip are uſed; but many of the laity, in different parts of the kingdom, have done the ſame; or, on theſe grounds, have become fixed diſſentients from our national eſtabliſhment. Several worthies whoſe names we have mentioned in our laſt number, have opened

their

their own houfes for public divine fervices; which muft tend to render the principles, on which they acted in refigning their preferments, more noticed and underftood. Several focieties, it is faid, have been formed in fome parts of the kingdom; and it hath become a leading object with others, (and no fmall number) which have before exifted in a ftate of feparation from our eftablifhed church, to conduct their devotional fervices in a ftrain which may afford an explicit and pointed teftimony to the divine unity, and to the fupreme godhead and unequalled dignity of the Father.

The fame fpirit of enquiry into this article, and of zeal for the pure worfhip of one God, the Father, hath appeared in Scotland. About five years fince, arofe at Montrofe, in that kingdom, under the aufpices of a liberal and learned layman,* a fociety of profeffed unitarian chriftians, fuch as never appeared before there. The like fpirit hath fpread itfelf to America; where the principal epifcopal church in Bofton hath laid afide its athanafian forms, and adopted Dr. Clarke's reformed liturgy.

They, who remember the ftate of religious enquiry and fentiments, on this head, about thirty or twenty years ago, and compare it with what now falls under their obfervation, muft know, " that " unitarian fentiments are gaining ground every " day. Every attempt to fupprefs them, by writ- " ing or otherwife, has hitherto been favourable to " their fpread, and we may be confident it ever will " be fo."†

B b 4   This

---

* Mr. Chriftie; who has publifhed a fet of Difcourfes on the Divine Unity, in which the fubject is treated with great compafs and judgement. For an account of the fociety at Montrofe, fee Mr. Lindfey's Hiftorical View, p. 551—560.

† Dr. Prieftley's Sermon on the Importance of Free Enquiry. p. 40.

This state of things is far more encouraging and favourable to those who are convinced that trinitarian worship is unscriptural, than were the circumstances in which Mr. Firmin, and the few unitarians of his day, found themselves. Our present unitarians find themselves a numerous and respectable body; not inferior to their christian brethren of the athanasian faith, in virtue and piety; equal to them, at least, in all kinds of science and learning; supported by the most able pens of the age, and the partizans of a *growing cause*. They are under much less temptation, therefore, to be shy of their sentiments, or to suppress them. Dissenting unitarian societies are so dispersed over the kingdom that most, who adopt unitarian principles, may be supposed to enjoy opportunities of joining some one, with which they may bear their testimony to the belief and worship of one God, the Father.

But, in any case, if they can find only a few like-minded with themselves on this point; if they have even no opportunity of extending the profession of what is, in their opinion, the truth, beyond the circle of their own family; in any case, sincerity in religious worship is their duty; to keep the commandments of God and the faith of Jesus, pure and undefiled, is their duty.

It may be permitted me, here, to lay before them the strong and serious remonstrances of Mr. Christie's pen, which have been laudably and forcibly recommended by his example.

" Some of the advocates for unitarianism (says this able writer) have given the most unequivocal proofs of sincerity by resigning church preferments, and submitting to great temporal inconveniences, for the sake of enjoying that inestimable treasure, a good conscience. And this brings one, naturally, to speak of the conduct of those who, being convinced of the one sole godhead of the Father, do yet continue to conform to trinitarian worship, and remain in churches where religious sentiments, diametrically opposite to their own, are the standard of doctrine, and constantly taught and inculcated. A conduct of this kind is justly censurable; particularly in laymen, who have little to sacrifice by acting up to the dictates of truth and sincerity.

"The fidelity we owe to God and his truth requires us to bear an open and consistent testimony to it; which we can never be said to do, while we statedly frequent those churches in which error is openly enforced and recommended. To speak in favour of the truth, is, no doubt, highly commendable, and tends to diffuse the knowledge of it in the world; but example has still a far more powerful effect. The edifying example of one or more persons, retiring, from conscientious motives, from the communion of a corrupt and erroneous church, will be far more efficacious, and make a deeper impression upon the greatest part of mankind, than the clearest and conclusive reasoning whatever.

"The difference of opinion betwixt unitarians and trinitarians is not of a light and trivial nature. It is not a verbal disputation, a poor play of words, a contest about ceremonies, forms, or church government; but a matter of the last importance. The honour and glory of God, the least part of which is greater than the greatest human affairs, are deeply concerned. The credit of the religion of Jesus is at stake. If ever there was a cause that would justify or require a separation from any church on earth, it is a conviction that the one true God, our heavenly Father, is there dishonoured, and his peculiar glory given to another.

"Far

"Far be it from me to pass any rash and uncharitable censures upon those who do this ignorantly, having no opportunity of being better informed, or from invincible prejudices that cannot be overcome. I acknowledge and admit the innocency of unavoidable error. But I am speaking just now to unitarians, whom God, in his providence, hath brought out of darkness into his marvellous light; and I am sure it is their duty to act in conformity to the light that God hath afforded them, by an open avowal of their principles, a resolute departure from those societies where false doctrines are taught and an unscriptural worship prevails; and thereby increasing the number of the true worshippers of the Father in spirit and in truth, and setting an instructive example of religious integrity to the world."*

These remonstrances apply with great force to those who, by education and long practice, and, perhaps, by interest, are fixed in a regular connexion with the established church; but they will apply with still greater force to dissenters, who have never yet been exposed to such powerful influence; who have never been in the habit of trinitarian worship, who may be supposed to have seen, and to have felt, a variety of objections to the worship, discipline, and constitution of a national church. *Their* minds, it might be imagined, must be fully open to these arguments; their ears not having been familiarized to trinitarian doxologies and prayers, their hearts must revolt from them as harsh and dissonant to all their ideas; *they*, from the consideration,

* Christie's Discourses on the Divine Unity, p. 280, 281. and a Free and Serious Address to the Christian Laity, especially such as, embracing Unitarian Sentiments, conform to Trinitarian Worship. Also, A Letter to a Layman, on Mr. Lindsey's Proposal for a Reformed English Church.

ration, in favour of non-conformity, drawn from the object of worship, muft derive a potent reafon in aid of all the other reafons that juftify their diffent; nay, a reafon, in itfelf, equal to them all in folemnity and importance. What fhall we fay, then, but lament the inconfiftency of human characters, the weaknefs of human virtue falling into thofe eftablifhed churches in the prayers of which praifes and addreffes to other perfons befides to the one God, the Father, are continually recurring? Their conduct doth not agree with their fentiments, nor with their former felves. It weakens the hands of thofe who would preferve a good confcience, and maintain the purity of chriftian worfhip; and it is throwing additional weight into the fcale of error and falfe worfhip, which is already borne down by the majority and emoluments of the world.

To adopt here a clofe and pointed remonftrance;

" That unitarian diffenters, already out of the church eftablifhed; that they, who have the bleffing of being free from all fuch fervitude and fubjection to human authority in the things of God, fhould voluntarily put themfelves under the yoke again, now fo much harder than that under which their forefathers groaned, but which, however, their honeft minds were not able to bear; is not, to fay the leaft, a thing eafily to be accounted for, or to be reconciled with any juft and right way of thinking. By going over to a church which they, as unitarians, are perfuaded is very corrupt in the grand point of the object of worfhip, they take the ready way to obftruct and prevent all reformation. For, wherefore complain or defire any thing amifs to be rectified, when it is no more than you can conform to without fcruple or uneafinefs?

" What language would Mr. Whifton have ufed concerning *fuch* diffenters, who did not refrain

from

from faying, with his wonted bluntnefs and honefty; "It is certainly much more neceffary for private perfons in the eftablifhed church to feparate from it, on account of thefe points of great moment, (viz. its athanafian doctrine and worfhip, &c.) than it was for many of thofe diffenters of old to feparate from the church of England, about (precompofed) forms of prayer, or furplices, or the crofs in baptifm."*

There is an awful paffage in the book of Revelations, which, at leaft in a degree, is applicable to the important fubject of the preceding reflections; and which, with the remark of Dr. Doddridge upon it, we would fubmit to the ferious attention of the reader, and fo conclude.

Rev. xiv. 9, 10, 11. *And the third angel followed them, faying, with a loud voice, If any man worfhip the beaft and his image, and receive his mark in his forehead and in his hand, the fame fhall drink of the wine of the wrath of God, which is poured out without mixture into the cup of his indignation; and he fhall be tormented with fire and brimftone, in the prefence of the holy angels, and in the prefence of the lamb. And the fmoke of their torment afcendeth up for ever and ever, and they have no reft day nor night, who worfhip the beaft and his image, and whofoever receiveth the mark of his name.*

—"When I ferioufly reflect on this text, and how directly the force of it lies againft thofe who, contrary to the light of their confciences, continue in the communion of the church of Rome, for fecular advantage, or to avoid the terror of perfecution, it almoft makes me tremble; and I heartily wifh that all others, who connive at thofe things in the difcipline and worfhip of *proteftant* churches which they, in their confciences, think to be finful remains of

* Mr. Lindfey's Hiftorical View. p. 464, &c.

of popifh fuperftition and corruption, (N.B. The ufe of the athanafian and nicene creeds owes its origin to the church of Rome, and a pope firft enjoined the trinitarian doxology) would ferioufly attend to this paffage, which is one of the moft dreadful in the whole book of God, and weigh its awful contents, that they may keep at the greateft poffible diftance, from this horrible curfe, which is fufficient to make the ears of every one that hears it, to tingle."*

* Doddridge's Family Expofitor, on Rev. xiv. 11. Note (g.).

TO THE EDITOR OF THE CHRISTIAN MISCELLANY.

SIR,

If you think the following " Axioms" deferving a place in your Mifcellany, you will oblige me by inferting them this month.

A CONSTANT READER.

Art. III. *Axioms of Morality and of Chriftianity.*

BY J. R. TOULMIN.

1. Although God caufes evil to be productive of good, yet this fhould be no motive to induce us to do evil that good may come.

2. To follow the fafhions of the world, is an introduction to all evil.

3. Neatnefs in drefs is commendable; but, when it becomes the chief object of our attention, it ought to be condemned.

4. Indecency in converfation is fhameful, and highly difgufting to true politenefs and fenfibility.

5. Youth is generally cenfured and laughed at by his youthful companions, when they fee him purfuing

fuing the paths of wifdom and virtue with alacrity and zeal. But let him not be difcouraged. If God be on his fide, who can be againft him ?

6. Thofe, who reprove with paffion for every trifle, in a little time will not be regarded when they reprove with *reafon*.

7. Sufpicion indicates a great depravity of mind; and fufpicious people are generally found to be difhoneft themfelves.

8. If we would be truly great, we fhould think nothing below our notice, nor any thing too high for our attainment.

9. Thofe, that are always ready to accufe other people of plagiarifm, do not reflect that the utility of their writings is to promote the good of others. The niceft difcernment cannot always diftinguifh fimilitude from artful imitation.

10. The utility of offering up our fupplications before the throne of God, is not to convince him of our wants, but to make a fenfe of our obligations to, and dependence upon him more deep and affecting on our own minds.

11. A modeft and humble perfon will look with as much regard on the meaneft labourer, as on the higheft of human potentates.

12 A wife perfon is not furprized at any thing.

13. Thofe, who delight in animofity and bloodfhed, do not confider this facred maxim;—" He, that is flow to anger, is better than the mighty; and he, that ruleth his fpirit, than he that taketh a city." In fhort, one nation rifing up in war againft another is an act of fuicide, and depriving ourfelves of the exiftence which the all-wife creator has imparted to us.

14. Ignorance is the fource of bigotry, narrowmindednefs, and mifguided zeal.

15. Religious

15. Religious controverſy is to promote right conduct, and the practice of univerſal holineſs, amongſt men.

16. Noble and excellent ſentiments can never be too often enforced ; and the oftener we repeat them, the more influence they will have on our lives and conduct.

17. Senſible people are not always good ; but knowledge without zeal is inexcuſable.

18. There is enough revealed in the ſcriptures for our happineſs in this preſent ſtate, if we make a proper uſe of it.

19. The true chriſtian and the hero are inſeparably connected with each other.

20. Every perſon ſhould live conſiſtently with that ſituation in which his Maker has placed him.

21. He, who has honeſt and good intentions, cares not what man may ſay of him, or do unto him. The approbation of his own conſcience is far better than the applauſes of the world.

The following " Obſervations," though (as may be ſeen from the date) they arrived very late in the month, are inſerted from a regard to impartiality.

Aʀᴛ. IV. *Obſervations on a paper entitled, " Remarks on the Means of promoting Religion and Virtue."*

ᴛᴏ ᴛʜᴇ ᴇᴅɪᴛᴏʀ ᴏꜰ ᴛʜᴇ ᴄʜʀɪsᴛɪᴀɴ ᴍɪsᴄᴇʟʟᴀɴʏ.

sɪʀ,

The title of your periodical work induced me to become a ſubſcriber to it ; and though I ſoon diſcovered that the principles you avowed and the doctrines you recommended were very oppoſite to thoſe which, as a clergyman of the church of England, I believe to be true, yet the ingenuity of ſeveral of the eſſays, where *ſentiment* was out of the queſtion,

has

has afforded me some pleasure. You must, however, suppose that I except out of this number a letter signed I. X. which appeared in your magazine for July, p. 297, in reply to some former correspondents. To the tendency of this letter I have strong objections, which, if your candour will permit me, I will proceed without farther preface to state.

In the first place, then, I object to the expression of your correspondent " teachers established by *law*." Does he mean to insinuate that these " established teachers" have no other support for the doctrine of the trinity than the authority of an act of parliament ?—Again, he says these " teachers will be " alarmed and irritated at the push made against " saint Athanasius; and having an army of saints " under their command, may think it requisite to " defend the good old cause (it really is such) in " the way lately done at Birmingham."—An illiberal reflection this indeed. As if, because the clergy of that place are supposed, by the dissenters in general and their friends, to have fomented or connived at the late disturbances, that, therefore, the clergy in all other places would also avail themselves of their influence over the multitude, and employ them for such bad purposes. Yet, illiberal as it is, I. X. boldly avows it; as appears by the manner in which he has filled up the chasm in the author he has quoted. But if this was really the disposition of the leading clergy, I would ask I. X. what it is that hinders them from gratifying it, and once more " arousing the Lion." He is their witness that it is not want of power, since he has declared that they have an army of saints under marching orders. Let him explain this, if he can; and, in the mean time, let me gently whisper in his ear,—if you are right in your assertion, how great is the folly and temerity of your party in daring the generals of your enemies to put their army in motion ! Should they open

the

the campaign, Birmingham may not be the only city given up to military execution. *Verbum fat fap.* I. X. however, nor his friends have any reafon to be alarmed on this account, for the gentlemen of the "*fable tribe*," as he civilly terms them, "are not in the humour," at prefent, to commence hoftilities. Though their army is numerous and well difciplined, their officers experienced, their artillery of the beft kind, and their arfenals ftored with all the neceffaries of war, they mean to act entirely on the defenfive; unlefs the enemy dare to invade their quarters. Then, indeed, the Lion will aroufe.

I could wifh to afk I. X. what authority he has for infinuating that the "poor fellows," who are guilty of the peccadillos he has enumerated, belong to the eftablifhed church. It is an injurious afperfion. I would advife him to perufe what the Rev. Mr. Burn has faid on this fubject in his admirable reply to Dr. Prieftley. "If," fays he, "they rank as members of any fociety, it muft be "of that which the fcriptures denominate the fyna- "gogue of Satan; and, unqueftionably, every "chriftian church muft difclaim with abhorrence "all religious connection with them." Their converfion, however, is to be wifhed; and, as I. X. charitably leaves them in the poffeffion of that true faith, without which they cannot be faved, it is not to be defpaired of. The Rules he has communicated would greatly affift in this pious work. Therefore, though I have the misfortune to differ from him *toto cælo* in every thing elfe, I very cordially join him in wifhing that Societies, like thofe he mentions, were eftablifhed in every town and village in the kingdom.

A NORTH-COUNTRY CURATE.

Aug. 23, 1792.

C c

P O E T R Y.

Art. V. *A Sonnet.*

WHO health with innocence can join,
Enjoys within a richer mine
Of folid peace, than all the ftore
Peruvian hills or rivers pour.

Nature to him her homage pays.
He reigns a king, without the blaze
Of glitt'ring pomp and empty ftate;
But is indeed a monarch great:

This empire is extended wide,
Its honours are to none denied;
For all by reafon may controul
The rebel paffions of the foul.

THE END.

E R R A T A.

Page 37, line 14, for *Sufferings,* read *Sufficiency.*
55, — 4, for *exacted,* read *exalted.*
129, — 10, for *poffeffion,* read *profeffion.*
281, — 15, for *mental,* read *mortal.*

Other Errata, which do not materially affect the fenfe, the reader is defired to correct himfelf.

www.ingramcontent.com/pod-product-compliance
Lightning Source LLC
Chambersburg PA
CBHW062034090426
42740CB00016B/2905